The CALVIN INSTITUTE OF CHRISTIAN WORSHIP LITURGICAL STUDIES Series, edited by John D. Witvliet, is designed to promote reflection on the history, theology, and practice of Christian worship and to stimulate worship renewal in Christian congregations. Contributions include writings by pastoral worship leaders from a wide range of communities and scholars from a wide range of disciplines. The ultimate goal of these contributions is to nurture worship practices that are spiritually vital and theologically rooted.

PUBLISHED

The Pastor as Minor Poet: Texts and Subtexts in the Ministerial Life
  M. Craig Barnes

Arts Ministry: Nurturing the Creative Life of God's People
  Michael J. Bauer

Touching the Altar: The Old Testament and Christian Worship
  Carol M. Bechtel, Editor

Resonant Witness: Conversations between Music and Theology
  Jeremy S. Begbie and Steven R. Guthrie, Editors

God against Religion: Rethinking Christian Theology through Worship
  Matthew Myer Boulton

From Memory to Imagination: Reforming the Church's Music
  C. Randall Bradley

By the Vision of Another World: Worship in American History
  James D. Bratt, Editor

Inclusive yet Discerning: Navigating Worship Artfully
  Frank Burch Brown

What Language Shall I Borrow? The Bible and Christian Worship
  Ronald P. Byars

A Primer on Christian Worship: Where We've Been, Where We Are, Where We Can Go
  William A. Dyrness

Christian Worship Worldwide: Expanding Horizons, Deepening Practices
  Charles E. Farhadian, Editor

Missional Worship, Worshipful Mission

Gathering as God's People,
Going Out in God's Name

Ruth A. Meyers

To Susan,
With gratitude
Ruth Meyers

WILLIAM B. EERDMANS PUBLISHING COMPANY

GRAND RAPIDS, MICHIGAN / CAMBRIDGE, U.K.

Published 2014 by
Wm. B. Eerdmans Publishing Co.
2140 Oak Industrial Drive N.E., Grand Rapids, Michigan 49505 /
P.O. Box 163, Cambridge CB3 9PU U.K.
www.eerdmans.com

Printed in the United States of America

19 18 17 16 15 14   7 6 5 4 3 2 1

Library of Congress Cataloging-in-Publication Data

Meyers, Ruth A., 1957-
    Missional worship, worshipful mission: gathering as God's people, going out in God's name /
    Ruth A. Meyers.
        pages   cm.   — (Calvin Institute of Christian Worship liturgical studies series)
    Includes bibliographical references.
    ISBN 978-0-8028-6800-8 (pbk.: alk. paper)
    1. Worship.   2. Missions — Theory.   3. Common good —
    Religious aspects — Christianity.   I. Title.

    BV15.M49   2014
    264 — dc23

                                                                    2014015927

For my students,

past, present, and future

in gratitude for the joy

of learning and teaching with them

Contents

Foreword

A generation ago, in many different kinds of congregations, public worship and mission were often treated as two largely independent endeavors in congregations and parishes of many different denominations. The church gathered for worship on Sunday and engaged in a variety of service or mission projects throughout the week. Each required its own committee, task force, volunteer group, or staff position. The worship or liturgy committee met on Monday nights. The outreach, evangelism, or missions committee met on Tuesdays. As a result, a generation ago, books on worship and mission — with only a few notable exceptions — could be neatly placed on quite different shelves in libraries and bookstores. Such books would be studied in quite different seminary classes and church workshops.

In our work at the Calvin Institute of Christian Worship over the past seventeen years, we have noticed how dramatically this separation has been challenged across the spectrum of denominations. We have seen a variety of authors, pastor, consultants, and theologians challenging churches, often passionately, to rethink the functional separation of worship and mission in the imaginations of many churchgoers and church leaders. This rethinking has been fueled by the rapid decline of established Christianity in many cultural contexts. At times, the results of this have been troubling, turning Sunday worship into a consumer-oriented religious buffet. At other times, the results have been inspiring, helping worshipers perceive the intimate connection between how God may be at work through the Lord's Supper and the church's soup kitchen. As with any sea change, it often takes several years, even decades, for common wisdom to emerge about both the theological imagination and the daily practices that will best reflect the gospel and sustain vital, healthy church life.

As we have reflected on this movement, we have noticed three tendencies which make this book particularly welcome.

First, recent efforts to unite worship and mission have emphasized innovation over tradition, unnecessarily pitting the two against each other, and dismissing time-honored wisdom about worship as a quaint relic of the past. Now there is much to be said for responding innovatively to the dynamic, changing cultural context all around us. But there is also much to be said for realizing that a missional vision is as old and storied as the church itself, and that when the church unites mission and worship in its theological imagination, it is living up to the best of what it always was meant to be. Then we are free to be responsive to a changing world without the need for a breathless (and altogether exhausting) quest for endless innovation. This book breathes with appreciation for both dynamic responsiveness and the wisdom of ancient practices. Like the traditional Akan symbol "Sankofa," this book reaches back to envision progress, and invokes memory to instill hope. It models an attitude of what many are now calling "traditioned innovation."

Second, recent efforts to articulate fundamental unity of worship and mission seem divided, starkly at times, between academically oriented texts oriented to missiological theory and practical books oriented to solving technical, programmatic problems in congregational life. What we have needed are people at home in both worlds, with the heart, soul, and expertise of a teacher to ground practical thinking in the best of academic reflection, and to convey the insights of the best academic theology in metaphors and images that stick. Ruth Meyers, with her memorable and vivid images of the spinning top and the Möbius strip, offers this bridge-building voice.

Third, discussions about missional Christianity seem to unfold in several, often disparate discussion pockets. To be sure, this missional emphasis can be found in a variety of contexts. As I was reading this manuscript by this Episcopal seminary professor from the Bay area in California, I happened to visit a Mennonite congregation in rural northern Indiana. During the sermon, the pastor challenged the congregation to "develop a missional imagination," noting the connection between this goal and the mission and vision of the Mennonite Church (USA) more broadly. Earlier in the same week, I was moved and challenged by a presentation by theological educators who are establishing peer learning opportunities among leaders of the 2,000 new immigrants — mostly Pentecostal — congregations in New York City. They, too, spoke compellingly of a missional vision, and described the ways that worship, service, prayer, justice, and fellowship overlap in congregational life. These references are illustrative of quite different pockets of interest in missional Christianity among mainline, evangelical, and Pentecostal communities. Yet often the vast differences in theology, liturgy, and practice in these denominational and geographical contexts make it very unlikely that many would ever hear an Episcopal seminary professor patiently explaining the rich potential of the *Book of Common Prayer* to shape worship that exudes healing centrifugal energy. This book has rich potential as a boundary-crossing book across the spectrum of North American denominations.

To be sure, the response to this book is likely to be quite different. If you are a lifelong Episcopalian (or a church with a similar liturgical tradition), you may discover new ways to appreciate what you have always done. If you are from a very different tradition of worship practices, you may actually discover in this book new practices to retrieve from the church's liturgical tradition, or, more deeply, an approach to public worship which will guide your choices about specific practices. All of us who read can rediscover the evocative ways that our participation in the worship life of the church helps us walk in step with the Holy Spirit, engaging God's active, transforming, redemptive work in the world with vigor and hope.

JOHN D. WITVLIET
Calvin Institute of Christian Worship
Grand Rapids, Michigan

Acknowledgments

This book is the result of many conversations and my experiences of worship in many communities over a number of years. I am grateful for all who have contributed to this book in various ways.

I have been privileged to develop my vocation as a teacher and scholar at Seabury-Western Theological Seminary, Evanston, Illinois, from 1995 to 2009, and since 2009 at Church Divinity School of the Pacific and the Graduate Theological Union, Berkeley, California. I am grateful to my colleagues and students for lively conversation and for encouragement, challenge, and critique as I have formed my understanding of missional worship. Over the years, several dioceses and congregations have invited me to lead conferences and workshops on the subject of missional worship, and each of those events helped me think more deeply about the relationship between worship and mission.

Several congregations graciously welcomed me for worship and gave me the opportunity to interview clergy and lay members: All Saints' Episcopal Church, Chicago, Illinois; Church of the Apostles, Seattle, Washington; Franklin Reformed Church, Nutley, New Jersey; Gloria Dei Evangelical Lutheran Church in America, Northbrook, Illinois; Holy Family Episcopal Church, Half Moon Bay, California; Holy Trinity Episcopal Church, Lansdale, Pennsylvania; St. Andrew Episcopal Church, Kokomo, Indiana; St. Andrew's Episcopal Church, Omaha, Nebraska; St. George's Episcopal Church, Austin, Texas; and the community of St. Hildegard, Austin, Texas. My home congregations — St. Augustine's Episcopal Church, Wilmette, Illinois, and All Souls Episcopal Parish, Berkeley, California — have been places of formation and sustenance.

My research trips were made possible by several grants: an "Evangelism in the 21st Century" grant from the Episcopal Evangelical Education Society in 1999, a theological research grant from the Association of Theological Schools in 2002, and a grant from the Conant Fund in 2008-2009. I am grateful to Seabury-Western Theological Seminary for giving me sabbatical leave to pursue my research.

This book was written at Ripon College Cuddesdon (near Oxford University, England) in Fall 2013, with the support of a grant from the Conant Fund. I thank the Board of Church Divinity School of the Pacific for supporting the study leave that enabled me to complete my work.

I am deeply indebted to the staff and students at Ripon College Cuddesdon for their warm hospitality and careful listening as I wrote this book. At the end of my stay, I had the opportunity to read portions of the manuscript to a group of students and faculty. Their eager reception of my work was very encouraging, and their questions and comments gave me additional insight. I want to give special thanks to Cathy Ross for arranging this lecture and to Tim Naish for hosting it.

My sabbatical leave during Fall 2013 also included trips to the Iona Community in Scotland and the Taizé Community in France, funded by a grant from the Conant Fund. I am grateful to Jo Love and Graham Maule of the Wild Goose Group for wonderful music, pastoral wisdom, and amazing storytelling during my week at Iona. While I was at Taizé, Brother John and Brother Jean-Marie each gave generously of their time in conversation with me, and I appreciate their insight and support.

Over the years, I have had occasion to publish results of my research, and some of those publications have been incorporated into this book. Portions of Chapter 1 appeared in earlier form in "Missional Church, Missional Liturgy," *Theology Today* 67 (2010): 36-50; "Unleashing the Power of Worship," *Anglican Theological Review* 92 (2010): 55-70; and "Mission," Chapter 20 in *The Study of Liturgy and Worship,* edited by Juliette Day and Benjamin Gordon-Taylor (London: SPCK, 2013), pp. 202-11. Some of Chapter 8 appeared in "The Promise and Perils of Liturgical Change," *Anglican Theological Review* 86 (2004): 103-14 and in "The Liturgical Formation of Children, Teens, and Young Adults," in *Worship-Shaped Life: Liturgical Formation and the People of God,* edited by Ruth A. Meyers and Paul Gibson (New York: Morehouse Publishing; Norwich, UK: Canterbury Press, 2010).

I presented some of the material in Chapters 2 and 3 at "Stirring the Waters: Reclaiming the Missional, Subversive Character of Baptism," a conference in June 2013 sponsored by the North American Association for the Catechumenate and Associated Parishes for Liturgy and Mission. Chapter 4 is revised from my lecture "A Priestly Offering: Intercessory Prayer in Public Worship," given at the 2009 Associated Parishes for Liturgy and Mission Colloquium at Church Divinity School of the Pacific: http://associatedparishes .org/colloquium.html. I am grateful to my fellow members of the Council of the Associated Parishes for Liturgy and Mission for these invitations to speak and for their encouragement and insight over the years.

The illustration of the spinning top in Chapter 1 was created by Constance Wilson. Jacob Bilich created the diagram of the Möbius strip. I am grateful to both of them, and to Rebecca Wilson, for taking my ideas and giving them strong visual form.

I am indebted to my colleagues in the North American Academy of Liturgy, especially members of the liturgy and culture seminar, who have offered wisdom and encouragement along the way. I am especially grateful to John Witvliet for helping me pursue publication of this work, reading and commenting on the manuscript, and agreeing to write the foreword.

Gil Ostdiek, OFM, offered invaluable guidance in my study of the relationship of mission and liturgy, and my colleague John Dally has provided inspiration and encouragment. My thanks to those who have read portions of the book as I was writing it and offered their comments and critique: Martha Baker, Steve Bevans, Tom Brackett, Phil Brochard, Jennifer Davidson, Paul Fromberg, James Harding, Tripp Hudgins, Brother Jean-Marie of Taizé, Brother John of Taizé, Tim Naish, Cathy Ross, Marilyn Salmon, Tom Schattauer, and Sylvia Sweeney. Special thanks to Liz Dowling-Sendor for serving as writing coach — editing and commenting on the manuscript, listening me into speech, and cheering me on to the finish. I am also very grateful to my editor at Eerdmans, Mary Hietbrink, for her careful reading of my text.

Finally but by no means least, my husband, Daniel Prechtel, has lived with this book for many years, enduring my absences for research trips and my distractedness as the book consumed my attention. Words cannot express the depth of my gratitude and affection.

RUTH MEYERS
Advent 2013

Introduction

"Worship and mission?" my dinner companion asked. "We don't usually think of those two things together, do we?" My companion, a pastor in the Lutheran Church of Denmark, was spending a few days at Ripon College Cuddesdon, near Oxford University in England, after attending a conference on the "Fresh Expressions" movement.[1] We'd had several conversations over meals in the college dining hall, and I knew that he was deeply interested in the church's engagement with the contemporary world. But he gave voice to a common perception: *worship* is considered an activity within the church, usually celebrated on Sunday morning as Christians have done for centuries, while *mission* is the way the church engages the world.

Worship and Mission: Is There a Connection?

Increasingly, a lively conversation about mission is underway. Christians have begun to view the church as a community engaged in mission and to recognize that mission takes place locally as well as globally. The term "missional," coined during the 1990s, expresses an understanding that mission is rooted in God's identity and purpose — that is, God's love for the world and

---

1. "Fresh Expressions," a movement and an ecumenical endeavor based in the United Kingdom, encourages and provides resources for new ways of being church in a changing world. See "Fresh Expressions," http://www.freshexpressions.org.uk/.

God's desire to restore all creation to wholeness and integrity. Rather than having its own mission, the church engages in God's mission (sometimes referred to with the Latin phrase *missio Dei*). By proclaiming and enacting God's creating and reconciling love for the world, the church participates in the mission of God.

While literature and Web sites about the "missional church" have proliferated over the past two decades, much less has been written about missional worship. As a scholar and teacher of worship, I have been pondering how to imagine worship from a missional perspective. Mission certainly takes place in the world, outside the church's assembly for worship. But I have come to believe that worship *itself* is an important locus of mission, a place and time where the people of God celebrate and participate in God's self-giving love for the sake of the world. Moreover, worship and daily life are interwoven in a dynamic relationship. God's steadfast love and merciful judgment infuse both worship and the world outside worship. The experience of God in worship forms people for participation in God's mission in the world, and encounters with the God of Jesus Christ in daily life shape participation in worship. This book uses the term "missional worship" to speak about patterns and understandings of worship as a form of participation in the mission of God. It also introduces a related term, "worshipful mission," to describe participation in God's mission in the world, underscoring the dynamic relationship between the assembly's worship and its members' engagement in God's work in the world.

New Understandings of Mission

My interest in mission took shape in the mid-1990s, shortly after I began teaching liturgy at Seabury-Western Theological Seminary in Evanston, Illinois. During my fourteen years on the faculty at Seabury (1995-2009), my understanding of missional church and missional worship developed through my work with my faculty colleagues and students. When I joined the faculty, Seabury had just begun its Doctor of Ministry program in congregational development. Students who came to this program were contending with challenges facing the church at the end of the twentieth century: a decline in church membership, difficulty in attracting new members, and the diminishing influence of the church in American society. Our students — clergy and lay leaders from throughout North America (and later from elsewhere in the world as well) — saw their ministry as cutting-edge. As they grappled with the changing context, they were introducing bold innovations as they worked to plant new congregations or revitalize existing ones. They came to our campus each summer weary from their struggles and eager to find new understandings and new resources that would strengthen them in their ministries.

I began teaching a session or two in the program and later developed an entire course on missional worship. Each of the program's courses included sessions taught by practitioners, parish clergy who were exploring new forms of worship and were eager to proclaim the good news, by word and by action, in their surrounding communities. My co-teachers and my students offered one another — and me — much practical wisdom and pushed me to think ever more deeply about the relationship between worship and mission.

In the late 1990s, after the congregational development program had been underway for a few years, the faculty undertook revision of the curriculum for the Master of Divinity, the core three-year program for those preparing for ordained pastoral leadership in the church. We began our work by considering issues facing the church at the close of the millennium. A core text in the Doctor of Ministry program, *Transforming Mission: Paradigm Shifts in Theology of Mission* (published in 1991) by the South African scholar David Bosch, offered a solid theological foundation for doctoral students as they reflected on their ministries. Those who taught in the Doctor of Ministry program urged the entire faculty to engage the conversation.

So we embarked on a collegial journey, traveling with Bosch through the New Testament and the history of Christianity to the emergence of postmodernity in the twentieth century. Our church-history faculty helped us explore Bosch's four major models of mission: mission to the Gentiles in the early church and Eastern Christianity, medieval Roman Catholicism, the Protestant Reformation, and the modern Enlightenment. Together we pondered Bosch's "elements of an emerging ecumenical missionary paradigm." Together, we began to understand what I believe is *the* critical insight in contemporary theologies of mission: mission is not something the church *does*, a program alongside other programs like Sunday school and the youth group. Rather, mission *defines* the church.

As a people called and sent by the God of Jesus Christ, we participate in God's mission. Bosch says it this way:

> We have to distinguish between *mission* (singular) and *missions* (plural). The first refers primarily to the *missio Dei* (God's mission), that is, God's self-revelation as the One who loves the world, God's involvement in and with the world, the nature and activity of God, which embraces both the church and the world, and in which the church is privileged to partici- pate. *Missio Dei* enunciates the good news that God is a God-for-people. *Missions* (the *missiones ecclesiae;* the missionary ventures of the church) refer to particular forms, related to specific times, places, or needs, of participation in the *missio Dei.*[2]

In short, mission is a matter of identity rather than program, a question first about *being* rather than *doing*. Mission is first and foremost God's activity, not of human origin.

Through studying Bosch and reflecting on the implications of his contem- porary model for mission, the Seabury faculty decided that from the begin- ning of their seminary experience, students in the Master of Divinity program would engage contemporary questions about mission. We designed a course called "Gospel Mission," to be taught by the entire faculty. The first year we offered the course, I overhead a student explain to one of our donors what he was learning in seminary: "I'm realizing that I'm called to be a missionary. My bishop expects me to go back home to Mississippi, and I knew that when I started. But I'm discovering that *that* work *is* mission: going to those rural ar- eas, preaching the gospel to the people I know so well. Mission isn't just about going away to some foreign land; it's living the gospel wherever God calls me."

Through my work with this student and many others in both the Master of Divinity and the Doctor of Ministry programs, I honed my understanding of mission. Like many Christians, I had associated mission with the church's work among those who were not baptized and who perhaps had never heard the gospel. Mission might take the form of saving souls, or it might be undertaken through activities such as teaching and medical work. I knew that my church,

---

2. David J. Bosch, *Transforming Mission: Paradigm Shifts in Theology of Mission* (Mary- knoll, N.Y.: Orbis Books, 1991), p. 10; emphasis in original.

the Episcopal Church, is legally incorporated as "the Domestic and Foreign Missionary Society," that missionaries from our church had been sent to Native American communities as well as to the nineteenth-century frontier, and that our church continues to send missionaries throughout the world.

My view of mission broadened considerably through my study and teaching. "Mission is a multifaceted ministry," writes Bosch, "in respect of witness, service, justice, healing, reconciliation, liberation, peace, evangelism, fellowship, church planting, contextualization, and much more." But, he continues, "even the attempt to list some dimensions of mission is fraught with danger, because it again suggests that we can define what is infinite."[3] Bosch insists that mission must be understood from the perspective of the mission of God, which establishes the church. Mission, he concludes, is "the good news of God's love, incarnated in the witness of a community, for the sake of the world."[4] Thus I have come to appreciate that mission is God's activity, a reconciling love made known in creation, in the incarnation, death, and resurrection of Jesus, and in the sending of the Spirit.

Worship and Mission: Making a Connection

What might mission understood in this way have to do with worship? Worship, like mission, proclaims and celebrates the good news of God's love, and worship is offered for the sake of the world. How might the concepts of worship and mission be brought into dialogue? What would worship be like in a congregation that came to view mission as living the gospel wherever God calls them?

When I began teaching in the Doctor of Ministry program, little had been written about the relationship between worship and mission. In 1966, British scholar J. G. Davies lamented, "Worship and mission are treated as two totally distinct objects of theological investigation."[5] His book *Worship and Mission* seeks to bridge that gap from a theological perspective, ex-

3. Bosch, *Transforming Mission,* p. 512.

4. Bosch, *Transforming Mission,* p. 519.

5. J. G. Davies, *Worship and Mission* (London: SCM Press, 1966; New York: Association Press, 1967), p. 9.

ploring the meaning of worship in terms of mission. Bosch says little about worship in his 1991 study of mission.[6] In 1999, a group of worship professors in Lutheran seminaries in the United States and Canada collaborated on a collection of essays published as *Inside Out: Worship in an Age of Mission.* The editor, Thomas Schattauer, acknowledges Davies' work and asserts that a separation of worship and mission "no longer characterizes the work of those concerned primarily with either the church's mission or its worship."[7] Schattauer's insightful analysis of different approaches to the relationship of mission and worship has exerted a significant influence on my thinking, and I discuss his work in more detail in Chapter 1.

Another core text in Seabury's Doctor of Ministry program, *Missional Church: A Vision for the Sending of the Church in North America,* a collaborative project of six scholars published in 1998, develops a theology of missional church and explores some of the practical implications of understanding mission as the mission of God in which the church participates. Although this book does not devote a chapter solely to worship, the chapter titled "Cultivating Communities of the Holy Spirit" includes brief sections about baptism and the Lord's Supper.[8] This book has also shaped my thinking, and I discuss it as well in Chapter 1.

Some of the researchers who collaborated on *Missional Church* joined others in a study of congregational models of the missional church; the result was *Treasure in Clay Jars: Patterns in Missional Faithfulness,* published in 2004. The authors describe a missional church as "a church shaped by participating in God's mission, which is to set things right in a broken, sinful world, to redeem it, and to restore it to what God has always intended for the

6. Near the end of his book, Bosch notes that some contemporary scholars added "liturgy" as an aspect of mission, and a few pages later he devotes one brief paragraph to worship (*Transforming Mission,* pp. 512, 517). The index has just one entry for "worship," with the subheading "Matthean meaning of"; "baptism" appears in the index with two subheadings: "Paul's understanding of" and "importance of rite of," the latter appearing in the chapter on medieval Roman Catholic approaches to mission (*Transforming Mission,* pp. 566, 576). But Bosch does not give sustained attention to worship in his lengthy section outlining "elements of an emerging ecumenical missionary paradigm."

7. Thomas H. Schattauer, "Liturgical Assembly as Locus of Mission," in *Inside Out: Worship in an Age of Mission,* ed. Thomas H. Schattauer (Minneapolis: Fortress Press, 1999), p. 1.

8. *Missional Church: A Vision for the Sending of the Church in North America,* ed. Darrell L. Guder (Grand Rapids: Wm. B. Eerdmans, 1998), pp. 159-66.

world."[9] They identify eight patterns found in a missional church, including "worship as public witness." Building on Schattauer's work, they include one chapter in their book that explores this pattern and offers examples of several churches whose worship is missional. Worship is mission, the authors explain, because it turns outward to the world: "Everything [the church] does has a public horizon." Worship declares God's reign, sustains the missional identity of the Christian community, and both motivates and permeates the public life of the congregation.[10]

Eastern Orthodox theology offers a distinctive perspective on worship and mission. In *For the Life of the World,* first published in 1963, liturgical scholar Alexander Schmemann explores the significance of worship as the foundation for a Christian approach to the world and to human life.[11] Ion Bria, a Romanian Orthodox theologian, describes "the extension of the liturgical celebration into the daily life of the faithful in the world" as "the liturgy after the liturgy."[12]

Two more recent books offer important contributions to the conversation about the relationship between worship and mission. In *Sent and Gathered: A Worship Manual for the Missional Church,* published in 2009, Clayton Schmit develops a theology of worship and in light of that theology offers principles for planning and celebrating worship in a missional church.[13] Schmit's key insight, evident in his book's title, is that the sending with which a worship service concludes is the pivotal moment that turns the assembly outward toward action in the world. *Worship and Mission after Christendom,* a 2011 book by Mennonite scholars Alan Kreider and Eleanor Kreider, considers the intersection of worship and mission in contemporary contexts, giving significant attention to Scripture and Christian history.[14] Both of these

---

9. Lois Y. Barrett et al., *Treasure in Clay Jars: Patterns in Missional Faithfulness* (Grand Rapids: Wm B. Eerdmans, 2004), p. x.

10. Barrett et al., *Treasure in Clay Jars,* pp. 100-116.

11. Alexander Schmemann, *For the Life of the World: Sacraments and Orthodoxy,* 2nd ed., revised and expanded (Crestwood, N.Y.: St. Vladimir's Seminary Press, 1973).

12. Ion Bria, *The Liturgy after the Liturgy: Mission and Witness from an Orthodox Perspective* (Geneva: WCC Publications, 1996), p. 20.

13. Clayton J. Schmit, *Sent and Gathered: A Worship Manual for the Missional Church* (Grand Rapids: Baker Academic, 2009).

14. Alan Kreider and Eleanor Kreider, *Worship and Mission after Christendom* (Scottdale, Pa., and Waterloo, Ontario: Herald Press, 2011).

books have also shaped my understanding of missional worship — that is, a theology of worship as a primary experience of God's mission. I draw on their work at various points in this book.

I also refer at several points to the work of Craig Dykstra, Dorothy Bass, and their collaborators on Christian practices — honoring the body, household economics, saying yes and saying no, keeping Sabbath, discernment, hospitality, testimony, shaping communities, forgiveness, healing, dying well, and singing our lives to God — which they define as "things Christian people do together over time to address fundamental human needs in response to and in light of God's active presence for the life of the world."[15] Though Dykstra and Bass do not use the term "mission," they understand practices as participation in God's work in the world: "Christian practices are set in a world created and sustained by a just and merciful God, who is now in the midst of reconciling this world through Christ. . . . When they participate in such practices, Christian people are taking part in God's work of creation and new creation."[16] Thus, by engaging in Christian practices, we participate in God's mission. Moreover, Christian practices in the world are directly connected to worship. "In public worship," Dykstra and Bass explain, "the Christian community takes all these gestures [of practices in the world] and performs them on a grand scale. . . . Worship distills the Christian meaning of the practices and holds them up for the whole community to see."[17]

Worshiping Communities

In addition to my study of mission and the relationship between worship and mission, my understanding of missional worship has developed in dialogue with several worshiping communities. During a sabbatical leave in 1999, I spent time with five congregations in the Episcopal Church that were

15. Craig Dykstra and Dorothy C. Bass, "A Theological Understanding of Christian Practices," in *Practicing Theology: Beliefs and Practices in Christian Life,* ed. Miroslav Volf and Dorothy C. Bass (Grand Rapids: Wm. B. Eerdmans, 2002), p. 18.

16. Dykstra and Bass, "A Theological Understanding of Christian Practices," p. 21.

17. Craig Dykstra and Dorothy C. Bass, "Times of Yearning, Practices of Faith," in *Practicing Our Faith: A Way of Life for a Searching People,* ed. Dorothy C. Bass, 2nd ed. (San Francisco: Jossey-Bass, 2010), p. 9.

experimenting with new forms of worship. To varying degrees, each of them was moving beyond officially approved texts of the 1979 *Book of Common Prayer* while maintaining continuity with Christian tradition. I wondered how their members perceived their worship, and I was curious about the processes by which each congregation was renewing its worship and the ways in which its worship was responding to contemporary cultural shifts. In addition to worshiping with each of these congregations, I interviewed the clergy and several lay members. While my questions were focused on their experiences of worship, I also asked each person how worship formed him or her as a Christian — that is, what impact worship had on his or her life as a follower of Christ.

Three years later, I returned to each congregation to discuss my findings from my first visit, worship once again with them, and learn more about their experiences of worship and their processes of worship planning and preparation. My observations of worship, along with my interviews of clergy and lay leaders, helped me discover ways in which these congregations made creative use of space, symbols, movement, music, and silence as well as texts. Each of these congregations showed a willingness to experiment, to try new forms and let go of those that did not engage worshipers. I did not discover new principles for different dimensions of worship (such as space and music) but instead found examples of how they applied sound liturgical principles in their particular contexts.

My visits in 1999 and 2002 focused on worship. What are the challenges and rewards of developing innovative worship? How does worship intersect with particular cultural contexts? As I reflected on my conversations, though, I was intrigued by what people thought about the significance of worship for Christian living. For many members of the congregations I studied, worship is formative and transformative and offers significant connections with their daily lives. Transformation usually was not associated with a particular form or aspect of worship but rather was brought about by the totality of the worship experience and the person's ongoing participation in the worshiping community. As I analyzed my interviews, I began to ponder the relationship between worship and mission and to develop an understanding of missional worship — that is, a theology of worship as a primary experience of participation in God's mission.

A year-long sabbatical in 2008-2009 gave me opportunities to worship with more congregations and talk with clergy and lay members. Then in the fall of 2013 I spent a week with the Iona Community in Scotland and several days with the Taizé Community in France. Both communities attract pilgrims from around the world, and worship resources, especially music, from these communities have spread to many churches in many different Christian traditions. Worshiping with these communities and talking with some of their leaders added further perspective to my theology of missional worship.

Missional Worship, Worshipful Mission

This book is intended for those who worship, including those who lead. I have come to believe that missional worship is integral to the lived experience of Christian communities. Because my theology is rooted in my experience of different worshiping communities, I have organized this book around a basic pattern of Christian worship, exploring the missional significance of primary actions of worship: gathering as God's people, proclaiming and responding to the Word of God, celebrating the Lord's Supper, and being sent forth to be God's people in the world. Clayton Schmit describes this fourfold pattern as the "historic wisdom" of the church at worship and shows how this pattern is evident in many different worshiping traditions.[18] God's mission is at the heart of all Christian worship, and throughout the book I seek to unfold the missional significance of actions of Christian worship that are common to many Christian traditions.

In Chapter 1, I explore the origins and meanings of "worship," "liturgy," "mission," and "missional," each of them key terms for a theology of missional worship. It's interesting to note that in its original secular use in the ancient Greek world, the term "liturgy" meant "work for the common good" or "public service." True liturgy turns outward for the sake of the world. Recovering this meaning of "liturgy" may help Christians appreciate the integral and dynamic relationship of mission and worship. I conclude Chapter 1 with two models for the relationship between mission and worship: a Möbius strip and a spinning top. These models offer different ways to imag-

---

18. Schmit, *Sent and Gathered,* pp. 57-78; see especially the comparative chart, p. 73.

ine missional worship and worshipful mission, and I return to these models throughout the book.

I use these two models to explore primary actions of worship in Chapters 2-7, which cover gathering, proclaiming and responding to the Word, praying for the world, enacting reconciliation, celebrating a meal, and going forth. This sequence comes from Justin Martyr's description of a Sunday assembly at Rome in the mid–second century, a pattern that many churches have followed over the course of the centuries.[19] Although some churches today structure their worship in other ways, each of these actions is part of worship in most churches, and reviewers of this text from other traditions have assured me that the material can be applied to other denominational contexts which may have a different structure of worship or use different terminology. For example, acts of reconciliation may occur at various points in worship; placing this chapter after the one on intercessory prayer reflects the order in the 1979 *Book of Common Prayer* of the Episcopal Church, my own worshiping tradition and so the one I know best. While not every church celebrates communion every Sunday, the chapter on "celebrating the meal" is relevant whenever it occurs.

In Chapter 8, "Preparing Missional Worship," I turn from the sequence of actions in worship to consider what I call "dimensions" of worship: people, space, time, objects, actions, texts, music, and silence. Although I focus on each of these aspects of worship in turn, I also know that preparing worship is always more than marking a checklist of component parts. Worship, the liturgical work for the common good, is a living reality whose source is God. My hope is that those who read this book will be inspired to return to that wellspring again and again and so find themselves caught up in the movement of God's mission, God's love for the world.

19. Justin Martyr, *I Apology 67*, in *The Apostolic Fathers with Justin Martyr and Irenaeus,* Vol. 1 of *Ante-Nicene Fathers,* ed. Alexander Roberts and James Donaldson, Christian Classics Ethereal Library, available at http://www.ccel.org/ccel/schaff/anf01.viii.ii.lxvii.html.

CHAPTER 1

Imagining Missional Worship

'Tis the gift to be simple, 'tis the gift to be free,
'tis the gift to come down where we ought to be,
and when we find ourselves in the place just right,
'twill be in the valley of love and delight.
When true simplicity is gained
to bow and to bend we shan't be ashamed,
to turn, turn, will be our delight,
till by turning, turning we come 'round right.

Shaker song, eighteenth century[1]

Missional worship is an understanding and practice of worship that engages worshipers in the mission of God, drawing them into God's self-offering of redemptive love through Christ and in the power of the Spirit. From this perspective, worship and mission are in a dynamic relationship. We can imagine not only missional worship but also worshipful mission. Both concepts are built upon contemporary understandings of mission and the missional church.

---

1. Shaker hymn, *The Hymnal 1982* (New York: Church Hymnal Corp., 1985), #554.

A Rising Church for a Risen Christ

On February 24, 1993, All Saints' Episcopal Church, located in the Ravenswood neighborhood of Chicago, handed out bags of groceries to about twenty people. From this small beginning on that cold winter night has grown a vibrant ministry that brings together members of the congregation, hungry neighbors, and volunteers from the neighborhood and beyond. Every week, a delicious hot meal is served for 120 or more people; neighbors and volunteers share stories and laugh and cry; and between 250 and 350 bags of groceries are distributed. Several times a year, the parish hall is transformed into an elegant four-star restaurant with waiters serving gourmet meals to hungry neighbors seated at beautifully decorated tables as live music plays in the background. Each year, they serve five to seven thousand hot meals and host eighteen to twenty thousand visitors to their pantry.[2]

As outreach ministry has grown, so too has the congregation. By 1992, membership and giving had dwindled to the point that the bishop decided to close the church. But when he met with the congregation to communicate that decision, the dedication and commitment he found convinced him instead to invite them to be reborn. From that meeting came a motto — "a rising church for a risen Christ" — and an image — a phoenix rising from the ashes. The bishop appointed a congregational development vicar. Today, over two hundred people worship at one of three services celebrated each Sunday, a non-profit organization administers the pantry and community kitchen, the parish has vibrant links with congregations in South Sudan and Mexico, and they continue a long-term commitment, begun after Hurricane Katrina in 2005, to rebuilding homes and restoring wetlands in New Orleans and coastal Louisiana.[3]

Worship has been integral to this renewal. As a congregation of the Episcopal Church, All Saints' celebrates the Eucharist each Sunday. They use the 1979 *Book of Common Prayer,* along with the officially authorized hymnal and other supplemental resources. Within this framework of the tradition,

---

2. All Saints' Episcopal Church, "Outreach in Our Community," available at http://www.allsaintschicago.org/outreach/outreach-in-our-community; Ravenswood Community Services, "Our Programs," available at http://www.ravenswoodcommunityservices.org/programs.

3. All Saints' Episcopal Church, available at http://www.allsaintschicago.org/.

All Saints' has developed a dynamic liturgy that is at the heart of their congregational life.

Sit down with a member of All Saints' for a conversation about their worship. She is likely to tell you that worship is fun, that they don't take themselves too seriously. She may tell you that worship connects them as a community or brings them closer to God. For one person, the Eucharistic prayer with its recitation of salvation history is especially meaningful. For another, the highlight is powerful preaching that calls the faithful to action. At some point in the conversation, she will probably begin talking about their pantry. Although outreach is seldom an explicit focus of the Sunday liturgy, it seems that members of All Saints' cannot think of worship without also considering their service in the world. As one member explained, "The engine that drives All Saints', but . . . doesn't come across in worship, . . . is our outreach."

What is it about worship, or outreach, or All Saints', that links worship and outreach for so many? How do other Christians understand the relation between worship and ministry in the world? That is, how do they understand the relation between worship and mission? Are these distinct spheres of Christian faith and life, or is there an intrinsic connection? All Saints' was one of the congregations I studied, and my conversations with members of the parish helped shape my understanding of missional worship.

Worship That Is Mission

In the workshops and classes that I have offered on the subject of missional worship, participants frequently asked, "How can I make my church's worship missional?" As I listened to these questions and probed more deeply, I realized that many people were asking about techniques. During the 1950s and 1960s, a grassroots liturgical renewal movement in several churches advocated specific worship practices in order to foster active participation in worship. In a liturgical-movement parish in the Episcopal Church, the altar would be moved away from the wall so that the priest could face the people when presiding at Holy Communion, a layperson rather than a priest would read the epistle at the communion service, the congregation would join in saying prayers usually said by the priest alone, gospel and offertory processions enhanced the celebration, and the bread would be "real" bread rather than wafers. In the context of my presentations about mission and worship, people seemed to be asking, "What specific worship techniques would characterize missional worship?"

As I struggled to answer the question, I began to realize that it is the wrong question. Missional worship is not about particular techniques but about an approach to worship and to Christian faith and witness in the world. In missional worship, the assembly understands its identity as a lively Christian community, staying in dialogue with its contemporary context while also drawing deeply from the well of tradition, confident in the enlivening power of the Spirit, proclaiming and celebrating the reign of God. Missional worship takes place in a missional congregation, one that is "shaped by participation in God's mission" and which "lets God's mission permeate everything that the congregation does — from worship to witness to training members for discipleship."[4]

A community's identity is thus key to both its public worship and its public works of justice and mercy, as Christian Scharen discovered in a 2004 study of three congregations located in downtown Atlanta, Georgia. Scharen rejects a linear model that claims that worship forms Christians who then embody their Christian commitment in works of justice and mercy in the world. Rather, Scharen concludes that people join a church "because they feel a fit between their vision of church and the vision embodied in the congregation's communal identity," worship embodies the congregation's identity and so deepens commitment, and that commitment is expressed in participation in public works that draw upon the gifts and skills of the congregation's members.[5] Although Scharen does not describe public works as missional, his understanding of the crucial role of identity lends support to an understanding that missional worship is not a matter of specific techniques but rather an approach to both worship and public work that is shaped by participation in God's mission. A congregation's missional identity is expressed and deepened in its public worship and its public works.

4. Lois Y. Barrett et al., *Treasure in Clay Jars: Patterns in Missional Faithfulness* (Grand Rapids: Wm. B. Eerdmans, 2004), p. x.

5. Christian Scharen, *Public Worship and Public Work: Character and Commitment in Local Congregational Life* (Collegeville, Minn.: Pueblo Books, 2004), pp. 221-26; quotation on p. 222.

Before exploring models for imagining the relationship between worship and mission, I want to examine contemporary understandings of "mission" and the relatively new term "missional" as well as the meaning of "worship" and a related term, "liturgy."

What Is Mission? What Does "Missional" Mean?

The word "mission" is derived from a Latin word meaning "to send." Not solely a religious term, it can refer more generally to a task or responsibility or function that a person undertakes. It is usually associated with a particularly significant calling. Businesses as well as churches today may develop a "mission statement" that spells out their core understanding of their identity and purpose.

Mission as a program of the church. Some Christians today understand mission as an activity of the church, bringing the gospel to the unchurched, whether through direct proclamation and efforts to grow the church, or by establishing social services such as hospitals and schools. In some traditions, mission is undertaken primarily to save souls, and the work of a missionary centers on preaching the gospel, making disciples (Matt. 28:19), and planting churches. Other churches understand mission as care for those in need, sometimes referring to their work as "outreach," in the belief that these acts of mercy will also lead unbelievers to faith. For these churches, Jesus' command to care for "the least of these" (Matt. 25:40, 45) is central to the gospel.

Whatever the approach, mission is carried out in response to the gospel. Missionaries, lay or ordained, travel, often to distant lands, to carry out their activities on behalf of a sending church. I recently heard a missionary speak about her work in Brazil. Trained as a nurse in England, she had gone to Brazil to work in a favela (a slum or shantytown). Her ministry there had included both nursing and more direct evangelizing — that is, both making disciples and caring for "the least of these." During the eight years she spent in Brazil, she met and married a Brazilian. Together, they had returned to England and were pursuing further education in preparation for missionary work in Africa.

Missionary activity such as this in recent centuries has resulted in the growth of Christianity around the globe to such an extent that the majority of Christians today live in Africa, Latin America, and Asia. If we understand mission as a response to Jesus' command to "make disciples of all nations" (Matt. 28:19), the missionary efforts of recent centuries have been wildly successful. The gospel has been proclaimed "to the ends of the earth" (Acts 1:8), women and men who had never heard the good news have responded enthusiastically, and Christianity is thriving in many places.

However, the model of missionary activity underlying this remarkable growth had significant flaws, despite the best intentions of missionaries and churches. Missionaries representing the dominant culture were sent to foreign lands, often accompanying social and political efforts to colonize those places. The missionaries brought with them not only the gospel but also their cultural norms, and all too often the gospel they proclaimed was bound up with those cultural values and expectations. In a study of historical models of mission, Stephen Bevans and Roger Schroeder offer a sympathetic description of this approach:

> Missionaries often found themselves in close relationship with colonialism and imperialism, which usually but not always . . . implied dependence and collaboration. The pervading spirit of manifest destiny and religious fervor instilled within them a desire to promote their culture and religion, a sense of responsibility for other peoples, a willingness to sacrifice and to trust, and a hope fueled by enthusiastic optimism. . . . In this way, proclamation and social "advancement," Christianity and "civilization," often went hand in hand. . . . Later generations would criticize them for their paternalism, superiority complex, and collaboration with imperialism, but *one should not overlook their dedication and sacrifice in proclaiming the gospel in the way that made sense to them as children of their time.*[6]

Bevans and Schroeder maintain that this attitude of missionary dominance and corresponding dependence shifted over the course of the twentieth century to one in which Christianity is "one religion among others in a pluralistic world."[7] While Christianity in the early twenty-first century is flourishing in many non-Western places, churches in Western countries are declining

---

6. Stephen B. Bevans and Roger P. Schroeder, *Constants in Context: A Theology of Mission for Today* (Maryknoll, N.Y.: Orbis Books, 2004), p. 221; emphasis added.

7. Bevans and Schroeder, *Constants in Context,* p. 242.

in membership and levels of participation, and their context in Europe and North America is described as post-Christian or post-Christendom. Christians in these countries are increasingly recognizing that if there is a mission field where the gospel is to be proclaimed, it is located not just in some distant land, but in their own neighborhood.

Accompanying the global growth of Christianity and the emergence of post-Christendom in the West has been a resurgence of theological reflection on mission. At the Brandenburg Mission Conference in 1932, Karl Barth argued that mission should not be understood "as a human activity of witness and service." Instead, Barth proposed, it is "primarily *God* who engages in mission by sending God's self in the mission of the Son and the Spirit."[8] This concept has come to be understood as *missio Dei* (the mission of God), and it has become widely embraced by Christians in many different church contexts.

Mission as the church's participation in the mission of God. Rather than approaching mission as a program, perhaps one of several programs of the church, contemporary theologians understand mission as rooted in God's identity and purpose, God's love for the world and God's desire to restore all things to unity. God is a missionary God, one who calls and sends people to participate in the divine mission. From this standpoint, the church does not have a mission, but rather God's mission has a church — that is, the church serves God's mission.

Reconceiving mission from the perspective of God's mission draws upon a dynamic understanding of the Trinity.[9] God is a communion of persons revealed in the sending of the Son and the sending of the Spirit. In Jesus and in the Spirit, Christians experience God's saving action, God's love for the world, and the church is drawn into this saving action. Catherine Mowry LaCugna explains: "Ecclesial life is a way of living in anticipation of the coming reign of God. . . . The mission, the 'being sent forth' of every Christian, is the same as the mission of Christ and the Spirit, to do the will and work of God, to proclaim the good news of salvation, to bring peace and concord, to justify hope in the final return of all things to God."[10]

---

8. Karl Barth, quoted in Bevans and Schroeder, *Constants in Context*, p. 290.

9. Bevans and Schroeder, *Constants in Context*, pp. 291-92.

10. Catherine Mowry LaCugna, *God for Us: The Trinity and Christian Life* (San Francisco: HarperSanFrancisco, 1991), pp. 401-2.

An early proponent of a Trinitarian foundation for mission was Lesslie Newbigin, a British missionary who served in India beginning in the mid-1930s and eventually became a bishop in the newly formed Church of South India. Drawing on his experience proclaiming the gospel in a largely non-Christian context, Newbigin argued that the Trinity is the necessary starting point for preaching to non-Christians: "One cannot preach Jesus even in the simplest terms without preaching him as the Son. His revelation of God is the revelation of 'an only begotten from the Father,' and you cannot preach him without speaking of the Father and the Son." An evangelist who is sensitive to those who hear the message will recognize that the Spirit has already been at work, preparing them to receive the gospel, and that same Spirit will continue to work in their lives after the evangelist departs.[11] Newbigin encouraged his readers to recognize that the mission therefore is God's:

> We are not engaged in an enterprise of our own choosing or devising. We are invited to participate in an activity of God which is the central meaning of creation itself. We are invited to become, through the presence of the Holy Spirit, participants in the Son's loving obedience to the Father. All things have been created that they may be summed up in Christ the Son. All history is directed towards that end. All creation has this as its goal. The Spirit of God, who is also the Spirit of the Son, is given as the foretaste of that consummation, as the witness to it, and as the guide of the Church on the road toward it.[12]

Upon his return to England in the 1970s, Newbigin began to challenge churches to recognize their emerging post-Christendom context and attend to the missionary encounter of the gospel with their culture. "Newbigin brought into public discussion a theological consensus that had long been forming among missiologists and theologians. He then focused that consensus on the concrete reality of Western society, as it [had] taken shape in [the twentieth] century."[13]

11. Lesslie Newbigin, *Trinitarian Faith and Today's Mission* (Richmond, Va.: John Knox Press, 1964), pp. 33-34.

12. Newbigin, *Trinitarian Faith and Today's Mission,* p. 78.

13. *Missional Church: A Vision for the Sending of the Church in North America,* ed. Darrell L. Guder (Grand Rapids: Wm. B. Eerdmans, 1998), p. 3.

The reflection on gospel and culture that Newbigin spurred in Great Britain was taken up by missiologists in the United States, leading to the emergence of the Gospel and Our Culture Network. In the 1990s, six leaders in that network collaborated on a study of mission in the post-Christendom context of North America. *Missional Church: A Vision for the Sending of the Church in North America* sets out an ecclesiology rooted in an understanding of *missio Dei*. In the introduction the authors explain, "Bishop Newbigin and others have helped us to see that God's mission is calling and sending us, the church of Jesus Christ, to be a missionary church in our own societies, in the cultures in which we find ourselves."[14]

To underscore the distinctiveness of this approach to mission — that is, mission rooted in the Trinitarian nature of God and as a matter of identity rather than an activity or program of the church — the authors introduced the term "missional." Since the publication of *Missional Church,* the term has come into widespread use, although it is not always employed in the same way, as another leader of the Gospel in Our Culture Network, Craig Van Gelder, noted in 2007:

> It is clear that confusion still exists over what the term *missional* really means. Some appear to want to use it to reclaim . . . the priority of missions in regard to the church's various activities. . . . The concept of a church being *missional* moves in a fundamentally different direction. It seeks to focus the conversation about what the church *is* — that it is a community created by the Spirit and that it has a unique nature, or essence, which gives it a unique identity. In light of the church's nature, the missional conversation then explores what the church *does.*[15]

Like Newbigin and like his colleagues in the Gospel in Our Culture Network, Van Gelder understands mission as God's reconciling work in the world, in which the church participates.

Rooted in a Trinitarian theology of God's mission, sending the Son and sending the Spirit, the missional understanding developed by Van Gelder

---

14. *Missional Church,* ed. Guder, p. 5.

15. Craig Van Gelder, *The Ministry of the Missional Church: A Community Led by the Spirit* (Grand Rapids: Baker, 2007), pp. 16-17.

and his colleagues links this Trinitarian understanding to the redemptive reign of God. In his person and his ministry, Jesus announced and inaugurated the presence of the reign of God, and Jesus' life, death, and resurrection now offer to all creation the possibility of being reconciled to God. Though the redemptive reign of God is not complete, the Spirit moves all things to their eschatological fullness, God's final consummation. Led by the Spirit, the missional church represents or bears witness to the reign of God that was manifest in Christ, as Newbigin explained:

> The church represents the presence of the reign of God in the life of the world, not in the triumphalist sense (as the "successful" cause) and not in the moralistic sense (as the "righteous" cause), but in the sense that it is the place where the mystery of the kingdom present in the dying and rising of Jesus is made present here and now so that all people, righteous and unrighteous, are enabled to taste and share the love of God before whom all are unrighteous and all are accepted as righteous.[16]

From Newbigin's perspective, proclamation of the reign of God has concrete implications for ministry. Christians enact God's reign in actions of justice and mercy and so offer a glimpse of God's love for all humanity.

Stephen Bevans and Roger Schroeder treat "liberating service of the reign of God" and "participation in the mission of the triune God" as distinct strains in contemporary missiology. To these, they add "proclamation of Jesus Christ as universal Savior," noting that this approach to mission is particularly strong in contemporary evangelical and Pentecostal theology. Pointing out strengths as well as limitations in each strain of missiological thought, Bevans and Schroeder propose a synthesis of these strains in what they term "prophetic dialogue":

> We believe that this rebirth in Christian mission commitment — with its elements of trinitarian vision, focus on the justice of God's reign, and witness to the uniqueness of Jesus Christ — might be best characterized in this new century as a commitment to prophetic dialogue. It must be *pro-*

---

16. Lesslie Newbigin, *The Open Secret: An Introduction to the Theology of Mission,* revised ed. (Grand Rapids: Wm. B. Eerdmans, 1995), p. 54.

phetic because the Church is obligated to preach always and everywhere, "in season and out of season" (2 Tim. 4:2), the fullness of the gospel in all its integrity. And it must be *dialogue* because of the imperative — rooted in the gospel itself — to preach the one faith in a particular *context.* Without dialogue, without a willingness to "let go" before one "speaks out," mission is simply not possible.[17]

Bevans and Schroeder identify six components of mission as prophetic dialogue: "(1) witness and proclamation; (2) liturgy, prayer, and contemplation; (3) commitment to justice, peace, and the integrity of creation; (4) the practice of interreligious dialogue; (5) efforts of inculturation; and (6) the ministry of reconciliation."[18] Though distinct from one another, these activities are also interrelated dimensions of the one mission, the mission of God in which the church participates.

What Is Worship?

Worship, writes Anglican theologian Evelyn Underhill, "is the response of the creature to the Eternal." She continues, "Worship is an acknowledgment of transcendence; that is to say, of a reality independent of the worshiper, which is always more or less deeply colored by mystery, and which is there first."[19] Underhill defines worship expansively, not even limiting it to human activity: "There is a sense in which we may think of the whole life of the Universe, seen and unseen, conscious and unconscious, as an act of worship, glorifying its Origin, Sustainer, and End."[20]

While Underhill offers a theological definition of worship, the original Old English word "worth-ship" meant more generally the act of giving worth or honor. It was not always used in reference to the divine. So, for example, in the sixteenth-century English marriage service, the groom's words when placing the ring on his bride's finger included "With my body, I thee wor-

17. Bevans and Schroeder, *Constants in Context,* p. 350.

18. Bevans and Schroeder, *Constants in Context,* p. 351.

19. Evelyn Underhill, *Worship* (London: James Nisbet & Company, 1936; reprint ed., New York: Crossroad, 1982), p. 3.

20. Underhill, *Worship,* p. 3.

ship."[21] To worship was to hold a person in high esteem and give honor to that person. Gradually, though, the proper object of worship came to be understood as God, and worshiping another person or thing is now commonly seen as a form of idolatry.

Worship can nonetheless be understood broadly, taking many forms and occurring in many places. It may be a response to a particular experience of the holy, perhaps a simple "thank you" in response to an awareness of God at work in our lives or a stunned silence as the awesomeness of God surrounds us in a holy moment. It is also a bodily activity. "O come, let us worship and bow down, let us kneel before the LORD, our Maker," says the psalmist (Ps. 95:6). In many religions, worshipers respond to the divine by bowing or kneeling, prostrating themselves or standing with upraised hands. In the New Testament, the Greek verb *proskynein,* which means "to bow down in homage or submission," is used in Matthew to refer to the actions of the women and the disciples when they encounter the risen Jesus (Matt. 28:9, 17) and in Revelation to describe the response to God and to the Lamb (e.g., Rev. 4:10; 5:14; 7:11; 11:16).[22]

Paul uses a different verb, *latreuein,* meaning "to serve," in his letter to the community in Rome: "I appeal to you therefore, brothers and sisters, by the mercies of God, to present your bodies as a living sacrifice, holy and acceptable to God, which is your spiritual worship" (Rom. 12:1). Yet this worship, too, is a bodily self-offering, presenting our whole selves to God, expressing our obedience to God through our relationships and actions in the world. Reflecting on this passage in the context of Romans 12–15, David Peterson concludes, "Acceptable worship involves effective ministry to one another within the body of Christ, love and forgiveness toward those outside the Christian community, right relationships with ruling authorities, living expectantly in the light of Christ's imminent return, and expressing love especially towards those with different opinions within the congregation of Christ's people."[23]

---

21. "Of Matrimony," *The Book of Common Prayer* 1549, available at http://justus.anglican .org/resources/bcp/1549/Marriage_1549.htm.

22. David Peterson, "Worship in the New Testament," in *Worship: Adoration and Action,* ed. D. A. Carson (Grand Rapids: Baker, 1993), pp. 52-53. Peterson also refers to other uses of *proskynein* in both the Old Testament and the New Testament.

23. Peterson, "Worship in the New Testament," pp. 69-70.

In this sense, all of life is worship, our self-offering in response to God's reconciling love — that is, God's mission in the world. Not only is worship missional, but mission is worshipful, a way in which we honor and glorify God. Hebrews 12 says, "Through Christ, then, let us continually offer a sacrifice of praise to God, that is, the fruit of lips that confess his name. Do not neglect to do good and to share what you have, for such sacrifices are pleasing to God" (Heb. 12:15-16). Reflecting on this passage, Miroslav Volf comments, "Christian worship consists both in obedient service to God and in the joyful praise of God."[24] Our offering of praise is integrally related to our offering of good works, all giving glory to God.

Underhill's definition reminds us that worship is always a response to God's initiative. We experience the divine as wholly other, an awesome mystery glimpsed, for example, in the beauty of a sunset or the embrace of a loved one, or in an overwhelming sense of presence that cannot be rationally explained. Christians believe that God is also revealed in the history of salvation — in particular, in creation, in the story of the people of Israel, in the incarnation, death, and resurrection of Jesus, and in the sending of the Holy Spirit. In worship, we remember what God has done for us, and by retelling our story, we are drawn together as the people of God. Worship is thus linked to mission, because in worship we encounter and respond to the Triune God, revealed in the sending of Jesus and the sending of the Spirit, and in worship we proclaim this good news of God's reign.

Miroslav Volf proposes that worship comprises both adoration, "words and symbolic actions that are directed to God," and action, "deeds directed toward the world." Adoration, Volf asserts, "is the well-spring of action." By praising God's work in creation and redemption, we align ourselves with God's character and purposes. Then, in action in the world, we cooperate with God, "working together" with God in God's field, God's building (1 Cor. 3:9). "Christian action in the world," says Volf, "leads to adoration of God. Action establishes conditions in which adoration of God surges out of the human heart."[25] We can think of this interplay of adoration and action as

---

24. Miroslav Volf, "Worship as Adoration and Action: Reflections on a Christian Way of Being-in-the-World," in *Worship: Adoration and Action,* ed. D. A. Carson (Grand Rapids: Baker, 1993), pp. 210-11.

25. Volf, "Worship as Adoration and Action," pp. 210-11.

missional worship and worshipful mission, all of it participation in God's mission of reconciling love.

Although we can understand all of life as worship, as our response to God and all that God has done and is doing in our lives, Christians usually think of worship as an activity in which the people of God participate at a fixed time each week, usually on Sunday, the Lord's Day. That is the primary sense in which I am using the term in this book.

Some Christians use a related term, "liturgy," to speak about their worship. In some traditions, this term has negative connotations, implying rituals performed by rote that constrain worshipers' free response to God. Yet every form of public worship has some structure: people gather, they undertake some activity in response to God (usually including praise and thanksgiving, proclamation, and prayer), and they go forth. Even in traditions that understand themselves as free churches, worship tends to follow a similar pattern from week to week.

We can understand liturgy as the structured body of texts and actions by which people worship God. Reformed theologian James Smith explains, "All Christian worship is liturgical in the sense that it is governed by norms, draws on a tradition, includes bodily rituals or routines, and involves formative practices."[26] In this sense, "liturgy" can refer to a particular form — for example, a communion liturgy — or the worship forms of a particular church — for example, Lutheran liturgy. However, a study of the origins of the term "liturgy" offers a much richer understanding, and it is to this that I now turn.

What Is Liturgy?

"Liturgy" is derived from the Greek word *leitourgia,* and many contemporary books and articles explain its meaning as "the work of the people." But *leitourgia* is formed not directly from *laos,* "people," but from *leitos,* which means "concerning the people or national community" — that is, "the public" or "the body politic." In the ancient Greek world, it was a technical political

---

26. James K. A. Smith, *Desiring the Kingdom: Worship, Worldview, and Cultural Formation* (Grand Rapids: Baker Academic, 2009), p. 152.

term used for services rendered for the body politic. One might build a road or an aqueduct, or supply equipment for the armed forces. Required by law to perform these "liturgies," some citizens did so grudgingly, while others offered their services freely and willingly. Gradually the term came to be used more generally for an act done in the service of another, not necessarily for the body politic (the *leitos*). It also began to be used to speak of service to the gods — that is, worship. When the Hebrew Scriptures were translated into Greek, *leitourgia* (as well as the cognate verb *leitourgein*) was used almost exclusively for the worship of God performed by the priests and Levites in the tabernacle or the temple; it was never used for service to another person. While the older political use disappeared entirely, it likely underlies the decision of the translators of the Hebrew Scriptures to use *leitourgia*. The service rendered by the priests and Levites was offered to God for the common good.[27]

The New Testament use of *leitourgia* builds on this earlier usage in several ways, although the word and its cognates appear infrequently, and translators often choose a word other than "liturgy" to translate the Greek term into English. "Service" is evident in Paul's use of the term in reference to his collection for the church in Jerusalem (Rom. 15:27; 2 Cor. 9:12). Perhaps Paul had in mind the older Greek usage of a work for the common good, since the collection is intended for the community. But Paul also uses *leitourgia* to speak of service to himself, explaining in his letter to the Philippians that Epaphroditus had risked his life to bring Paul the gift that the Philippians could not (Phil. 2:30).[28]

Leitourgia and its cognates appear several times in Hebrews as the author contrasts the ongoing service of the priests in the temple with Jesus' self-offering. Jesus has attained a "more excellent liturgy" (Heb. 8:6; a phrase frequently translated as "more excellent ministry"), of which he himself is the "liturgist" (*leitourgos;* Heb. 8:2). With the fulfillment of the priestly ministry — that is, the liturgy — in Christ, Christians can now enter confidently into the sanctuary by the blood of Jesus (Heb. 10:19). No longer needing priests, the new community itself is a priesthood (1 Peter 2:9). By offering sacrifices

---

27. H. Strathmann, *"Leitourgeō, leitourgia, leitourgos, leitourgikos,"* in *Theological Dictionary of the New Testament,* Vol. IV, ed. Gerhard Kittel, ed. and trans. Geoffrey W. Bromiley (Grand Rapids: Wm. B. Eerdmans, 1967), pp. 215-22.

28. Strathmann, *"Leitourgeō, leitourgia, leitourgos, leitourgikos,"* p. 227.

of praise and sacrifices of good works (Heb. 13:15-16), Christians join with Christ in mission.

A new, more spiritualized meaning of "liturgy" also begins to emerge in the New Testament. Writing to the Philippians (Phil. 2:17), Paul connects *leitourgia* with *thusia,* "sacrifice." The passage can be translated in different ways, referring to the faith of the Philippians as a sacrifice offered to God, a sacrifice to which Paul will add through his martyrdom, or to Paul's missionary work as a service offered to establish the faith of the Philippians.[29] In his letter to the Romans, Paul describes himself as a "liturgist" (*leitourgos,* usually translated as "minister" or "servant") to the Gentiles, performing a "priestly service of the gospel" in which the Gentiles are an offering to God, accomplished through Christ (Rom. 15:16). Here, the language of priestly service in the temple is applied to the proclamation of the gospel.[30] In each of these uses, "liturgy" refers to Christian work in the world, joining in God's mission of reconciliation.

A more explicit use of "liturgy" in reference to a gathering for worship appears in Acts 13:2. A group of prophets and teachers at Antioch are engaged in a "liturgy" (*leitourgounton,* translated variously as "worshiping" or "serving"), resulting in a missionary call that sends Barnabas and Saul on a journey.[31] Here, "liturgy" leads to mission, sending apostles to preach the good news.

A gradual shift occurred during the early centuries of Christianity. Christian writers used *leitourgia* and the verb *leitourgein* to speak of service, whether rendered to God or to the community. But gradually the concept of priesthood from the Hebrew Scriptures came to be transferred to Christian clergy, and increasingly the term came to refer to the action of worship, particularly the Eucharist. In Eastern Orthodox churches, "Divine Liturgy" became a common term for the Eucharist, while in Western Christianity, the term fell out of common use until the twentieth century.

---

29. Strathmann, *"Leitourgeō, leitourgia, leitourgos, leitourgikos,"* p. 227. For different interpretations of the verse, compare "Your faith in the Lord and your service are like a sacrifice offered to him. And my own blood may have to be poured out with the sacrifice" (Phil. 2:17, CEV); "even if I am poured out like a drink offering upon the altar of service for your faith, I am glad" (Phil. 2:17, CEB).

30. Strathmann, *"Leitourgeō, leitourgia, leitourgos, leitourgikos,"* p. 230.

31. Strathmann, *"Leitourgeō, leitourgia, leitourgos, leitourgikos,"* p. 228.

In the twentieth century, leaders of the liturgical renewal movement that swept through many Western Christian churches revived the use of the word "liturgy." Virgil Michel, an early Roman Catholic leader of the liturgical movement in the United States, explained it in this way: "The word *liturgy* according to its etymology means a public work or service."[32] Many leaders of the liturgical movement took note of this original Greek meaning of the term "liturgy." But the phrase that took hold in popular imagination, and continues to be widely repeated, is "the work of the people." Massey Shepherd, the leading liturgical scholar in the Episcopal Church in the 1950s and 1960s, emphasized that the entire congregation, not just the ministers, participate in liturgy: "[Liturgy] is literally the 'work of the people' in their common life of prayer. It involves a responsible and active participation by all the worshippers, the congregation no less than the ministers."[33] Shepherd, like Michel and many others, does discuss the root meaning of "liturgy" as "public service." But this concept has not entered the popular imagination as a way to understand liturgy. Many books and articles to this day continue to repeat the rallying cry of the liturgical movement, which Shepherd himself used: "Liturgy is the work of the people!" In my seminary classes and in workshops for laity and clergy alike, when I ask participants what "liturgy" is, the response comes, "The work of the people."

Explaining liturgy as the people's work, an activity that by its very nature demands the active participation of all the faithful, was an important insight at a time when many Christians in different worshiping traditions, lay and ordained, approached worship as the job of a few vested leaders for a largely passive spectator congregation. Eventually, this concept was incorporated into official formularies. The 1979 *Book of Common Prayer* of the Episcopal Church directs, "In all services, *the entire Christian assembly participates* in such a way that the members of each order within the Church, lay persons, bishops, priests, and deacons, fulfill the functions proper to their respective orders, as set forth in the rubrical directions for each service."[34] In the Roman

32. Virgil Michel, *The Liturgy of the Church, According to the Roman Rite* (New York: Macmillan, 1937), p. 1.

33. Massey H. Shepherd, *The Worship of the Church* (Greenwich, Conn.: Seabury Press, 1952), p. 49.

34. *The Book of Common Prayer and Administration of the Sacraments and Other Rites*

Catholic Church, the 1963 *Constitution on the Sacred Liturgy* of the Second Vatican Council urged that "all the faithful should be led to that fully conscious and active participation in liturgical celebrations which is demanded by the very nature of the liturgy."[35]

Understanding that liturgy requires every Christian to participate fully is an important insight for missional theology. Just as worship services are not the work of a few leaders on behalf of the entire congregation, so also participation in God's mission in the world is the responsibility of every Christian.

However, it is time to retire the definition of liturgy as "the work of the people."

The phrase "the work of the people" emphasizes the people who gather, those who proclaim and respond to the Word and offer intercession, the assembly that celebrates a holy meal. By not also turning our attention beyond ourselves to the need of the world for God's reconciling love, continuing to think of liturgy as "the work of the people" impoverishes our celebrations. In this book, when I use the term "liturgy," I have in mind *both* the structured ritual activity that involves texts and actions, using symbols, speech, song, and silence, *and* the assembly's work for the common good, its public service as a gathered community and as the people of God in the world. Liturgy as work for the common good is thus a form of participation in the mission of God.

Both "liturgy" and "worship" can be understood in relation to mission. I turn now to two models that relate mission and worship more explicitly.

Model One: Worship and Mission: Closing the Loop

Lutheran liturgical scholar Thomas Schattauer identifies several approaches to the relationship of public worship and mission. We can view worship and mission as *separate spheres* of action, worship taking place inside the church, and mission occurring in the world outside the church. When instead wor-

---

and Ceremonies of the Church, Together with The Psalter or Psalms of David (New York: Church Hymnal Corp., 1979), p. 13; emphasis added.

35. *Constitution on the Sacred Liturgy (Sacrosanctum Concilium)*, par. 14 (4 December 1963), available at http://www.vatican.va/archive/hist_councils/ii_vatican_council/documents/vat-ii_const_19631204_sacrosanctum-concilium_en.html.

ship is used as an instrument of mission, Schattauer explains, worship can be a form of *evangelism,* used to present the gospel to those who do not know Christ, or it can be a platform from which to *call people to action in the world,* whether service or social or political action. Finally, Schattauer says, we can understand *worship as mission,* enacting and signifying God's mission for the life of the world.[36]

As I pondered these approaches, I discovered a simple visual aid to understanding these different possible relationships of mission and worship.[37] This aid requires only a blank, letter-sized sheet of paper and a pen or pencil and a piece of tape, if desired, to preserve the work. Cut or tear a half-inch strip down the long side of the piece of paper. On one side of the strip of paper, write the phrase "public worship." On the other side, write "mission."

Worship and mission as separate spheres of action. Hold the strip of paper in front of you, one end in each hand, with the phrase "public worship" facing you and "mission" facing away. Imagine that each side stretches as far as you can see, and you will get a sense of what Schattauer calls a "conventional" approach to the relationship. The strip of paper separates these different activities. Worship is what we the church do inside; it nourishes and strengthens us for the mission we engage in outside the church doors. Schattauer explains this approach: "Worship serves the purpose of mission, not because it directly accomplishes the tasks of evangelical proclamation and diaconal service but because it offers access to the means of grace that propel the individual and the community as a whole into such activity. Worship and mission, however, remain distinct activities within clearly demarcated spheres of the church's life."[38]

Many Christians understand worship in this way. They "go to church" in order to be formed as Christians and empowered for their service in the world. For some, this is primarily an individual experience, a personal encounter with God that infuses the worshiper with the grace, mercy, and love of God and gives them the strength to carry out their daily activities.

36. Thomas H. Schattauer, "Liturgical Assembly as Locus of Mission," in *Inside Out: Worship in an Age of Mission,* ed. Thomas H. Schattauer (Minneapolis: Fortress Press, 1999), pp. 1-3.

37. Parker Palmer, "Finding Your Soul," *Spirituality and Health,* September/October 2004, pp. 38-43.

38. Schattauer, "Liturgical Assembly as Locus of Mission," p. 2.

Others emphasize the communal dimension, understanding liturgy as "the work of the people" that builds up the Christian community and sends the assembly into action in the world. *The Use of the Means of Grace,* a 1997 statement on the practice of Word and sacrament by the Evangelical Lutheran Church in America, declares, "In every gathering of Christians around the proclaimed Word and the holy sacraments, God acts to empower the Church for mission."[39]

Understood in this way, the worship undertaken within the church is vital for the mission that takes place in the world. But this is not the only way to understand the relationship.

Worship as evangelism. Take the strip of paper and bring the ends together, putting "public worship" on the outside. In this approach, worship is "a stage from which to present the gospel and reach out to the unchurched and irreligious."[40] Mission, the motivation for worship, which we usually imagine as happening outside the church, is actually at the inside of our circle, while worship is the outward face of the church, drawing people into relationship with Christ. In this approach, mission is viewed as the work of making disciples and so is the driving force for worship. Worship takes the form of seeker services, designed to meet the needs and desires of those outside the church.

The contemporary seeker-service phenomenon was popularized by Willow Creek Community Church, founded in 1975 in the Chicago area. At Willow Creek, worship takes place in a large auditorium, bare of Christian symbols. Services are highly choreographed, using multimedia presentations. Simple lyrics set to rock music are projected on screen, allowing worshipers to join in as they choose. High production values are essential. After opening its primary campus in South Barrington, Illinois, a suburb of Chicago, in 1981, Willow Creek soon began to draw thousands of worshipers each Sunday, and beginning in 2001, the congregation opened six branch campuses in and around Chicago.[41] Visitors began to come to Willow Creek from

39. Evangelical Lutheran Church in America, *The Use of the Means of Grace: A Statement on the Practice of Word and Sacrament* (Minneapolis: Augsburg Fortress Press, 1997), Principle 51, p. 56.

40. Schattauer, "Liturgical Assembly as Locus of Mission," p. 2.

41. A brief history is found on the Willow Creek Web site: "Willow History," available at http://www.willowcreek.org/aboutwillow/willow-whistory.

around the country, eager to learn about their success in creating evangelistic worship.

In a research study that began in 2004, Willow Creek asked how people grow spiritually and what role church activities play in this spiritual growth. The results astonished the leadership. More than 25 percent of the respondents described themselves as "stalled" in their spiritual growth or "dissatisfied" with the church. Those who were dissatisfied tended to be the more spiritually mature, regularly attending worship, participating in small groups, volunteering at church, and maintaining personal spiritual practices such as prayer and Bible study. Sixty-three percent of these dissatisfied members were thinking of leaving the church.[42]

As a result of their study, the Willow Creek leadership decided to change their weekend services to meet the needs of those who were more spiritually mature.[43] Their language is telling: again and again, they write of "meeting needs" and worship having "value."[44] Their concern for making disciples is evident, but their approach views worshipers as consumers and the church, particularly its leadership, as the purveyor of goods, albeit spiritual goods rather than material ones.

Willow Creek did not invent the use of worship as a tool for evangelism. The impulse for such worship was already evident in frontier worship that developed in the United States and its territories during the nineteenth century. "The essential discovery of the frontier churches was a form of worship for the unchurched, a need none of the other traditions had yet dealt with seriously," explains United Methodist scholar James White.[45] As the American frontier moved westward, a significant number of the population were unchurched. Building on the Scottish Presbyterian model of sacramental seasons, ministers began to hold camp meetings that gathered people from miles around for several days of preaching, leading to the baptism of converts and the celebration of the Lord's Supper. In 1801, a camp meeting held at Cane Ridge, Bourbon County, Kentucky,

---

42. Greg L. Hawkins and Cally Parkinson, *Reveal: Where Are You?* (Barrington, Ill.: Willow Creek Association, 2007), pp. 46-47, 50-54.

43. Hawkins and Parkinson, *Reveal*, p. 66.

44. Hawkins and Parkinson, *Reveal*, pp. 64-73.

45. James F. White, *Protestant Worship: Traditions in Transition* (Louisville: Westminster John Knox Press, 1989), p. 171.

drew a crowd estimated between 10,000 and 25,000. White comments, "The extraordinary success of this meeting despite its isolated location . . . guaranteed the continuation of the camp meeting as a form of both mission and worship."[46]

The evangelistic impulse to use worship to reach out to those who do not know Christ or have left the church is commendable. In recent decades, Willow Creek and other megachurches have been highly effective at attracting people to worship. The leaders of Willow Creek and those in churches large and small who have emulated their style of seeker-friendly worship have listened carefully to the contemporary culture and fashioned worship that is accessible and attractive to religious seekers. But as Willow Creek's own research showed, moving people beyond a seeker service to active Christian discipleship and sustaining the commitment of those disciples have proved challenging.

At its best, seeker-friendly worship uses public worship as the church's primary interface with the world. Mission, understood as a commitment to preach the gospel to the ends of the earth, is inside the circle, the driving force for worship. A primary goal of this worship is to bring people from the worship on the outside to become disciples.

Worship as a call to mission. For a different perspective on worship as an instrument of mission, separate the ends of your strip of paper, then re-join them in the opposite way, so that "mission" is now on the outside and "public worship" is inside. In this approach, worship is "a platform from which to issue the call to serve the neighbor and rally commitment for social and political action."[47]

Many congregations employ this approach in preaching that calls the assembly to acts of mercy and justice, or announcements during worship that call attention to action in the world. For some, this call to public work in the world is a predominant theme of worship. The mission statement of Central Presbyterian Church in Atlanta, which describes itself as a congregation "at work in the city of Atlanta," underscores the congregation's commitment to social justice informed and inspired by worship: "We come as to a wellspring, bringing our thirst and emptiness, only to discover that our cup is filled by

46. White, *Protestant Worship*, p. 173.
47. Schattauer, "Liturgical Assembly as Locus of Mission," p. 2.

the living Word, Who sends us to be with those in need and to call forth God's justice in a chaotic world."[48] In a study of the relationship of worship and ethics, Christian Scharen describes worship in this congregation: "The whole progression of the order of service revolves around the Word: first gathering, then proclaiming, then responding to and sealing of the Word, and finally bearing and following the Word into the world."[49] Certainly there is some understanding of worship as an activity separate from mission in the world, but in this congregation and others like it, the worship serves more directly as a call to action. There has been some effort to bring mission and worship together, as we have represented with the ends of our strip of paper joined to form a circle.

As with seeker-friendly worship, using worship to call the assembly to service and social action has its limitations and challenges. Too narrow a political or social agenda can constrict a congregation's vision. A different drawback was becoming evident in one congregation I studied. Their worship employed seeker-friendly elements while also serving as an occasion for outreach groups to promote their ministries and encourage members to participate in social service activities. They were finding, however, that leaders of the different ministries were competing for time and attention during Sunday worship.

These two approaches, worship as evangelism and worship as a call to mission, go some way toward bringing public worship and mission more directly into relationship with each other. Yet simply bringing the two ends of the paper together still leaves worship on one side and mission on the other. The final approach we will explore using our strip of paper brings them into a more integrated and dynamic relationship and so serves as one model for missional worship.

Worship as mission. To envision this relationship of mission and worship, separate the two ends of your ring of paper. On one side (it matters not whether it is the "mission" side or the "public worship" side), write the letters "A" in the top left corner, "B" in the bottom left, "C" in the top right, and "D" in the bottom right. Now hold your strip of paper in two hands, give it a half-

---

48. Central Presbyterian Church, Atlanta, "Mission Statement," available at http://www.cpcatlanta.org/mission.

49. Scharen, *Public Worship and Public Work*, pp. 185-86.

twist, and join the short ends, matching "A" to "D" and "B" to "C."[50] Holding your strip of paper together with the fingers of one hand (or after taping the ends together), put a finger on "public worship" and trace it along the strip. Eventually, you will come to "mission," and as you continue you will return to the word "public worship." The form you have created is a Möbius strip, which has only one side.

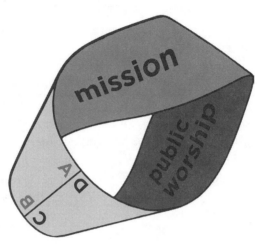

On our Möbius strip, which illustrates one model for the relationship between mission and worship, worship and mission flow into and out of one another, public worship becoming mission, which becomes public worship, which becomes mission, in an ongoing dance. Schattauer explains, "The liturgical assembly is the visible locus of God's reconciling mission toward the world. The seemingly most internal of activities, the church's worship, is ultimately directed outward to the world."[51]

The mission of God is God's movement outward toward the world, a love for the world evident in creation and in covenant with Israel, a passion revealed in the life, death, and resurrection of Jesus. Through the Spirit, God calls together a community whose identity is rooted in the mission of God, a community that participates in God's mission, embodying God's healing,

50. For directions on making a Möbius strip, see "How to Make a Möbius Strip," available at http://www.wikihow.com/Make-a-Mobius-Strip.

51. Schattauer, "Liturgical Assembly as Locus of Mission," p. 3.

reconciling, and saving love for the world, and proclaiming the good news of God's reign.

When worship *is* mission, the assembly embodies and inhabits worship in such a way that ritual texts and patterns come alive, for people today, through speaking and singing, in symbols and actions. Such worship turns outward, for the sake of the world. It is true liturgy, in the deepest sense of the word: work for the common good, a public service. Responding to God's self-offering, the people of God offer praise and proclamation and prayer on behalf of all creation. The 1997 statement of the Evangelical Lutheran Church in America, *The Use of the Means of Grace,* said it this way: "By God's gift, the Word and the sacraments are set in the midst of the world, for the life of the world."[52]

In worship, the people of God come together — assemble — as a community. Far more than a collection of individuals, they gather as a local assembly, in a particular place and at a particular time. Together, they represent the whole people of God, throughout the world and over time. For example, in the Eucharistic prayer, the assembly joins saints and angels and the whole company of heaven in proclaiming God's praise with the song "Holy, Holy, Holy Lord." The assembly's communion with one another manifests the communion they have with God in Jesus Christ and anticipates the fullness of communion that is God's promise, the new creation in which the world is reconciled to God (2 Cor. 5:17-20).

Worship is also a symbolic activity. Always more than what appears on the surface, worship uses basic elements of everyday life — water, bread, wine, oil. Through the purposeful action of the assembly in their encounter with God, these common things reveal the mystery of God. Water, for example, with a power that is both life-giving and death-dealing, recalls the waters of creation over which the Spirit breathed, the waters of the Red Sea through which the Israelites escaped from slavery, and the waters of the Jordan River in which Jesus was baptized. With symbolic language and symbolic acts, the assembly enters and enacts the truth of God's reign. "The church in its assembly around word and sacrament enacts a ritual symbol of God's gracious purpose for the world and so participates in God's world-encompassing mission."[53]

---

52. Evangelical Lutheran Church in America, *The Use of the Means of Grace,* Application 51B, p. 56.

53. Schattauer, "Liturgical Assembly as Locus of Mission," p. 13.

Worship that is mission shapes a people for mission. In acts of praise and thanksgiving, the assembly acknowledges God as the source of life, as one involved in the world, and most especially as the one who sends the Son and the Spirit. Worship thus turns hearts and minds, bodies and souls to God and acknowledges God's abiding love for the world and ultimate sovereignty over the world.

Understanding mission as God's movement toward the world means recognizing that God is at work in the world, even before we do anything. Worship thus engages the local context by drawing upon the language and thought patterns of the local culture, acknowledging and celebrating where God is at work as well as lifting up those places desperately in need of God's healing mercy. Water, bread, wine, and oil, the primary symbols of worship, are the stuff of everyday life, and their use in worship not only can speak vividly in the assembly but also can enable members of the community to make connections between worship and everyday life. Craig Dykstra and Dorothy Bass explain, "We use the familiar elements of everyday life — food, water, oil, embrace, word — to proclaim and celebrate what God is doing in the world and in our lives. Worship distills the Christian meaning of the practices and holds them up for the whole community to see."[54] Receiving the bread of life in the assembly's Eucharist, for example, may enable worshipers to recognize Christ in ordinary meals. "Give us this day our daily bread," we pray, recognizing God's providence in giving daily sustenance.

At All Saints' Church in Chicago, we find examples of all four approaches we have explored using our strip of paper. For some members of the congregation, worship is formative, enabling them to grow as individual Christians and strengthening the community. Although this is suggestive of an approach that separates mission and worship, for most worshipers at All Saints' the connections between worship and mission are more fluid than the clear delineation between worship as an inside activity and mission as an outside activity.

The use of worship as a call to mission is evident in preaching that calls the assembly to acts of mercy and justice, but worship at All Saints' does

54. Craig R. Dykstra and Dorothy C. Bass, "Times of Yearning, Practices of Faith," in *Practicing Our Faith: A Way of Life for a Searching People,* ed. Dorothy C. Bass, 2nd ed. (San Francisco: Jossey-Bass, 1997, 2010), p. 9.

not function primarily to spur mission activity. At times, All Saints' uses worship intentionally for evangelism. For example, an annual pet blessing at the principal Sunday service has brought numerous visitors over the years, some of whom go on to become active members of the congregation.[55] Yet, although there are several such creative liturgies each year with an explicitly evangelical purpose, this strategy is not the primary approach to worship at All Saints'.

What of worship *as* mission, the model of the Möbius strip in which worship is mission is worship . . . ? Certainly there is an inchoate sense among many members of All Saints' that both worship and outreach — that is, mission understood as acts of mercy — are integral to life in this community. Is worship itself a locus of mission, enacting and signifying God's reconciling love for the world? In my interviews with members of All Saints', one worshiper explained that the God she encounters in worship is "very much a part of everything and very willing . . . to be there in all of these different sometimes humorous and sometimes sad and sometimes joyful occasions and ways." Another described her experience in this way: "God is . . . loving, and caring, and present and in the world around us. But I think [our worship is also] more three-dimensional — if you have any thoughts of being angry at God, or struggling with this crazy world we have and what does it mean that there's a God that created this. . . . It definitely feels like there is a place to [struggle with those questions], and that's valued and valid." By manifesting God's fierce love for the world in all its complexities, worship at All Saints' is itself mission, just as the congregation's food pantry and relationship with a congregation in Sudan are also mission. That is, their worship is missional and their mission is worshipful.

Model Two: Missional Worship: A Different Spin

With the simple visual aid of a strip of paper, we have explored different approaches to the relationship of mission and public worship: worship and mission as separate spheres of action; worship as evangelism; worship as a

---

55. All Saints' Episcopal Church, "Special Services," available at http://www.allsaintschicago .org/services/special-services.

call to mission; and worship *as* mission. In each of these approaches, "public worship" and "mission" are treated as equivalent categories, and we have discovered how these two aspects can be brought together, like a Möbius strip, so that worship is mission is worship. . . . However, Bevans's and Schroeder's model of mission encourages us to recognize that the two concepts are not of the same order, two spheres of activity that intersect. Rather, public worship, or liturgy, is a subset of the larger category that is "mission." Building on the work of other contemporary missiologists, Bevans and Schroeder point out that mission is multidimensional.[56]

I find this model a helpful complement to Schattauer's claim that liturgy is a locus of mission. It reminds us that worship is not the only place where mission is enacted — that is, where the church participates in the mission of God. At first I imagined this as a field, a circle, if you will, with different elements within it (witness and proclamation; liturgy; prayer and contemplation; work for justice, peace, and the integrity of creation; interreligious dialogue; efforts of inculturation; and reconciliation). But as I reflected further, I realized that the relationships are more complex. In the *Constitution on the Sacred Liturgy* of the Roman Catholic Church, the Second Vatican Council declared,

> The liturgy is the summit toward which the activity of the Church is directed; at the same time it is the font from which all her power flows. . . . From the liturgy, therefore, and especially from the Eucharist, as from a font, grace is poured forth upon us; and the sanctification of [humanity] in Christ and the glorification of God, to which all other activities of the Church are directed as toward their end, is achieved in the most efficacious possible way.[57]

In other words, public worship has a unique place in the life of the church. In worship, through the forms and structures of liturgy, the church's identity is expressed and shaped.

---

56. Bevans and Schroeder, *Constants in Context,* pp. 350-51.

57. *Constitution on the Sacred Liturgy,* par. 10. I am indebted to my colleague Jon Nilson for reminding me of this statement and helping me grasp its significance for my work on liturgy and mission.

Rather than a circle with different elements, imagine mission as a spinning top, with worship as the axis, surrounded by other dimensions of mission. Here, public worship is at the core of missional life. The dynamic energy of the spinning top flows into and out of this core. Public worship sends us out from the center, into the world, to be God's people in the world. There we are caught up in other aspects of mission. Romanian Orthodox theologian Ion Bria writes of the "liturgy after the liturgy": "liturgy reshapes the social life of Christians with a new emphasis on the sharing of bread, on the healing of brokenness, on reconciliation and on justice in the human community."[58] Then the spinning top draws us back in to the center, shaped by our encounters with the God of Jesus Christ in the world, cognizant of the hurts and hungers of our broken world. We bring with us into worship all of those experiences, offering them to God, singing our praise, discovering anew God's judgment and mercy, seeking healing and forgiveness. As we noted earlier, Miroslav Volf explains that our adoration of God — that is, the assembly's worship — is integrally connected to action in the world, to the other dimensions of mission that Bevans and Schroeder delineate.

As shown in the diagram, in the innermost core of this top are baptism and communion, which constitute the church. Baptism, a gift of God rooted in the ministry of Jesus, incorporates us into the body of Christ and into the mission of God.[59] "We have been buried with Christ by baptism into death," writes Paul to the church in Rome, "so that, just as Christ was raised from the dead by the glory of the Father, so we too might walk in newness of life" (Rom. 6:4). The authors of *Missional Church* underscore the significance of baptism for mission: "The practice of baptism introduces persons into a radically new kind of social relationship; no longer isolated individuals, they have become brothers and sisters adopted into the body of Christ to live a communal life as a sign of God's reign in the midst of

58. Ion Bria, *The Liturgy after the Liturgy: Mission and Witness from an Orthodox Perspective* (Geneva: WCC Publications, 1996), p. 21.

59. "Baptism," par. 1, *Baptism, Eucharist, and Ministry,* Faith and Order Paper No. 111 (Geneva: World Council of Churches, 1982), available at http://www.oikoumene.org/en/resources/documents/wcc-commissions/faith-and-order-commission/i-unity-the-church-and-its-mission/baptism-eucharist-and-ministry-faith-and-order-paper-no-111-the-lima-text?set_language=en.

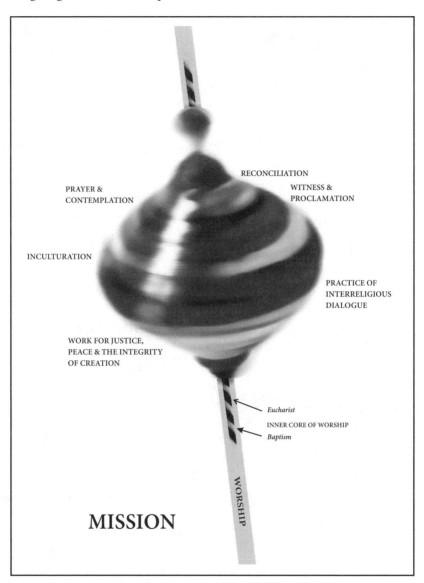

RECONCILIATION

PRAYER &
CONTEMPLATION

WITNESS &
PROCLAMATION

INCULTURATION

PRACTICE OF
INTERRELIGIOUS
DIALOGUE

WORK FOR JUSTICE,
PEACE & THE INTEGRITY
OF CREATION

Eucharist

INNER CORE OF WORSHIP

Baptism

WORSHIP

MISSION

human history."[60] Through the Lord's Supper, Christians are reconstituted as the body into which they were initiated at baptism. "Eternal God, heavenly Father, you have graciously accepted us as living members of your Son, our

60. *Missional Church,* ed. Guder, p. 161.

Savior Jesus Christ," Episcopalians pray after receiving communion.[61] That is, having become members of Christ's body in baptism, in the Eucharist we are once again united with Christ. The ecumenical statement *Baptism, Eucharist, and Ministry* declares unequivocally, "The eucharist embraces all aspects of life." The document continues,

> The eucharistic celebration demands reconciliation and sharing among all those regarded as brothers and sisters in the one family of God and is a constant challenge for appropriate relationships in social, economic, and political life (Matthew 5:23f.; 1 Corinthians 10:16f.; 1 Corinthians 11:20-22; Galatians 3:28). All kinds of injustice, racism, separation, and lack of freedom are radically challenged when we share in the body and blood of Christ.[62]

This dynamic relationship of worship and mission, with Eucharist at the center, sending people out into the world only to gather them once again as the people of God, to feast on the body and blood of Christ, is well illustrated by the practice of the Love Feast in the Church of the Brethren. Gilbert Bond explains that believers will celebrate the Love Feast only when members of the community have been reconciled to one another and to God. Rather than mediating grace, the Love Feast manifests the Christ who is already present in the community. Only members of the community can participate in the feast. It begins with a foot-washing, during which every member of the community has his or her feet washed and washes another's feet. Once feet are washed, the community shares an *agape* meal (the "love feast"), which includes prayer and the reading of Scripture. Finally, participants share the bread and the cup. If members of the community are not reconciled to one another and to God, they do not celebrate the Love Feast.[63] In the Church of the Brethren, the Love Feast enacts and manifests the reconciliation that is God's mission in the world.

Bond relates the experience of a Church of the Brethren community in

---

61. *The Book of Common Prayer* 1979, p. 365.

62. "Eucharist," par. 20, *Baptism, Eucharist, and Ministry.*

63. Gilbert I. Bond, "Liturgy, Ministry, and the Stranger," in *Practicing Theology: Beliefs and Practices in Christian Life,* ed. Miroslav Volf and Dorothy C. Bass (Grand Rapids: Wm. B. Eerdmans, 2002), pp. 145-46.

the midst of an impoverished urban neighborhood in Chicago. Members of the church had attempted to serve their neighbors by distributing food provided by a federal government surplus program. The government requirements, however, created great resentment among the recipients, resulting in conflict with members of the church. So the church made the painful decision to close its food distribution ministry, recognizing that the ministry, though well-intentioned, distorted its relationships with those in need. Eventually, recognizing the need for reconciliation with their neighbors, they contacted some of those who had once lined up for government surplus food and invited them to a meal. That event, over time, led to members of the church and neighbors preparing meals for one another and praying together. Then neighborhood children began coming to church. Bond summarizes the intersection of mission and worship in this challenging work: "If we carried the logic of our most powerful, liturgical enactments to their conclusion, we could define our practice of encountering the stranger as an effort to create the conditions that would enable us to wash one another's feet. Receiving from those we were supposed to serve, from those outside of our community, stretched, painfully, the boundaries of our understanding of ourselves and our perception of others."[64]

Baptism and communion are not the entirety of the worship core of our spinning top. Like the Church of the Brethren, some churches do not celebrate the Lord's Supper every Sunday, although a growing number of churches are doing so, and some of those that do not have weekly celebrations are increasing the frequency of their celebrations. The weekly public worship of a Christian community, whether or not it is a celebration of communion, is a participation in God's mission, a public service offered on behalf of the whole world. The people of God gather, drawn into the core of the spinning top, the heart of God's mission. Assembling as a people who have been in action in the world and carrying with them the needs and hopes of the world, the assembly offers praise, proclaims the good news of God's steadfast mercy and abiding love, and joins in the intercession of Christ. Then the assembly goes forth, the Spirit leading them out of the core of the top into action in the world, to continue to participate in the mission of God.

In addition to worship on Sunday, the Lord's Day, some Christians gather

---

64. Bond, "Liturgy, Ministry, and the Stranger," p. 147.

daily, others one or more times a week, for worship that is not sacramental. From the earliest centuries of the church, Christians prayed several times a day at set hours as an expression of the biblical injunction to "pray without ceasing" (1 Thess. 5:17). At first, daily prayer was most often offered at home, but by the fourth century, when Christianity had become an accepted religion in the Roman Empire, morning prayer and evening prayer were public offices intended for the whole people of God. Over the course of the Middle Ages, monastic communities of women and men expanded their daily prayer to include eight offices celebrated at set hours through the day and night. This provided a rhythm of worship and work for members of those communities but left most ordinary Christians without daily opportunities for worship.

Today, many churches or movements within and across churches encourage Christians to pray daily, and some provide texts for such prayer.[65] In my diagram of the spinning top, I have placed "prayer and contemplation" outside the core because they are activities that take place apart from the public worship of a community. Bevans and Schroeder believe that "the life of prayer of anyone can be a truly missionary act . . . prayer for those engaged in the church's work of crossing boundaries, for peoples struggling with injustice and poverty, for fragile communities of faith, for victims of human-caused or natural disasters — this is a valid way of being caught up in the saving and redeeming mission of God in the world."[66] Nor is this personal prayer limited to intercession. By singing God's praise and offering thanks for God's work in the world, we re-orient our lives to God and become better able to align ourselves with God's purposes, revealed especially in God sending Jesus and sending the Spirit.

Such personal prayer, however, is not distinct from the public worship that is at the heart of mission. In the dynamic movement of the spinning top,

---

65. See, for example, *Ancient Christian Devotional: A Year of Weekly Readings,* ed. Cindy Crosby and Thomas C. Oden (Downers Grove, Ill.: InterVarsity Press, 2007, 2009, 2011); David Adam, *The Rhythm of Life: Celtic Daily Prayer* (Harrisburg, Pa.: Morehouse, 2007); *The Daily Prayer of the Church,* ed. Philip H. Pfatteicher (Minneapolis: Lutheran University Press; Delhi, N.Y.: American Lutheran Publicity Bureau, 2005); The Northumbria Community, *Celtic Daily Prayer: Prayers and Readings from the Northumbria Community* (New York: HarperCollins, 2002); Daily Prayer, *The Book of Common Worship* (Louisville: Westminster John Knox Press, 1993), pp. 489-595.

66. Bevans and Schroeder, *Constants in Context,* p. 367.

energy flows into and out of the core, so that public worship informs our personal prayer throughout the week, and personal prayer, even when we pray alone, is always offered in communion with other Christians and so draws us back into public worship. A similar movement is at play with other aspects of mission as well. For example, witness and proclamation, sometimes called "evangelism," take place in the world as individual Christians live as disciples, as faith communities such as All Saints' in Chicago respond to the needs of the world, and as church bodies such as the United Methodist Church or the Roman Catholic Church challenge unjust systems. But public worship also incorporates witness and proclamation. The very fact that we gather week by week is itself a witness, and proclamation of the good news of Jesus is an integral component of worship. Moreover, we bring with us into public worship our experiences of evangelism in the world, offering thanksgiving for the ways we have found God at work and offering intercession for the needs of the world we have been addressing. Then, sent once more into the world, we bring with us the promise of God's reign that has been proclaimed in worship. This dynamic movement of different aspects of mission into and out of public worship is operative with every element of mission, and we will explore this more thoroughly in the chapters that follow.

The source of energy for all of these components — the public worship that is at the core of mission and the other actions of mission in the world — is God. Just as a top cannot spin on its own but needs someone to get it started, so also mission requires an animating force. Imagine God setting the top spinning, gathering us for the sacrifice of praise in public worship, sending us out of the center for the sacrifice of good works, then gathering us once again, in an ongoing dance of missional worship and worshipful mission. We experience and discern God's grace and mercy, God's reconciling love, and we respond with both action in the world and adoration in public worship. Just as a top eventually loses energy and slows, so too our participation in God's mission from time to time loses momentum. At these times, as always, God is at work, breathing new life into dry bones, calling and sending us to witness to the good news of God's reconciling love for the world.

We turn, then, to the actions of public worship. Understanding that, like our Möbius strip, worship is mission is worship . . . and cognizant of the dynamic energy that sends Christians into the world, like our spinning top, I begin with the gathering of the people of God.

CHAPTER 2

Gathering in the Name of God

On the day called Sunday, all who live in cities or in the country gather together to one place.

Justin Martyr, mid–second century[1]

Open our lips, O God,
And our mouths shall proclaim your praise.

Iona Abbey Worship Book[2]

The two models of mission I introduced in Chapter 1 point to the dynamic interaction of worship and mission. Christians participate in God's mission in the world, boldly bearing witness in word and deed to the good news of God's love for the world, and listening humbly, willing to learn from all they encounter and so grow in their knowledge of God's abundant mercy and love. Then God calls them together again into an assembly, to receive anew God's lavish blessings and to offer praise and intercession in response.

Roman Catholic writer Gregory Augustine Pierce proposes that Chris-

1. Justin Martyr, *I Apology* 67, in *The Apostolic Fathers with Justin Martyr and Irenaeus*, Vol. 1 of *Ante-Nicene Fathers*, ed. Alexander Roberts and James Donaldson, Christian Classics Ethereal Library, available at http://www.ccel.org/ccel/schaff/anf01.viii.ii.lxvii.html.

2. Opening responses, The Morning Service, *Iona Abbey Worship Book* (Glasgow: Wild Goose Publications, 2001), p. 15; see Psalm 51:15.

tians view this gathering as "coming back," returning from the previous celebration from which they were sent forth in mission. He emphasizes that everyone in the assembly is sent in mission: "The mission is to the world, including our jobs, our families and friends, our community and civic involvements."[3]

This chapter considers the assembly's gathering: what brings people to worship, what constitutes the assembly, and what particular acts may comprise a liturgical gathering. The assembly shifts from worshipful mission in the world to missional worship. In the spinning top that is mission, the energy is drawing us into the center; in the Möbius strip, we are moving into worship yet always engaged in mission.

Who Gathers?

On Sunday, in towns and cities around the world, people make their way to church, to join the Christian worship of God as Christians did in Rome during the second century. Some who gather today have made this journey week after week, while others are venturing into a church building for the first time. The gathering for worship begins here, as people travel from many directions to arrive at a designated place for worship.

Those who have been doing this for many years may experience this as routine, what they always do without consciously thinking about it. Sometimes it's a challenge to get children ready or to battle inclement weather; I recall a snowy Sunday morning in New Jersey when my parents bundled up my two brothers, my sister, and me, all under the age of six, and pulled us to church on sleds because the roads were not plowed. Often, regular worshipers go eagerly, anticipating the joy of offering praise to God and reconnecting with their sisters and brothers. On occasion, a regular worshiper is reluctant. In a congregation that had just changed its worship patterns as it added another Sunday morning service, one mother reported, "I didn't want to come to church on Sunday. I was a little freaked out by all the changes, and I thought it was going to be chaos. . . . I went into the girls' bedroom and

---

3. Gregory F. Augustine Pierce, *The Mass Is Never Ended: Rediscovering Our Mission to Transform the World* (Notre Dame: Ave Maria Press, 2007), pp. 42-43.

told my daughter Isabel, 'We're not going to church today.' She proceeded to melt down into complete hysterics, sobbing and wailing. 'All right, all right, I'll get ready,' I said, sighing." Once at church, this mother discovered that it hadn't changed as much as she had feared, and her daughter was enthusiastic about her experience. She concluded, "It just might be that the things that are jarring to me will wake me up a little more, make me more aware of who I am and where I am."[4]

Many regular worshipers do not consider deliberately each week whether to go to church or why they go. But if asked, they will tell you what is meaningful, why they bother to return week after week. The young mother whose daughter convinced her to go explained, "Singing the Lord's Prayer every week is one of the highlights, not just of my Sundays, but of my whole week."[5] My own daughter once commented that the intercessions were especially significant for her because it was the time she felt most connected to the world, most aware of God's concern for the needs of the world.

The highlight may differ for each worshiper, yet each comes to worship in response to God's call, drawn from offering good work in the world into the offering of praise and intercession in the assembly (Heb. 13:15-16). All of them are participating in God's mission in a weekly rhythm that gathers them, then sends them forth, then gathers them once again a week later. We can imagine them in the spinning top that is mission, being drawn into the center, then sent out, week after week.

Those who are coming for the first time or for the first time in a long time may be more intentional in their decision. Perhaps they are in the midst of a major life crisis — the loss of a job or the death of a loved one. Perhaps someone invited them. Maybe they are simply curious, noticing for the first time the sign outside the church building, or hearing music from within. These too, we believe, come in response to God, whether deliberately seeking divine comfort, mercy, and love or unable to explain the stirring in their souls that brings them to the threshold of a worshiping community. They have been touched by the reconciling love of God or newly awakened to their

---

4. Danielle Gabriel, "Voice from the Pew," *The Pathfinder,* All Souls Parish Newsletter, Berkeley, Calif., 12 September 2013, available at http://www.allsoulsparish.org/about_all_souls/pathfinder/?entry_id=953.

5. Gabriel, "Voice from the Pew."

hunger to know this mystery, and so their participation in the worshiping community is in some way the fruit of God's mission in the world.

An Invitation to Gather

In their analysis of the ways outsiders come to worship, Alan Kreider and Eleanor Kreider point out that outsiders often encounter Christianity first in contexts other than worship: "Christians must leave their buildings and structures and enter a space where they are not in control and where surprise and new discovery can happen." From experiences and relationships that form outside the church building and apart from worship — over a common meal, for example, or a common project — outsiders may gain the courage and curiosity to cross the threshold into worship.[6]

Although some unchurched people find their way into Christian worship without first encountering Christianity in another context, Christian communities today cannot expect that newcomers will seek them out for worship. Rather, witness and proclamation are essential elements of mission in the world.[7] After the resurrection the risen Christ assures his disciples, "You will receive power when the Holy Spirit has come upon you; and you will be my witnesses in Jerusalem, in all Judea and Samaria, and to the ends of the earth" (Acts 1:8). When the Spirit descends on the day of Pentecost, according to Acts, Peter is inspired to preach, and in response, three thousand people welcome his message and are baptized (Acts 2:14-41). Peter's sermon and the disciples' subsequent witness to the risen Christ, Lesslie Newbigin points out, are responses to God's initiative: "The initiator, the active agent, is the Lord who is the Spirit."[8] The Gospel of Matthew reports an even more explicit command from the risen Jesus: "Go therefore and make disciples of all nations, baptizing them in the name of the Father and of the Son and of the Holy Spirit, and teaching them to obey everything that I have

---

6. Alan Kreider and Eleanor Kreider, *Worship and Mission after Christendom* (Scottdale, Pa., and Waterloo, Ontario: Herald Press, 2011), pp. 225-27.

7. Stephen B. Bevans and Roger P. Schroeder, *Constants in Context: A Theology of Mission for Today* (Maryknoll, N.Y.: Orbis Books, 2004), pp. 352-61.

8. Lesslie Newbigin, "Cross-Currents in Ecumenical and Evangelical Understandings of Mission," *International Bulletin of Missionary Research* 6, no. 4 (October 1982): 147.

commanded you" (Matt. 28:19-20). Yet, Newbigin emphasizes, the process of bringing people to faith "is always the contagion of a joy that cannot but communicate itself, rather than the consciousness of a duty that must be discharged, a burden that must be carried."[9]

Those from evangelical and Pentecostal churches as well as some other Protestant churches tend to speak of evangelism rather than (or in addition to) witness and proclamation. The Lausanne Covenant, adopted in 1974 at the International Congress on World Evangelization organized by a committee headed by Billy Graham, describes the work of evangelism:

> To evangelize is to spread the good news that Jesus Christ died for our sins and was raised from the dead according to the Scriptures, and that as the reigning Lord he now offers the forgiveness of sins and the liberating gifts of the Spirit to all who repent and believe. Our Christian presence in the world is indispensable to evangelism, and so is that kind of dialogue whose purpose is to listen sensitively in order to understand. But evangelism itself is the proclamation of the historical, biblical Christ as Savior and Lord, with a view to persuading people to come to him personally and so be reconciled to God. . . . The results of evangelism include obedience to Christ, incorporation into his Church, and responsible service in the world.[10]

This view of evangelism makes clear that its sole purpose is not to grow the church, whether through an increase in Sunday attendance or by addition to the membership roll. Rather, true evangelism is a witness to the gospel that invites people to hear the gospel message and respond with a change of heart and a change of life. This new life in Christ is sustained through participation in the community of faith. Acts reports of those baptized on the first Pentecost, "They devoted themselves to the apostles' teaching and fellowship, to the breaking of bread and the prayers" (Acts 2:42). Thus evangelism can result in growth of the church, the participation of newcomers in Sunday worship.

9. Newbigin, "Cross-Currents in Ecumenical and Evangelical Understandings of Mission," p. 148.

10. "The Lausanne Covenant," par. 4, available at http://www.lausanne.org/en/documents/lausanne-covenant.html.

Evangelism can take the form of personal witness not only in words but even more through faithful Christian discipleship. In early fourth-century Egypt, a peasant named Pachomius found himself in prison after being kidnapped and conscripted for military service. People he didn't know brought food and water to him and his fellow prisoners. He asked who they were and why they were helping. The explanation came: these are Christians, who "are merciful to everyone, including strangers." The experience of this compassionate service made a deep impression on him. When Pachomius was released, he sought out a church and there received instruction and was baptized. Later he became a key figure in desert monasticism.[11] By enacting God's love for the prisoners, the Christians who ministered to Pachomius engaged in worshipful mission. The conversion of Pachomius was not the purpose of their witness but rather a result of it.

In the contemporary church, Episcopal priest Stephanie Spellers calls for "radical welcome," which she describes as "the spiritual practice of embracing and being changed by the gifts, presence, voices, and power of The Other: the people systemically cast out of or marginalized within a church, a denomination, and/or society."[12] From her study of congregations she identified as moving toward radical welcome, Spellers gives an example from the priest at All Saints' Episcopal Church in Chicago: "We have about 120 people here every Tuesday night for a Community Kitchen, our version of a Soup Kitchen. There's great conversation and a meal. So when our associate Bridget was ordained, she invited a whole bunch of that crew to the service. They came to the church then, and they're still coming. We had a Newcomers' party, and they parked their [shopping] baskets right next to someone's Subaru and came right in."[13] When worship is mission, the witness to the gospel that occurs in different contexts leads to the radical welcome of outsiders to the assembly for worship, for in fact no one is finally outside the mercy of God.

Witness to the gospel occurs not only through acts of mercy and justice undertaken by individuals and by particular communities of faith. The church as an institution also bears witness to the gospel. In my own church,

11. Alan Kreider, *The Change of Conversion and the Origin of Christendom* (Harrisburg, Pa.: Trinity Press International, 1999), pp. 19-20.

12. Stephanie Spellers, *Radical Welcome: Embracing God, The Other, and the Spirit of Transformation* (New York: Church Publishing, 2006), p. 6.

13. Bonnie Perry, cited by Spellers in *Radical Welcome*, p. 75.

the Episcopal Church, I recently chaired the commission responsible for developing resources for blessing same-sex relationships. Turmoil about human sexuality has rocked the Episcopal Church for a number of years, and some have attributed a precipitous decline in membership to the church's growing welcome of lesbian and gay members and the willingness of some to bless the lifelong committed relationships of same-sex couples. Early in the process of developing official resources, with four colleagues helping to lead this work I journeyed to Phoenix, Arizona, to make a presentation to the Episcopal Church House of Bishops. As my friend Susan later said, there was some nibbling at the bread of anxiety over breakfast as we made our final preparations. That evening, our session with the bishops having gone very well, we gathered for a working dinner. It was a lively conversation punctuated by much laughter. As we began our dessert, a busboy came over to our table. "Excuse me," he said. "I really hate to disturb you, but I couldn't help but overhear your conversation."

Uh-oh, I thought. *Here it comes. We're going to get blasted for the church blessing same-sex relationships.*

The busboy continued, "I'm gay. I didn't think there was any church that would welcome me rather than condemn me. Thank you. You've given me new hope."

Deeply moved, my table companions and I assured the busboy that he was not intruding and thanked him for telling us his story. Then we went back to our dessert. A few minutes later our server came to our table. "I hope it was okay that Michael came over," she said. "You see, he's been in the kitchen crying because he was so moved. I encouraged him to come talk to you." We assured her it was fine. She continued, "I was raised Catholic, but it didn't fit anymore, and I've stopped going to church. Where can I go in Phoenix?" We explained that we were all from out of town and didn't know the Episcopal Church in Phoenix. One of my colleagues handed the server a business card and encouraged her to get in touch. "I'll find you a church," she assured the young woman.

As our server walked away, my table companions and I looked at one another in amazement. The bishops had encouraged us to consider the missional implications of blessing same-sex relationships. Here we were, that same day, engaging in mission, proclaiming the good news without even trying. We didn't have long to comment about what was happening, though, because a third restaurant staffer, this time the supervisor, came to our table. "I know that staff aren't supposed to interrupt diners, and I apologize. But we've been listening to you this weekend, and you have offered us so much hope. I finally found a church home a couple of years ago, and I was going every Sunday. Then I brought a friend who's gay, and the church wouldn't welcome her. So I stopped going. Where can *I* go to church?"

We were stunned. We had gathered for a meal, a celebration for a job well done after breakfasting on the bread of anxiety. We encountered three restaurant staff members who feasted on the crumbs of our conversation. The living bread that they found gave them new hope and a promise of God's abundant love. That same living bread fed us, my table companions and me, who had journeyed to Phoenix with some trepidation, charged as we were to lead the Episcopal Church to a new welcome of same-sex couples.[14] The response of our waitstaff made clear that our witness was not just a personal witness; rather, we represented the institution that is the Episcopal Church. They trusted that within the church we could identify a worshiping community that would welcome them. Our engagement with the restaurant staff was an act of worshipful mission, giving glory to God by witnessing to God's boundless love.

Beyond specific acts of witness, the church's gathering for public worship week by week is itself a witness and so a participation in the mission of God. Sometimes this witness is especially profound. "In the 1970s and 1980s . . . under the burden of despotic and totalitarian [Communist] regimes, the *Kyrie eleison* of the modest and sometimes hidden Sunday liturgy was the only collective cry for truth, love, and mercy," writes Romanian Orthodox theologian Ion Bria.[15] Whether or not the local circumstances are especially dire, every place in the world is desperately in need of the healing and reconciling love of God. God responds by calling together people who gather for Christian worship Sunday after Sunday. These assemblies bear witness to

14. I am grateful to my colleague Susan Russell for her reflections on this experience in "A Missional Moment (AKA 'Dessert with a Side of Evangelism')," *An Inch at a Time: Reflections on the Journey*, 19 September 2010, available at http://inchatatime.blogspot.co.uk/2010/09/missional-moment-aka-dessert-with-side.html.

15. Ion Bria, *The Liturgy after the Liturgy: Mission and Witness from an Orthodox Perspective* (Geneva: WCC Publications, 1996), p. 22.

the gospel and so enact and signify God's mission, the movement of God's reconciling love into the world.

Assembly

Far more than a collection of individuals, the people of God gather as a local assembly in a particular place and at a particular time. They represent the whole people of God throughout the world and over time. The communion of members of the assembly with one another manifests the communion we have with God in Jesus Christ and anticipates the fullness of communion that is God's promise, the new creation in which the world is reconciled to God (2 Cor. 5:17-20). "The purpose of the church is essentially symbolic: in its very existence as a community in Christ, the church points to the kingdom of God as the ultimate shape of reality. . . . The gathering of people into this symbolic representation of God's purposes for the world is the church's part in the *missio Dei,*" writes Thomas Schattauer.[16] Eastern Orthodox theologian Alexander Schmemann emphasizes that the very act of gathering forms a people, a community. He explains that as they journey from their homes, "they are now on their way to *constitute* the church, or to be more exact, to be transformed into the church of God. They have been individuals . . . and now they have been called to 'come together in one place,' to bring their lives, their very 'world' with them and to be more than what they were: a *new* community with a new life."[17]

In a statement of principles for renewing worship at the beginning of the twenty-first century, the Evangelical Lutheran Church in America made a deliberate choice to use the term "assembly" to refer to the gathering of the church in worship. "This word expresses the nature of the church as *ekklesia,* a biblical word for the church that has at its root the meaning 'called out.'"[18] In ancient Greece, *ekklesia* referred to an assembly summoned by a herald,

16. Thomas H. Schattauer, "Liturgical Assembly as Locus of Mission," in *Inside Out: Worship in an Age of Mission,* ed. Thomas H. Schattauer (Minneapolis: Fortress Press, 1999), p. 13.

17. Alexander Schmemann, *For the Life of the World: Sacraments and Orthodoxy,* 2nd ed., revised and expanded (Crestwood, N.Y.: St. Vladimir's Seminary Press, 1973), p. 27.

18. Evangelical Lutheran Church in America, *Principles for Worship,* Renewing Worship, vol. 2 (Minneapolis: Augsburg Fortress Press, 2002), p. vi; emphasis in original.

while in the Greek translation of the Hebrew Scriptures the term was used to speak of the people or congregation of Israel. In the New Testament, *ekklesia* is the church of God called together in Christ.

"Assembly" (the original meaning of the Greek word *ekklesia*) can mean simply a gathering or coming together, but it can also describe a deliberative body empowered to make decisions. The political connotations of "assembly" — a legislative assembly has power to effect change — suggest that the people who gather for worship have agency — that is, they have power to think, to discern, and to act.[19] A liturgical assembly is not a passive meeting of individuals concerned with their personal salvation but rather a purposeful gathering of a community called together by God for the sake of the world. The assembly at worship performs liturgy, public service on behalf of the whole creation, and so participates in God's mission. Roman Catholic educator and theologian Michael Warren underscores the significance of calling the gathering for worship an assembly: "Restoring in any deep way the political dimensions of how we come together calls for more than updated liturgical choreography; it will involve fundamental changes in the way each person conceives of the self as an agent in an agent-full assembly."[20]

While liturgy requires the participation of the entire assembly acting together in purposeful response to God, an assembly nonetheless needs a leader, someone who can convene the gathering and orchestrate the actions of the entire body. In the current worship book of the Evangelical Lutheran Church in America, that leader is called the "presiding minister."[21] The term suggests that this minister has a particular role without implying that only one minister, the leader of the assembly, is acting. The Episcopal Church's 1979 prayer book, while saying that "the entire Christian assembly participates" in all services, uses the term "celebrant" to refer to an ordained minister who leads worship.[22] Episcopalian liturgical scholar Louis Weil com-

---

19. John Addison Dally, *Choosing the Kingdom: Missional Preaching for the Household of God* (Herndon, Va.: Alban Institute, 2008), pp. 81-82.

20. Michael Warren, *At This Time, in This Place: The Spirit Embodied in the Local Assembly* (Harrisburg, Pa.: Trinity Press International, 1999), pp. 86-87.

21. Evangelical Lutheran Church in America, *Evangelical Lutheran Worship* (Minneapolis: Augsburg Fortress Press, 2006).

22. *The Book of Common Prayer and Administration of the Sacraments and Other Rites*

ments, "An awareness emerged [among liturgical theologians] that the term 'celebrant' should not be limited to the ministry of the presider since it is the entire assembly who are 'celebrants' in the liturgical action."[23] John Dally, an Episcopal priest in Chicago, tells of his conversations with his congregation about the terms "celebrant" and "presider." Their discussions inspired the lay leaders of the congregation to write an identity statement that was printed in their worship leaflets:

> We are the assembly, the people called out by our baptisms to proclaim God's reign of love and justice breaking into a world of hate and injustice. Together, we make eucharist, blessing and eating bread and wine as Jesus commanded us in order to be strengthened by his living presence for our own lives of Christian witness. Everyone present today is a celebrant of the eucharist; our worship is led by lay and ordained presiders.[24]

This identity statement offers a vision of an assembly that understands its agency. In this assembly, baptism is the wellspring that empowers the people. Within this assembly, some of the baptized step forward to lead, enabling the entire assembly to celebrate and so to participate in God's mission as they worship.

Baptismal Identity

Baptism defines the Christian community and is the foundation of its identity as those who participate in God's mission. Yet in our post-Christendom context, some of those who come to worship will not be baptized. What is the significance of baptism? Why does it matter?

As Acts tells the story, the descent of the Spirit on the day of Pentecost leads to three thousand people being baptized in response to Peter's sermon, and those who were baptized "devoted themselves to the apostles' teaching

---

and Ceremonies of the Church, Together with The Psalter or Psalms of David (New York: Church Hymnal Corp., 1979), p. 13.

23. Louis Weil, *Liturgical Sense: The Logic of Rite* (New York: Seabury Books, 2013), p. 15, n. 3.

24. Dally, *Choosing the Kingdom*, p. 84.

and fellowship, to the breaking of bread and the prayers" (Acts 2:42). Baptism leads to ongoing participation in the life of the Christian community, centered in worship, and baptism defines the community of believers.

The frequent references to baptism in the New Testament suggest that the earliest Christian communities knew well the significance of baptism for Christian life, for participation in God's mission. "We have been buried with [Christ] by baptism into death," writes Paul to the church in Rome, "so that, just as Christ was raised from the dead by the glory of the Father, so we too might walk in newness of life" (Rom. 6:4). To Titus is written, "[God] saved us . . . through the water of rebirth and renewal by the Holy Spirit" (Titus 3:5). In the waters of baptism, believers are cleansed and transformed, becoming a part of the body of Christ who are empowered to participate in Christ's ministry of self-giving love. When Justin Martyr, writing during the mid–second century, says that "all who live in cities or in the country gather together to one place,"[25] he is referring to all of the Christians in the area — that is, all who were baptized.

Today, many churches are rediscovering the significance of baptism for Christian mission. Grace Episcopal Church in Kirkwood, Missouri, recently installed a new baptismal font. The previous one, a marble pedestal font, was on wheels with a tow rope attached. When it came time for baptism, the font was wheeled out from a corner and set into place at the head of the aisle where all could see the baptism. In its place is a large block of black granite standing about forty inches high at the entrance to the worship space. Carved into the top of this granite slab is a basin large enough to immerse an infant. Water circulates continuously, bubbling up into the basin and flowing down the sides into a drain at the floor.

The first time the new font at Grace Church was used, the candidate was five years old. Following the sermon, the entire assembly was invited to process to the church entrance around the font. Most did so. When it came time to administer the water, the priest took a large bowl, scooped up water from the font, and poured it over the boy's head. People gasped in astonishment, experiencing in a new way the radical transformation that baptism signifies. Three times the water came: "I baptize you in the name of

---

25. Justin, *I Apology* 67.

the Father [water is poured], and of the Son [more water], and of the Holy Spirit [even more water]."[26]

Water is always flowing in the font. As people pass by when they enter for worship, adults trail their fingers through the water. Young children eagerly run forward to touch the water flowing down the sides of the font. At first, adults tried to prevent them from doing this, but the priest has encouraged them to allow young and old to engage the water when they assemble for worship. "Let the little children come . . ." (Mark 10:14) to receive living water. At Grace Church in Kirkwood, baptism is being pulled out of the dusty corners of Christian life so that it can become a source of power welling up, cleansing and transforming people and drawing them into the mission of God.

Five hundred years ago, the reformer Martin Luther said of baptism: "Just as the truth of this divine promise, once pronounced over us, continues until death, so our faith in it ought never to cease, but to be nourished and strengthened until death by the continual remembrance of this promise made to us in baptism."[27] Here and elsewhere in Luther's writing there is a strong baptismal spirituality, an awareness of the ongoing effect of baptism in Christian life, a sense of comfort and power in knowing that the covenant established by God in baptism is the foundation for mercy and forgiveness throughout one's life.

Baptism is significant not only for individual Christian believers. Through the waters of baptism God forms a new community, the body of Christ. In this community, division is overcome and God creates "one new humanity" (Eph. 2:18). "In Christ Jesus you are all children of God through faith," Paul tells the Galatians. "As many of you as were baptized into Christ have clothed yourselves with Christ. There is no longer Jew or Greek, there is no longer slave or free, there is no longer male and female; for all of you are one in Christ Jesus" (Gal. 3:27-28). James Smith explains that baptism "cuts against the hierarchies of privilege."[28] By welcoming all to worship

26. "Grace Celebrates All Saints' Sunday," *Grace Episcopal Church: News and Events,* 4 November 2012, available at http://www.gracekirkwood.org/2012/11/grace-celebrates-all-saints-sunday/.

27. Luther, *The Babylonian Captivity of the Church* 3.5, available at http://www.lutherdansk.dk/Web-babylonian%20Captivitate/Martin%20Luther.htm#_Toc58730607.

28. James K. A. Smith, *Desiring the Kingdom: Worship, Worldview, and Cultural Formation* (Grand Rapids: Baker Academic, 2009), p. 184.

without distinction, Christian assemblies today enact and embody God's all-embracing love and so participate in the mission of God.

This radical welcome was challenging for the earliest Christian communities. Paul sternly rebukes the church at Corinth because their practices do not reflect their reconciled humanity in Christ: "When you come together, it is not really to eat the Lord's supper. For when the time comes to eat, each of you goes ahead with your own supper, and one goes hungry and another becomes drunk" (1 Cor. 11:20-21). Paul urges them to wait for one another when they assemble to share a meal in memory of Jesus. The letter of James challenges similar distinctions in the assembly: "Do you with your acts of favoritism really believe in our glorious Lord Jesus Christ? For if a person with gold rings and in fine clothes comes into your assembly, and if a poor person in dirty clothes also comes in, and if you take notice of the one wearing the fine clothes and say, 'Have a seat here, please,' while to the one who is poor you say, 'Stand there,' or, 'Sit at my feet,' have you not made distinctions among yourselves, and become judges with evil thoughts?" (James 2:1-4).

What of our assemblies today? Is there a place for all, without distinction? Do those who lead reflect the diversity of the congregation? Does the assembly signify the new humanity in Christ in which divisions of race, ethnicity, class, gender, sexual orientation, age, and all other categories are overcome? God's mission extends to all; none are outside the reach of the gospel.

Stephanie Spellers describes the effects of the radical welcome in Christ that shatters barriers:

> People on the margins will enter and discover resonances, time-honored wisdom and beauty in the congregation's received tradition, even as they share love and stories and engage in ministry as part of the gathered body. But the existing community will also experience conversion, hearing with new ears the wisdom brothers or sisters bring from the margins, trying on new practices, engaging God from a different perspective, and expanding what is possible, normative, essential, or holy for Christian life in their context.[29]

"Conversion" usually refers to the change of heart and change of mind that lead to baptism, to incorporation into the body of Christ. Spellers encourages

29. Spellers, *Radical Welcome*, pp. 72-73.

us to recognize that conversion occurs not only in those coming to know Christ for the first time but also in the entire body. Mission understood as prophetic dialogue is always open to experiencing God's love in new and surprising places, to know ever more fully God's abundant grace and mercy. Such conversion may be a sudden dramatic experience, or it may unfold gradually over the course of Christian life.

In a study of the process and patterns of conversion in different eras of Christian history, Alan Kreider concludes that conversion encompasses behavior, belief, and belonging. Conversion during the earliest centuries of Christianity involved a radical change in behavior, conforming one's life to Christ, embodying God's love, and participating in God's mission of reconciliation. Conversion also meant coming to believe in Jesus, incarnate, crucified, and risen, and that in him, God's reign of justice, peace, and love was manifest. Learning the Apostles' Creed, with its summary of Christian belief, became part of preparation for baptism. After an intensive time of formation that fostered both a change of belief and a change of behavior, converts were baptized and so belonged to the community, joining its participation in God's mission in the world, engaging in actions such as those of the Christians who ministered to Pachomius and his fellow prisoners.[30]

Beginning in the fourth century with the conversion of Constantine, Christianity became publicly acceptable in the ancient Mediterranean world, and eventually became the official religion of the Roman Empire. As Christendom emerged in Europe, Christian belief, behavior, and belonging came to be expected and even compulsory for all people. According to Kreider, "Christendom's uniform belief, its homogeneous belonging, and its common behavior in significant measure spread because they were made into an offer people couldn't refuse."[31]

For the past century or more, these patterns of common belief, belonging, and behavior have been breaking down, and increasingly Europe, North America, and other Western societies are post-Christendom cultures.[32] Ryan Bolger, who teaches at Fuller Seminary in Pasadena, California, describes

---

30. Kreider, *The Change of Conversion and the Origin of Christendom,* pp. xiii-xvii, 1-32.

31. Kreider, *The Change of Conversion and the Origin of Christendom,* p. 97.

32. For an analysis of how the United States is and is not a post-Christendom society, see Kreider and Kreider, *Worship and Mission after Christendom,* pp. 259-63.

post-Christendom as "that social space where there is a Christian memory, but that memory no longer affects how people make meaning with their lives."[33] This dual reality — the memory of Christianity that continues to infuse our culture and the simultaneous loss of that memory as the organizing principle pervading every aspect of our lives — has profound consequences for Christian life. Freed from our enmeshment with the surrounding culture, we can claim our distinctive Christian identity as the people of God, formed by the life, death, and resurrection of Jesus Christ, called and sent to embody the reign of God and so to participate in the mission of God. Freed from the all-embracing worldview of Christendom, we can forge a strong baptismal identity, allowing baptism to become the force that animates Christian faith and life.

Baptism thus can create a strong center for the assembly, even as people who are not baptized may also come to worship. Baptism, available to all without distinction, includes a commission to be in relationship with all for whom Christ died, to enact God's reconciling love for all humanity. By opening the doors of the assembly to all, baptized and unbaptized alike, the community of believers announces that God's love is for all.

Some communities intentionally design worship to welcome non-Christians. In Chapter 1, I discussed worship as evangelism, in which worship is "a stage from which to present the gospel and reach out to the unchurched and irreligious."[34] Contemporary seeker services, like nineteenth-century camp meetings, often focus on attracting large crowds in order to introduce them to the gospel. A more recent movement, sometimes called emerging or emergent church, has a very different scale. The assembly is usually small in number, built around a core community that identifies with the life of Jesus and seeks to embody and practice the reign of God in all aspects of life — that is, to live missionally.[35] In some emerging churches, worshipers gather around a meal in a house church, while others assemble for ser-

---

33. Ryan K. Bolger, preface to *The Gospel after Christendom: New Voices, New Cultures, New Expressions,* ed. Ryan K. Bolger (Grand Rapids: Baker Academic, 2012), p. xxv.

34. Schattauer, "Liturgical Assembly as Locus of Mission," p. 2.

35. In *Emerging Churches: Creating Christian Community in Postmodern Cultures* (Grand Rapids: Baker Academic, 2005), Eddie Gibbs and Ryan K. Bolger analyze the core practices of emerging churches, based on their study of these churches and their pastors in the United States and the United Kingdom.

vices of Word and prayer, and still others celebrate communion each week. In these communities, belief, belonging, and behavior are fluid. In a study of emerging churches in England and the United States, Anglican bishops Mary Gray-Reeves and Michael Perham report, "We experienced corporate behavior and the theology conveyed through the liturgy as easy to pick up in emergent churches, and could see how this contributed to a deeper sense of belonging. Likewise, it encouraged participation in liturgical behavior that allows people new to the faith to engage in what believing Christians say and do. . . . Emergent churches allow believing and behaving to meld together over time."[36]

While emergent churches cultivate a practice of welcoming strangers and seeker services are intentionally designed for outsiders, other, more settled forms of church life also attract newcomers. Alan Kreider and Eleanor Kreider point out that what outsiders see and experience "is immensely important, for the church of whatever size and sociological form is meant to be a demonstration of God's mission in action." They continue, "Unfortunately, in many congregations in Britain and the United States, they can see worship that is decayed and de-spirited, out of tune with God's mission. . . . But in other churches of every size and many sorts, the outsiders can encounter worship that is alive and attuned to the character and purposes of God."[37]

Those who are baptized, James Smith writes, "are chosen and commissioned as God's image bearers . . . [and] empowered to be witnesses of a coming kingdom and charged with the renewal of the world."[38] Recovering the significance of baptism for Christian life, pulling it out of the dusty corners of Christian life, is an important aspect of developing missional worship. This involves not just the baptismal ritual itself but also catechesis that cultivates transformed belief and behavior, drawing outsiders into the fullness of Christian life and participating in God's mission, in which the assembly is sent into the world and then gathered each week for worship.

David Bosch understands the entire community to be the primary

---

36. Mary Gray-Reeves and Michael Perham, *The Hospitality of God: Emerging Worship for a Missional Church* (New York: Seabury Books; London: SPCK, 2011), p. 75.

37. Kreider and Kreider, *Worship and Mission after Christendom*, p. 233.

38. Smith, *Desiring the Kingdom*, p. 185.

bearer of mission. He explains, "Laypersons are no longer the scouts who, returning from the 'outside world' with eyewitness accounts and perhaps some bunches of grapes, report to the 'operational basis'; they *are* the operational basis from which the *missio Dei* proceeds. . . . In the New Testament dispensation the Spirit (just as the priesthood) has been given to the whole people of God, not to select individuals."[39]

Bosch describes the ministry, or "service," of laypeople as a ministry in the world, offered in the context of daily living. When we view worship as a locus of mission, where the assembly enacts and signifies God's mission of reconciliation, then we must recognize that the entire assembly is the bearer of mission in worship as well as in the world. Reflecting on the description of the community in Acts 2 — "They devoted themselves to the apostles' teaching and fellowship, to the breaking of bread and the prayers . . . all who believed were together and had all things in common; they would sell their possessions and goods and distribute the proceeds to all, as any had need" (Acts 2:42-45) — Don Saliers points out the dynamic interplay of the first-century community's participation in mission: "The servanthood *within and for* the gathered community at prayer flowed into the servanthood *to and from* their daily life, including to those outside the community."[40] This is a community formed by baptism (Acts 2:41) and called through baptism to a life of worship and service. Worship and mission then flow into and out of one another, part of a seamless whole, like our Möbius strip or our spinning top.

Sunday

At least as early as the second century, Christians have assembled for worship on Sunday. Writing in the middle of the second century, the Greek apologist Justin Martyr explained, "Sunday is the day on which we all hold our common assembly, because it is the first day on which God, having wrought

39. David J. Bosch, *Transforming Mission: Paradigm Shifts in Theology of Mission* (Maryknoll, N.Y.: Orbis Books, 1991), p. 472.
40. Don E. Saliers, *Worship as Theology: Foretaste of Glory Divine* (Nashville: Abingdon Press, 1994), p. 181; emphasis in original.

a change in the darkness and matter, made the world; and Jesus Christ our Savior on the same day rose from the dead."[41] Each of the four Gospels reports that some of the women who followed Jesus went to his tomb early in the morning on the first day of the week, that is, Sunday. Gathering to celebrate the resurrection on Sunday came to be a core Christian practice.

However, the first followers of Jesus may have gathered regularly to remember Jesus on Friday evening, the beginning of the Jewish Sabbath. (In the Jewish calendar, days extend from sunset to sunset; see Genesis 1.) Jews customarily observed the Sabbath with a ritual meal. Other followers of Christ, especially Gentile communities, may have assembled to share a meal and a ministry of the Word after the Sabbath was over, at the beginning of the first day of the week (that is, Saturday evening). Eventually, the Saturday evening gathering was transferred to Sunday morning.[42]

The earliest weekly assemblies took the form of a ritual meal. Many of the Gospel accounts of the disciples' encounters with the risen Christ report that he shared a meal with them. On the evening of the day of Christ's resurrection, two disciples walking to Emmaus encountered a stranger on the road, one who interpreted the unsettling and puzzling experiences of Jesus' crucifixion and the discovery of the empty tomb in light of the Hebrew Scriptures. They prevailed upon the stranger to join them for a meal, and the stranger took bread, blessed and broke it, and gave it to them. "Then their eyes were opened, and they recognized him." Returning to Jerusalem, they reported to the community gathered there that Jesus "had been made known to them in the breaking of the bread" (Luke 24:13-35). For the first followers of Jesus, meals shared in his memory made him present to them and united them in communion with him. "The cup of blessing that we bless, is it not a sharing in the blood of Christ? The bread that we break, is it not a sharing in the body of Christ?" (1 Cor. 10:16).

Beginning in the second century, Christians shifted their weekly practice from sharing a full meal to sharing instead just a fragment of bread and a sip of wine. Scholars are not certain of the reason for this change. Perhaps the logistics of a meal became too difficult as communities grew, or perhaps

---

41. Justin, *I Apology* 67.

42. Paul F. Bradshaw, *Early Christian Worship: A Basic Introduction to Ideas and Practice* (Collegeville, MN: Liturgical Press, 2010), pp. 46-48, 84-85.

the Roman authorities banned evening gatherings for meals. Whatever the cause, by the middle of the third century, the weekly Christian assembly was no longer an evening meal but rather a symbolic sharing of bread and wine more like the Eucharist as we know it today, and Christians celebrated this ritual on Sunday morning.[43]

For the first three centuries of Christianity, nearly all the evidence that scholars have found indicates that Christians regularly celebrated the Eucharist only on Sundays and a few saints' days as those began to emerge in local churches. Liturgical scholar Paul Bradshaw concludes, "During the rest of the week the Church was dispersed and hidden, as its individual members went about their life and work in different places. But on Sunday the Church came together and revealed itself in the celebration of the Eucharist, with each member occupying his or her proper place in the assembly."[44] Worship on Sunday thus came to be an important mark of identity for Christians, signifying their communion with one another in the body of Christ and so enacting their participation in God's mission.

Even more, because it is the "Lord's Day," Sunday has eschatological significance, pointing toward the reign of God in the age to come. "I was in the Spirit on the Lord's day," says John at the beginning of Revelation (Rev. 1:10). Designating Sunday as the Lord's Day acknowledged both the present reality of Christ's reign and the promise of the age to come, when Christ would be Lord over all. Alexander Schmemann writes, "The seventh day points beyond itself toward a new Lord's Day — the day of salvation and redemption, of God's triumph over his enemies."[45] The eschatological character of Sunday is emphasized in designating it as the eighth day, the day that goes beyond the seven-day cycle of the week, as Justin explained in his *Dialogue with Trypho*: "For the first day after the Sabbath, remaining the first of all the days, is called, however, the eighth, according to the number of all the days of the cycle."[46] As the first day of the week, Sunday is the day of creation ("the first day on which God, having wrought a change in the darkness and matter,

---

43. Bradshaw, *Early Christian Worship*, pp. 46-47.

44. Bradshaw, *Early Christian Worship*, p. 85.

45. Schmemann, *For the Life of the World*, p. 50.

46. Justin Martyr, *Dialogue with Trypho* 41, in *The Apostolic Fathers with Justin Martyr and Irenaeus*, Vol. 1 of *Ante-Nicene Fathers*, ed. Alexander Roberts and James Donaldson, Christian Classics Ethereal Library, available at http://www.ccel.org/ccel/schaff/anf01.viii.ii.lxvii.html.

made the world"[47]), and as the eighth day it is the day of new creation. The non-scriptural *Epistle to Barnabas*, written near the end of the first century, explained that the eighth day is "the beginning of another world," and so "we also celebrate with gladness the eighth day in which Jesus also rose from the dead, and was made manifest, and ascended into Heaven."[48] Because of the joyous character of this day, celebrated in anticipation of the reign of God, early Christian communities were instructed not to kneel for prayer or to fast on Sundays.[49]

The practice of assembling for worship on Sunday has thus been handed down to us as a core Christian practice and so unites us to Christians of all times and places. We gather not just as a particular group of people in a particular place on Sunday but also as part of the universal body of Christ. Alan Kreider and Eleanor Kreider emphasize that this gathering is essential for the church's life because it aligns our lives with the mission of God.[50] When we gather for worship, together we remember who God is for us and among us, and we remember who we are before God. When we gather for worship, we are reassembled as the body of Christ that is called and sent in the power of the Spirit to continue participation in God's mission of reconciliation. Without worship, the church is just one among many worthwhile service organizations who contribute to the greater good of the world. Worship enables Christians to situate their actions of justice and mercy in the context of God's judgment of and mercy for the world.

Worship and Culture

Gathering involves more than people arriving in a designated place at a designated time. The pattern of gathering and the particular texts, music,

---

47. Justin, *I Apology* 67.

48. *Epistle to Barnabas* 15:8-9, in *Apostolic Fathers*, ed. Kirsopp Lake, Loeb Classical Library (1912), Early Christian Writings, available at http://www.earlychristianwritings.com/text/barnabas-lake.html.

49. Bradshaw, *Early Christian Worship*, p. 86; Paul F. Bradshaw and Maxwell E. Johnson, *The Origins of Feasts, Fasts, and Seasons in Early Christianity* (London: SPCK; Collegeville, Minn.: Liturgical Press, 2011), pp. 16-17, 25-26.

50. Kreider and Kreider, *Worship and Mission after Christendom*, p. 151.

symbols, and actions used for this first movement of worship vary from one community to the next, as they have varied over the course of Christian history. The differences reflect not only the heritage of diverse Christian traditions but also the dynamic interplay between Christian worship and culture. God's mission concerns who we are and where we live, and so worship, as one element of mission, must engage with the culture(s) of the worshiping community. But not every aspect of our culture accords with the gospel; the prophet Isaiah reminds us that God's ways are not our ways (Isa. 55:8). Moreover, God's mission crosses all human divisions and boundaries and so is beyond all human cultures.

In recent decades, scholars and teachers of liturgy have introduced the term "inculturation" to describe the relationship of worship and culture. Roman Catholic theologian Anscar Chupungco defines inculturation as "the process whereby the texts and rites used in worship by the local church are so inserted in the framework of culture that they absorb its thought, language, and ritual patterns."[51] He continues, "Only those cultural elements that can harmonize with the nature of the liturgy are to be incorporated into the liturgy, and they should be able to communicate adequately the Christian message. . . . There must be reciprocity and mutual respect between the liturgy and culture. . . . Liturgical inculturation does not inflict violence on culture; rather, it works according to the cultural patterns whether of language and rite or of time and space."[52]

The relationship between worship and culture is complex. The 1996 Nairobi Statement of the Lutheran World Federation identifies four aspects of this relationship. Worship, the statement asserts, is transcultural, contextual, countercultural, and cross-cultural.

Worship as transcultural. Some elements of worship transcend particular cultural expressions. According to the Nairobi Statement, "The use of this shared core liturgical structure and these shared liturgical elements in local congregational worship . . . are expressions of Christian unity across time, space, culture, and confession."[53] We have seen how Sunday has been *the* day

---

51. Anscar Chupungco, *Liturgies of the Future: The Process and Methods of Inculturation* (Mahwah, N.J.: Paulist Press, 1989), p. 29.

52. Chupungco, *Liturgies of the Future,* pp. 31-32.

53. Lutheran World Federation, "Nairobi Statement on Worship and Culture," par. 2.3.

for Christian worship, especially the celebration of the Eucharist, since the early centuries of Christianity,[54] and we have discussed baptism as a core Christian practice that shapes identity. In later chapters, we will explore other transcultural elements of worship.

Worship as contextual. Some elements of Christian worship reflect the values and patterns of the local culture. The Nairobi Statement, echoing Chupungco's definition of inculturation, stresses that local cultural practices can be used "insofar as they are consonant with the values of the gospel."[55] For example, in the late 1990s, St. Nicholas Episcopal Church in Elk Grove Village, a suburb of Chicago, began to use the exchange of the peace at the beginning of its worship. Though the Episcopal Church *Book of Common Prayer* sets the exchange of the peace in the middle of the Eucharist, St. Nicholas Church decided to place it at the beginning in order to reflect the common North American practice of greeting one another when gathering for an event. This cultural practice is consistent with a gospel value of hospitality.

Worship as countercultural. Not every element of a culture is consonant with the gospel. "Some components of every culture in the world are sinful, dehumanizing, and contradictory to the values of the gospel," declares the Nairobi Statement.[56] Worship must resist and challenge those elements of culture that are contrary to the gospel message of God's reconciling love, maintaining or recovering "patterns of action which differ intentionally from prevailing cultural models."[57] In North America, singing together, particularly with live accompaniment or without any accompaniment, is uncommon. "Happy Birthday" is one of the few exceptions. When the assembly sings together to begin its worship, it engages in a countercultural practice that can unite worshipers in a harmony of voice, building up the body of Christ as well as glorifying God.

Worship as cross-cultural. Cross-cultural elements of worship remind us that Jesus, the Savior of all, "welcomes the treasures of earthly cultures into the city of God. . . . The sharing of hymns and art and other elements of worship across cultural barriers helps enrich the whole church and strengthen

54. A few churches, such as Seventh-Day Adventists, do not keep Sunday as the Lord's Day; instead, Saturday is their day of worship.

55. Lutheran World Federation, "Nairobi Statement on Worship and Culture," par. 3.1.

56. Lutheran World Federation, "Nairobi Statement on Worship and Culture," par. 4.1.

57. Lutheran World Federation, "Nairobi Statement on Worship and Culture," par. 4.2.

the sense of the *communio* of the church."[58] The Nairobi Statement urges communities to exercise understanding and respect when using elements of different cultures. In the gathering, music may include songs from other cultures, whether the culture of Christians living in a different century or a contemporary culture in a distant part of the world or the culture of a nearer neighbor.

Worship as multicultural. The Nairobi Statement does not address the subject of different local cultures. Yet some congregations are themselves multicultural, with members representing several distinct cultures — for example, Asian and Euro-American. For these assemblies, what is contextual for one member will be cross-cultural for another. Intentionally incorporating elements from different cultures into worship signals that all are welcome, all are part of the body of Christ.[59]

How the Assembly Gathers

As was true for the earliest followers of Christ, gathering for worship today is an occasion for joy. Clayton Schmit points out, "The mood is typically celebratory, as God's people re-assemble for fellowship and centering."[60] In the gathering, members re-unite with one another and turn their attention to the worship of God, remembering that God is worthy to receive our praise and glory, responding to God's call to us.

In his discussion of the space for worship, United Methodist liturgical scholar James White underscores that gathering is an encounter with both God and neighbor: "In recent years liturgists have become more sensitive to the need for *gathering space,* in which the people come together to discern the body of Christ. [The gathering] may be the most important single action of worship, and failure to take it seriously could have dire consequences, as Paul warns (1 Corinthians 11:29). Gathering space . . . marks the transition

58. Lutheran World Federation, "Nairobi Statement on Worship and Culture," par. 5.1.

59. In *One Bread, One Body: Exploring Cultural Diversity in Worship* (Bethesda, Md.: Alban Institute, 2003), C. Michael Hawn develops principles for multicultural worship based upon case studies of four multicultural congregations in the United Methodist Church.

60. Clayton J. Schmit, *Sent and Gathered: A Worship Manual for the Missional Church* (Grand Rapids: Baker Academic, 2009), p. 161.

from the world outside to the community gathered in Christ's name inside. Worshipers come to meet their God and immediately encounter their neighbor in this space."[61]

The gathering begins informally as people cross the threshold into the church building and its worship space. Regular members enter with confidence because they know where to go and what to expect. They acknowledge their fellow worshipers with a few words of greeting, a nod or a smile, perhaps a hug. If there is a baptismal font with water in it, they may trail their fingers in the water like some worshipers at Grace Church in Kirkwood, Missouri; some may make the sign of the cross on themselves. These regular worshipers find a seat, often the exact place they return to week after week.

Outsiders, especially those who have little experience with Christian worship, enter with some uncertainty. Thomas Long stresses the importance of hospitality to strangers. "Vital and faithful congregations," says Long, "make planned and concerted efforts to show hospitality to the stranger." He continues, "People need to be welcomed into God's house, recognized and known by name, and joined with others in offering their lives to God in acts of mission."[62] Congregations enacting God's mission will show hospitality to all who come to worship, outsiders and regulars alike. Such hospitality, says Christine Pohl, "is first a response of love and gratitude for God's love and welcome to us."[63] In North American contexts, some who come to worship for the first time may be eager to engage those they meet, while others will need more space, the opportunity to take a place at the edges of the assembly.[64] Though these newcomers may want to be known by name, as Long claims, many will not want to be publicly singled out in the assembly.

At Trinity United Church of Christ, a large congregation on Chicago's south side, the worship space is abuzz as people gather and greet one another.

---

61. James F. White, "The Spatial Setting," in *The Oxford History of Christian Worship*, ed. Geoffrey Wainwright and Karen B. Westerfield Tucker (New York and Oxford: Oxford University Press, 2006), pp. 799-800.

62. Thomas C. Long, *Beyond the Worship Wars: Building Vital and Faithful Worship* (Herndon, Va.: Alban Institute, 2001), p. 35.

63. Christine D. Pohl, *Making Room: Recovering Hospitality as a Christian Tradition* (Grand Rapids: Wm. B. Eerdmans, 1999), p. 172.

64. For an account of an assembly where some people deliberately choose the edges, see Bevans and Schroeder, *Constants in Context*, p. 365.

Official greeters wearing name tags and other members of the congregation welcome visitors and help them find a place in the assembly. Worship begins slowly with announcements, prayer, and song as people continue to enter and the choir processes to its place. Then the presiding minister greets the assembly more formally and asks members of the assembly to greet their neighbors and offer God's blessing to one another. Later, after prayer, song, and the reading of Scripture, the pastor asks visitors to stand. Ushers distribute cards to these newcomers, where they can fill in their names and contact information and indicate what ministry or contact they desire. Newcomers who complete the card and turn it in after the service receive a CD giving information about the congregation. Once ushers have distributed the cards, the pastor asks members to greet the visitors. As members welcome the visitors, the members greet one another as well. This pattern of gathering is an effective form of hospitality, welcoming long-time members and strangers alike. Those who are visitors can be personally acknowledged and known by name without finding themselves in the spotlight. Like the exchange of the peace at the beginning of worship at St. Nicholas Episcopal Church, the greetings at Trinity United Church of Christ are a contextual form of worship. The various elements of the gathering connect people to each another as worshipers who offer God's blessing and draw the assembly together to praise God.

In addition to greeting one another, the gathering turns the attention of the assembly to God. A call and response taken from Scripture, such as "Open our lips, O God/and our mouths shall proclaim your praise" (Ps. 51:15), unites the voices of the assembly as it begins the praise of God. Since the Early Middle Ages, the hymn *Gloria in excelsis* ("Glory to God in the highest," the song of the angels at the birth of Jesus; Luke 2:14) has been part of the gathering in Western churches,[65] and it continues to be used in many liturgical churches. Other entrance songs serve equally well to unite the assembly in praise. In our praise, we acknowledge and respond to God, who first loved us, and our praise flows from our experience of God's love

---

65. For further discussion of the historical development of the texts and acts of the gathering in Western churches, see John Baldovin, "The Introductory Rites: History of the Latin Text and Rite," in *A Commentary on the Order of Mass of The Roman Missal: A New English Translation, developed under the auspices of the Catholic Academy of Liturgy,* ed. Edward Foley et al. (Collegeville, Minn.: Liturgical Press, 2011), pp. 115-23.

not only in our lives today but also in the ways God has acted in the history of salvation, and from our anticipation of God's new creation.[66] Our praise thus aligns us with God's mission in the world.

Some Christians also include an acknowledgment of sin as they come to worship. "Cleanse the thoughts of our hearts by the inspiration of your Spirit,"[67] Anglicans pray in the "Collect for Purity" that first appeared (in Latin) in the eighth century in a collection of prayers from the deacon Alcuin of York. The ancient acclamation "Lord, have mercy" *(Kyrie eleison),* originally a response to intercessory petitions in worship, is sometimes used today as a response to brief penitential prayers: "God, through Jesus Christ, will judge the secret thoughts of all: Lord, have mercy./Lord, have mercy./ Not everyone who says to me, 'Lord, Lord,' will enter the kingdom of heaven: Christ, have mercy./Christ, have mercy./Let anyone who has an ear listen to what the Spirit is saying to the churches: Lord, have mercy./Lord, have mercy."[68] (Chapter 5 of this book explores the practice of confession of sin.)

In many churches the gathering actions of worship conclude with the prayer of the day, sometimes called a "collect" (pronounced with an emphasis on the first syllable). This prayer draws together, or collects, all that members of the assembly bring. In the classical structure of a collect, the prayer first addresses God, often including a specific attribute or action of God — for example, "O God, who wonderfully created, and yet more wonderfully restored, the dignity of human nature." In one brief phrase, the assembly recalls who God is and what God has done and is doing in the world. The prayer then asks for God's action: "Grant that we may share the divine life of him who humbled himself to share our humanity, your Son Jesus Christ." Having acknowledged God's gracious love for the world, the assembly asks to participate in that wondrous love. Finally, a collect concludes with a doxology, a brief final statement of praise offering the prayer in the name of the Triune God: ". . . who lives and reigns with you, in the unity of the Holy Spirit, one God, for ever and ever."[69]

66. Kreider and Kreider, *Worship and Mission after Christendom,* pp. 152-54.

67. *The Book of Common Prayer* 1979, p. 365.

68. Church of England, *Common Worship: Times and Seasons* (London: Church House Publishing, 2006), p. 35.

69. Collect for the Second Sunday after Christmas Day, *The Book of Common Prayer* 1979, p. 214.

Philip Kenneson points out that "prayer is not simply a speaking to God, but a deep and abiding communion with God. Such communion requires that we both listen to God and open ourselves up to the transforming power of God's Spirit."[70] When the first movement of worship, the gathering, concludes with the collect, the prayer of the day, the assembly has come together, re-united in communion with God and one another, prepared to listen to God, to hear once again the stories of God's love for the world and the promise of God's new creation.

Worship proceeds from gathering the assembly to proclaiming and responding to the Word. In the proclamation and response to the Word, the assembly hears again the good news of God's love for the world and remembers its identity as participants in the mission of God, drawn into God's self-offering of redemptive love through Christ and in the power of the Spirit. In the next chapter we will explore this good news.

70. Philip Kenneson, "Worship, Imagination, and Formation," in *The Blackwell Companion to Christian Ethics,* ed. Stanley Hauerwas and Samuel Wells (Oxford and Malden, Mass.: Blackwell Publishing, 2004), pp. 61-62.

CHAPTER 3

Proclaiming and Responding to the Word of God

The memoirs of the apostles or the writings of the prophets are read, as long as time permits; then, when the reader has ceased, the president verbally instructs, and exhorts to the imitation of these good things.

Justin Martyr, mid–second century[1]

For the Word of God in Scripture,
for the Word of God among us,
for the Word of God within us,
Thanks be to God.

Iona Abbey Worship Book[2]

The assembly gathers in response to God's call, its initial activities reuniting its members with one another and turning their attention to God. Worship continues as the assembly proclaims and responds to the Word, hearing once again the stories of God's work in human history and God's promises of new creation. Worshipers feast on the Word, savoring it as a gift from God

---

1. Justin Martyr, *I Apology 67*, in *The Apostolic Fathers with Justin Martyr and Irenaeus*, Vol. 1 of *Ante-Nicene Fathers*, ed. Alexander Roberts and James Donaldson, Christian Classics Ethereal Library, available at http://www.ccel.org/ccel/schaff/anfo1.viii.ii.lxvii.html.

2. *Iona Abbey Worship Book* (Glasgow: Wild Goose Publications, 2001), p. 18.

and pondering how to interpret the Word in Christian life. Through this proclamation and response, worshipers hear an account of God's mission in the past and the promises of the fullness of the reign of God yet to come, and they are summoned to participate in the mission of God in the present.

In this chapter, I explore the story of God's mission as told in Scripture and consider which particular stories are told in the assembly. Turning from proclamation to response, I discuss not only the sermon but also silence and the use of a creed as forms of response.

"The Memoirs of the Apostles, and the Writings of the Prophets"

Worship, the Nairobi Statement tells us, is transcultural, incorporating elements that transcend particular cultural expressions and so uniting believers across time, space, culture, and confession. The proclamation of Scripture in the Sunday assembly is one such element.

Since the first century, the followers of Jesus have read Scripture at worship, as was Jewish practice. Luke reports that Jesus begins his ministry by teaching in the synagogues. On the Sabbath, he reads from the scroll of the prophet Isaiah, "The Spirit of the Lord is upon me" (Luke 4:16-18; see Isa. 61:1). When Paul and Barnabas visit the synagogue in Antioch, both the law and the prophets are read (Acts 13:15). As Jesus' followers began to meet in their assemblies apart from the synagogue, they continued the practice of reading Scripture.

Already in the first century, reading in the assembly may have extended beyond the Hebrew Scriptures. At the end of a letter to the church in Thessalonika, Paul directs, "Greet all the brothers and sisters with a holy kiss. I solemnly command you by the Lord that this letter be read to all of them" (1 Thess. 5:26-27). The letter to the Colossians concludes with this instruction: "And when this letter has been read among you, have it read also in the church [*ekklesia*] of the Laodiceans; and see that you read also the letter from Laodicea" (Col. 4:16). The letters of Paul and other church leaders were intended to be read aloud, and this may have occurred when the followers of Jesus assembled for worship. Paul exhorts the church in Corinth, "When you come together, each one has a hymn, a lesson, a revelation, a tongue, or an interpretation. Let all things be done for building up" (1 Cor. 14:26). Paul

Bradshaw has proposed that Paul may be describing an early form of a ministry of the Word, which occurred during the assembly for a meal and would have been quite different from synagogue study of the law and the prophets.[3]

In addition to reading Scripture and letters from Paul and others, the followers of Jesus also told the stories of Jesus during their assemblies. In the earliest days, eyewitnesses spoke of their experiences. As others learned the stories, they, too, repeated them in the assembly. Justin Martyr notes this practice in his description of the Sunday assembly at Rome during the second century: "The memoirs of the apostles or the writings of the prophets are read."[4] The "memoirs of the apostles" are the narratives that we now know as the Gospels, which by the time of Justin were being written down, while the "writings of the prophets" may refer to readings from the Old Testament prophets. By the fourth century, the Four Gospels became the canonically accepted stories of Jesus, while some of the letters became part of the larger canon of Christian Scripture.

Scripture: The Story of God's Mission

In 1966, historian J. G. Davies explained the relationship between mission and the reading of Scripture in the assembly in this way: "The Bible is the record of a sending God; consequently, to read from it, in the course of worship, is to present the hearers with an account of the *missio Dei* in the past, which becomes a summons to participate in it in the present."[5] As Davies suggests, this is not only a historical account, something that occurred long ago and far away; it is also a story that comes alive for us today. When Scripture is proclaimed in the assembly, worshipers encounter the living God and so are drawn into God's mission.

The Bible tells the story of God's mission from the beginning of creation to the promised new creation. As contemporary Trinitarian theologies have emphasized, God's very essence is to be in relationship, a relationship that

3. Paul F. Bradshaw, *Eucharistic Origins* (New York and Oxford: Oxford University Press, 2004), pp. 69-72.

4. Justin, *I Apology* 67.

5. J. G. Davies, *Worship and Mission* (London: SCM Press, 1966; New York: Association Press, 1967), p. 130.

extends beyond God's self to all of creation. Theologian Catherine LaCugna describes "the comprehensive plan of God reaching from creation to consummation, in which God and all creatures are destined to exist together in the mystery of love and communion."[6] We know who God is through our glimpses of God's work in the world, God's self-expression.

"In the beginning," Genesis tells us, "God created the heavens and the earth" (Gen. 1:1). God speaks, and the world comes into being. The Gospel of John begins by reiterating the creation story: "In the beginning was the Word, and the Word was with God, and the Word was God. . . . All things came into being through him, and without him not one thing came into being" (John 1:1-2). The creation accounts in the first chapters of Genesis tell of a God who is active, whose love flows outward and is manifest in the richness of creation. Human beings, created in the image of God, have the capacity for relationship with God. But to participate in this divine giving and receiving of love, humanity must have the freedom to choose to respond to God, a freedom that includes the possibility of turning away from God, of harming one another, and of acting contrary to God's desire for creation. The story of creation is followed quickly by the story of the Fall, acknowledging the reality of sin and evil and the resulting distortions and destruction.

Yet this is only the beginning. Scripture tells us again and again of God's desire and God's mission to restore us to union with God, with one another, and with all creation. Eleanor Kreider and Alan Kreider emphasize that God acts not with compulsion or coercion but by sending. "Sending *(missio)*, not compelling, is God's *modus operandi*."[7] Again and again, we find a dynamic of calling and sending. God calls Abram and Sarai and sends them to a distant land, promising to make their descendants a great nation (Gen. 12:1-2). God calls Moses and sends him to lead the people of Israel out of slavery in Egypt (Exod. 2:1-12). As the Israelites wander in the wilderness, God calls them to be "a priestly kingdom and a holy nation" (Exod. 19:6). When the people of Israel continue to stumble, to turn their backs on God, to oppress those who are poor or in need, God sends a succession of prophets whose

6. Catherine Mowry LaCugna, *God for Us: The Trinity and Christian Life* (San Francisco: HarperSanFrancisco, 1991), p. 223.

7. Alan Kreider and Eleanor Kreider, *Worship and Mission after Christendom* (Scottdale, Pa., and Waterloo, Ontario: Herald Press, 2011), p. 48.

mission is to call the people back to justice and righteousness. God calls Jeremiah when he is still a youth, despite Jeremiah's protests that he does not know how to speak. "You shall go to all to whom I send you, and you shall speak whatever I command you" (Jer. 1:7). Isaiah receives a vision of God's glory, and one of the seraphim touches his lips with a burning coal, purifying him. When God asks for a messenger, Isaiah replies, "Here am I; send me" (Isa. 6:8). Nor is this mission limited to particular prophets. The later chapters of Isaiah sketch a vision of a future with God in which God's house is a "house of prayer for all nations" (Isa. 56:6). In this promised age to come, God "will send survivors to the nations . . . to the coastlands far away that have not heard of my fame or seen my glory; and they shall declare my glory among the nations" (Isa. 66:19). Israel is sent to be a light to the nations, a sign of God's grace, mercy, and love for all creation, and so to participate in God's mission, restoring the world to unity with God and one another.

"In the last times," says an ancient prayer, "you [God] sent to us a savior and redeemer . . . who is your inseparable Word, through whom you made all things, and in whom you were well pleased."[8] In sending Jesus, God's own self enters human history; the Word becomes flesh (John 1:14). Through the incarnation, life, death, and resurrection of Jesus, God acts to restore humankind to right relationship with every creature and with God.[9] In the particular flesh of Jesus, we see who God is for the whole world. Theologian Leonardo Boff explains that the incarnation "shows the Trinity's eternal design: to bring all beings into its communion through the mediating of the Son and the driving force of the Holy Spirit."[10]

In his ministry, Jesus calls others and sends them to participate in his mission. Matthew, Mark, and Luke report that Jesus calls together the Twelve and sends them to heal the sick and proclaim the good news (Matt. 10:5-15; Mark 6:7-13; Luke 9:1-6). Luke adds a second narrative (Luke 10:1-12) that extends this commissioning beyond the inner circle of the Twelve to seventy others. The message is similar: heal the sick and announce that the reign of

---

8. "The Anaphora of *The Apostolic Tradition*," in *Sacraments and Worship: The Sources of Christian Theology*, ed. Maxwell E. Johnson (Louisville: Westminster John Knox Press, 2012), p. 194.

9. LaCugna, *God for Us*, pp. 292-96.

10. Leonardo Boff, *Trinity and Society*, trans. Paul Burns (Maryknoll, N.Y.: Orbis Books, 1988), p. 186.

God has come near. These messengers, like the Twelve, are to travel light, without a bag or purse or extra clothes, and they are to receive the hospitality offered by the people of each town they visit. Mission is always dialogical, requiring openness to the other, emptying oneself as Christ emptied himself (Phil. 2:5-11).[11] With mission comes the possibility of rejection; Jesus tells those he sends, "Whenever you enter a town and they do not welcome you, go out into its streets and say, 'Even the dust of your town that clings to our feet, we wipe off in protest against you. Yet know this: the kingdom of God has come near'" (Luke 10:10-11). Jesus himself experiences that rejection, culminating in his death on a cross.

After his death and resurrection, Jesus continues to send messengers. Mary Magdalene has been called "apostle to the apostles" because Jesus sends her from the garden where she encounters the risen Jesus to tell this good news to the disciples (John 20:11-18). The risen Jesus also sends other disciples. Matthew reports that Jesus tells the eleven disciples to go to the people of all nations, to make them disciples (Matt. 28:18-20). In John's Gospel, the risen Jesus appears to disciples who are cowering behind closed doors and tells them, "As the Father has sent me, so I send you" (John 20:21). The disciples are thus called to participate in Jesus' mission, to join in his acts of love and mercy and in his proclamation that the reign of God has come near.

The Johannine narrative introduces another key aspect of God's mission: the sending of the Holy Spirit. During the Last Supper, according to John, Jesus promises, "The Holy Spirit, whom the Father will send in my name, will teach you everything, and remind you of all that I have said to you" (John 14:26). When the risen Jesus appears to the disciples, he breathes on them, bestowing the Holy Spirit (John 20:22). Luke tells another story: the dramatic descent of the Spirit with a rushing wind and tongues of fire on the day of Pentecost (Acts 2:1-11).

Just as the Word was with God from the beginning, so too the Spirit is present at creation. The Hebrew word for spirit, *ruach,* can also mean "wind" or "breath," and this is the word used in Genesis to speak of God's action at the beginning of creation: "a wind [*ruach*] from God swept over the face of the waters" (Gen. 1:2). The Spirit is present among the people of Israel,

---

11. Stephen B. Bevans and Roger P. Schroeder, *Constants in Context: A Theology of Mission for Today* (Maryknoll, N.Y.: Orbis Books, 2004), pp. 348-49.

especially in the prophets. "The spirit of the Lord GOD is upon me," says the prophet Isaiah (Isa. 61:1). This same Spirit comes upon Mary, and the child she bears is holy, the Son of God (Luke 1:35). The Spirit descends on Jesus at his baptism (Matt. 3:13-17; Mark 1:9-11; Luke 3:21-22), and, according to Luke, Jesus begins his ministry "filled with the power of the Spirit" (Luke 4:14).

The Holy Spirit, says Catherine LaCugna, is always the "Spirit-of . . . the Spirit of God, Spirit of Christ, Spirit of the Christian community."[12] This Spirit "is God's outreach to the creature, and also the way back to God (Ephesians 2:18)."[13] Leonardo Boff summarizes the New Testament portrayal of the work of the Spirit:

> The Spirit is seen as the *power of the new* and of a *renewal* in all things . . . the Spirit in the New Testament is the *memory* of Jesus' deeds and words. . . . The Spirit makes us live as sons and daughters in our following of the incarnate Son, preventing us from forgetting the simplicity, humility, prophetic courage, will to serve others, and intimate relationship with the Father that characterized the Son. The Spirit's . . . mission is to *liberate* from the oppressions brought into being by our sinful state.[14]

God, through Christ, sends the Spirit, who acts in Christians and in the community that is the body of Christ, animating its activities and drawing the world into communion with God and into participation in God's mission. The New Testament tells the beginning of that story, particularly in the book of Acts, as the community of Jesus' followers, in response to the Spirit, spreads from Jerusalem to Judea and Samaria and throughout the ancient Mediterranean world.

Scripture, both Old Testament and New, also leans toward the future: "God's mission is to bring . . . God's redemptive reign. God's mission is . . . to bring new creation (Isaiah 65:17; 66:22; Galatians 6:15). God's mission is to make all things new (Colossians 1:20; Revelation 21:5) — humans with 'hearts of flesh' in a right relationship to God (Ezekiel 36:26), humans reconciled to their bitterest enemies (Isaiah 19:23-24), and the whole creation restored as

12. LaCugna, *God for Us*, p. 298.
13. LaCugna, *God for Us*, p. 297.
14. Boff, *Trinity and Society*, pp. 192-95; emphasis in original.

a place where justice is at home (2 Peter 3:13)."[15] Again and again, Jesus announces that the reign of God has come near. In the synagogue at Nazareth, Jesus reads from the prophet Isaiah: "The Spirit of the Lord is upon me, because he has anointed me to bring good news to the poor . . . to proclaim the year of the Lord's favor" (Luke 4:18-19; Isa. 61:1-2). After reading this prophecy, Jesus announces to those in the synagogue, "Today this scripture has been fulfilled in your hearing" (Luke 4:21). In his ministry, Jesus embodies and enacts the reign of God. When the disciples of John the Baptist ask Jesus, "Are you the one who is to come, or are we to wait for another?" Jesus responds, "Go and tell John what you hear and see: the blind receive their sight, the lame walk, the lepers are cleansed, the deaf hear, the dead are raised, and the poor have good news brought to them" (Matt. 11:3-5). Moreover, Jesus calls his followers and sends them to join him in proclaiming and embodying the reign of God, as Episcopalian theologian John Dally explains: "Jesus was asking his preachers . . . both to announce and to enact the kingdom of God by their words, by the meals they shared, and by their acts of healing and exorcism."[16]

When Scripture is proclaimed in the assembly, worshipers enter this stream of salvation history and come to understand themselves as participants in this story and actors in the performance of God's mission. Lutheran scholar and bishop Craig Satterlee describes Christian worship as a river: "Like a mighty river, the life and history of Israel, the saving work of Jesus, and the mission of the early church as these events are proclaimed in Scripture, are connected to one another and to the church's worship as the single, continuing story of God's saving activity in Jesus Christ."[17] In the worship of the Iona Community in Scotland, the leader who proclaims the Scripture concludes by saying, "for the Word of God in Scripture, for the Word of God among us, for the Word of God within us,"[18] linking the proclamation of Scripture in the assembly with God's presence in the world and in the worshipers.

The proclamation of Scripture thus informs and cultivates worshipers' identities as participants in the mission of God, drawn into God's self-offering of redemptive love through Christ and in the power of the Spirit.

---

15. Kreider and Kreider, *Worship and Mission after Christendom*, p. 46.

16. John Addison Dally, *Choosing the Kingdom: Missional Preaching for the Household of God* (Herndon, Va.: Alban Institute, 2008), p. 48.

17. Craig Satterlee, "Worship Is Mission," *Alban Weekly*, 19 January 2009, p. 2.

18. *Iona Abbey Worship Book*, p. 18.

Alan Kreider and Eleanor Kreider add that the narrative of salvation history must also be told because it is an "odd story," one that can be overwhelmed by conventional stories if it is not told and retold. The Bible's story is odd, say Kreider and Kreider, because "it has values that are upside down. God works not primarily through kings and superpowers but through marginal people and an insignificant nation. . . . [The story] assumes that God is present and active in the world [and] intervenes in human history with unpredictable displays and miracles . . . [and] it makes claims upon those who tell it."[19]

When Scripture is proclaimed in the assembly, worshipers become attuned to God's ways of acting, God's surprising grace. Jim Fodor elaborates: "From the Word of God Christian life inherits its peculiar character, discovers its orientation, and continually receives nourishment and power. Indeed, it is from the hearing of God's Word repeatedly read in public worship that a life of faith takes on something of its measured rhythms and cadences, its distinctive orchestration, but also its peculiar vision."[20] By telling and retelling the biblical stories, the assembly is, over time, shaped by these stories and empowered to participate in God's mission, as Orthodox theologian Alexander Schmemann explains: "[The proclamation of Scripture] transforms the human words of the Gospel into the Word of God and the manifestation of the kingdom. And it transforms the [person] who hears the Word into a receptacle of the Word and a temple of the Spirit."[21] Having received Christ anew and embodying the Spirit, worshipers then enact Christ's presence in the world, propelled from worship into other activities of mission, as in our spinning top.

What Story Do We Tell?

Scripture from Genesis to Revelation tells us of God's mission — that is, God's action from creation to new creation. Yet in any given worship service, only a portion of Scripture can be read. Over the centuries, Christians have

---

19. Kreider and Kreider, *Worship and Mission after Christendom*, pp. 67-69.

20. Jim Fodor, "Reading the Scriptures: Rehearsing Identity, Practicing Character," in *The Blackwell Companion to Christian Ethics*, ed. Stanley Hauerwas and Samuel Wells (Oxford and Malden, Mass.: Blackwell Publishing, 2004), p. 141.

21. Alexander Schmemann, *For the Life of the World: Sacraments and Orthodoxy*, 2nd ed., revised and expanded (Crestwood, N.Y.: St. Vladimir's Seminary Press, 1973), p. 33.

taken different approaches to deciding what Scripture to read on any given occasion.

Justin Martyr, writing during the second century, tells us that "the memoirs of the apostles or the writings of the prophets are read as long as time permits."[22] There is no fixed reading assigned for the regular Sunday assembly. It is likely that this community employed a *lectio continua* approach to reading Scripture: a book of the Bible is read sequentially, the reading beginning each week where the reader had ended the week before. A different approach, *lectio selecta,* is evident in a paschal homily of Melito, a second-century bishop of Sardis, which begins, "We have just read from the scriptures the story of the Exodus of the Hebrews."[23] Rather than reading whatever came next in Scripture, for the annual paschal celebration the assembly at Sardis selected Exodus 12, the story of the Passover, and in his homily, Melito used the theological motifs of Passover and exodus — deliverance from slavery, redemption, new life — as key interpretive lenses for understanding the significance of Jesus' death and resurrection.

Over the course of the Middle Ages, the church in the West gradually developed a lectionary with fixed readings for every Sunday and feast of the year. Some churches of the Reformation, particularly Anglican and Lutheran churches, continued to follow a lectionary, while other Protestant churches developed their own practices for deciding which passage(s) of Scripture to read each week. Today, many churches use the *Revised Common Lectionary,* a version of the three-year lectionary first developed in the Roman Catholic Church after the Second Vatican Council.[24]

The lectionary provides a systematic pattern of readings that are shared by many churches, thus uniting believers from different places. Lutheran

22. Justin, *I Apology* 67.

23. Melito, "Homily on the Pasch," in *Springtime of the Liturgy: Liturgical Texts of the First Four Centuries,* by Lucien Deiss, trans. Matthew J. O'Connell (Collegeville, Minn.: Liturgical Press, 1979), p. 99.

24. For a brief history of lectionaries in Christian history, including the development of the *Revised Common Lectionary,* see the introduction to Consultation on Common Texts, *The Revised Common Lectionary: Twentieth Anniversary Edition,* by Fred Kimball Graham (Minneapolis: Fortress Press, 2012), pp. ix-xxv. For a list of churches using the *Revised Common Lectionary* in 1998, see Consultation on Common Texts, "Worldwide Usage of the Revised Common Lectionary," available at http://www.commontexts.org/rcl/usage.html.

liturgical scholar Jann Boyd Fullenwieder, while appreciating many aspects of this ordered reading of Scripture, also urges ongoing reflection on and critique of a lectionary. Though the selection of texts comes from beyond a particular pastor and congregation and has been received by wider church bodies, not just particular local churches, it is still, Fullenwieder reminds us, "a culturally influenced creation and must be understood as a communal editing of the Bible for the purposes of public worship." Preachers and assemblies might consider critical questions such as the following: "What is not included in these selected readings? By what principle of interpretation have certain narratives and figures been omitted from public hearing? Who benefits from the inclusions, and who benefits from the exclusions? Do the texts maintain the raw, confrontational oddness of the varied texts through which God speaks? Or is the colorful, cursing and blessing, embarrassing, scandalous activity of God and God's people tailored to please us? Is there an authentic representation of the tremendous cultural diversity through which the word of God comes to us in the Bible?"[25]

One such analysis, undertaken by Episcopalian Jean Campbell in the late 1980s, found that scriptural texts about women and those presenting feminine images of God were "omitted, optional, or alternative" in the three-year lectionary. For example, in Matthew's and Mark's accounts of an unnamed woman at Bethany anointing Jesus just before his last supper (Matt. 26:6-13; Mark 14:3-9), the Evangelists conclude with Jesus saying, "Wherever this good news is proclaimed in the whole world, what she has done will be told in remembrance of her." But in the 1979 Episcopal lectionary, that text appeared only as an alternative reading for Monday in Holy Week.[26] The lectionary overlooked the surprising and perhaps scandalous action of an anonymous woman who stands behind Jesus and pours oil over his head, as ancient prophets stood to anoint kings of Israel.[27] By omitting this story,

25. Jann E. Boyd Fullenwieder, "Proclamation: Mercy for the World," in *Inside Out: Worship in an Age of Mission,* ed. Thomas H. Schattauer (Minneapolis: Fortress Press, 1999), pp. 30-31.

26. Jean Campbell, "The Feminine as Omitted, Optional, or Alternative Story: A Review of the Episcopal Eucharistic Lectionary," in *How Shall We Pray? Expanding Our Language about God,* ed. Ruth A. Meyers (New York: Church Hymnal Corp., 1994), pp. 57-68.

27. The Consultation on Common Texts, the ecumenical North American body that developed the 1992 *Revised Common Lectionary,* made a deliberate effort to include biblical

the lectionary muted the participation of women in salvation history and their equality before God evidenced, for example, in Paul's statement that "in Christ Jesus . . . there is no longer male and female" (Gal. 3:26-28).

Whatever system is used, churches taking a missional approach to worship will be attentive to selecting Scripture in a manner that over time presents the narrative arc of salvation history. God's ways are not our ways, the prophet Isaiah reminds us (Isa. 55:8-9), and the public reading of Scripture must enable the assembly to be shaped by the stories of God, who exalts the humble and casts down the mighty, who calls an insignificant people to be a light to the nations, who deigns to become human and dies on a cross, who breathes new life into a frightened and dispirited people, whose Spirit strengthens and renews. By hearing these peculiar stories, the assembly re-aligns itself with the mission of God. James Smith explains the importance of being confronted with the full narrative scope of Scripture: "We begin to absorb the plot of the story, begin to see ourselves as characters within it; the habits and practices of its heroes function as exemplars, providing guidance as we are trained in virtue, becoming a people with a disposition to 'the good' as it's envisioned in the story."[28]

Unless a congregation reads systematically through the entire Bible (a process that would take years of reading on Sundays, since the Bible contains more books than there are Sundays in a year), only a selection can be read, even over a long period of time. "Given the significance of the Bible in the life of God's people," Lutheran scholar Clayton Schmit declares, "it seems advisable that congregations draw deeply from the well of Scripture during worship by hearing from several portions of the Bible."[29] The three-year common lectionary provides a way to read through a significant portion of the Bible over the course of several years and so engage the full sweep of Scripture, the story of God's mission from creation to new creation.

The three-year lectionary is structured around the feasts and seasons

---

stories of women and feminine images of God. Mark's story of the unnamed woman is now part of the passion gospel appointed on Palm Sunday in lectionary Year B. See Consultation on Common Texts, *The Revised Common Lectionary* (Nashville: Abingdon Press, 1992), p. 46; and Graham, introduction to the *Revised Common Lectionary,* pp. xxii-xxiii.

28. James K. A. Smith, *Desiring the Kingdom: Worship, Worldview, and Cultural Formation* (Grand Rapids: Baker Academic, 2009), p. 196.

29. Clayton J. Schmit, *Sent and Gathered: A Worship Manual for the Missional Church* (Grand Rapids: Baker Academic, 2009), p. 176.

of the liturgical year. Whether or not a church follows the lectionary, an assembly that celebrates these feasts and seasons can over time encounter much of the biblical narrative of salvation history. The two cycles, Christmas and Easter, allow communities to focus on different aspects of the paschal mystery of Jesus' incarnation, death, and resurrection, and to view these as part of the overall arc of salvation history.

Though the liturgical year thus commemorates many of the events in Jesus' life, it is not a systematic exposition of Jesus' life-story, from birth to baptism and ministry and on to passion, death, resurrection, and ascension. Rather, over the course of several centuries, Christians identified key elements of the story of Jesus that were important to celebrate, and they filled in the calendar of readings bit by bit. The three-year lectionary, developed with a view of the entire liturgical year as it had emerged over the course of many centuries, offers a systematic plan of readings suitable for the different occasions.

Moreover, every feast and season, every celebration, also celebrates the totality of God's mission of reconciliation.[30] We can imagine the year as a jewel with many facets. As we go through the year, we attend first to one facet, then another, yet the entire jewel is always present. For example, biblical scholar Raymond Brown's book *An Adult Christ at Christmas* presents the Christmas stories of Jesus' birth as summaries of the entire gospel and links these stories as well to Old Testament narratives of God's saving work in Israel.[31] By keeping the liturgical year, Christian assemblies celebrate both particular events in the life of Jesus and the fullness of God's saving work, and they come to understand their lives as part of the grand — and odd — story of God's love for the world.

Learning the Story

In today's assemblies, we cannot assume that everyone is Christian or even familiar with Scripture. A pastor whose congregation had revitalized its

---

30. Benjamin Gordon-Taylor, "Time," in *The Study of Liturgy and Worship: An Alcuin Guide,* ed. Juliette Day and Benjamin Gordon-Taylor (London: SPCK, 2013), p. 114.

31. Raymond Brown, *An Adult Christ at Christmas: Essays on the Three Biblical Christmas Stories — Matthew 2 and Luke 2* (Collegeville, Minn.: Liturgical Press, 1978).

worship in a way that was attracting many unchurched people reports a startling exchange with one of these newcomers: "Pastor, there's just one thing I don't understand about your worship. What are they doing when they stand up and read from that book?" We dare not underestimate the need for teaching the basics of the Bible in our post-Christendom world. The assembly needs to know *that* there is a story, a narrative of salvation history from Genesis to Revelation, in addition to coming to know the contours of that story.

A missional assembly might present the full story of God's saving work and invite reflection on the significance of this story for people today. For example, in April 2013, the Bexley Seabury Federation sponsored "Restoring the Biblical Imagination." One workshop, "The Bible for Nones[32]: Sights and Sounds of Scripture," offered an imaginative vision of the narrative arc of Scripture. Participants entered a chapel to find three installations: "Building the Temple," "Losing the Temple," and "Waiting for the City." Each installation included art, music, and text; each presented several short passages of Scripture (one or two verses) posted on sign boards; and each offered an activity. "Building the Temple" featured scriptural passages about the Old Testament stories of the formation of Israel and the creation of the Temple, and the New Testament narratives of the gathering of the disciples. These were juxtaposed with contemporary images of new relationships — for example, wedding pictures. A table held a set of children's building blocks, and a sign near it invited, "Build something." From "Building the Temple" at the entrance to the chapel, participants could move to the altar and pulpit area to experience "Losing the Temple." Here they found pictures and stories of tragedies such as school shootings and the attacks on September 11, 2001, along with scriptural passages about the exile of the Israelites to Babylon and Jesus' passion and crucifixion. "Write something," a sign said, and participants could respond by writing in a blank book. The final station, "Waiting for

---

32. Since the 1960s, scholars of religion have used the term "nones" to describe those who report that they have no religion or no religious preference. The Pew Research Center prefers "religiously unaffiliated," a term which they believe is more accurate, since "the absence of a religious affiliation does not necessarily indicate an absence of religious beliefs or practices." See "'Nones' on the Rise: One-in-Five Adults Have No Religious Affiliation," p. 7, Pew Forum (2012), available at http://www.pewforum.org/files/2012/10/NonesOnTheRise-full.pdf.

the City," was placed at the baptismal font, a large immersion font with running water. Scriptural passages here spoke of the New Jerusalem and the promised new creation. At this installation, a sign invited participants to "Eat something" from a basket of broken bread.

In the event program, the introduction to the "Bible for Nones" workshop explained, "The poet Mary Karr once said that trying to speak about faith to people who don't share it is 'like doing card tricks on the radio.' Too often, biblical studies creates a similar communication problem, stockpiling information about the writing and interpretation of the Bible when study after study has shown that the religiously non-affiliated don't want information; they want to connect to the tradition with their hearts." After participants had an opportunity to experience the installations, we gathered for a conversation with the workshop presenters. Most people had made some visceral connection with at least one of the movements. But we also acknowledged that those who participated in this workshop were believers with a strong religious affiliation. How would people with no religious affiliation experience the movements? What would the brief excerpts of Scripture mean to them?

Though set in a chapel, the installation was not an act of formal worship, yet a similar creative presentation of Scripture would be possible in a worship setting. Worship in some emerging churches does invite members of the assembly to respond actively to Scripture, in a manner similar to that of the installations at this workshop. In a study of churches in the United States and the United Kingdom, Anglican bishops Mary Gray-Reeves and Michael Perham report on the use of "stations" or "open space" in worship. At Church of the Apostles in Seattle, a Lenten service offered three stations, each responding to one of the appointed readings for the week. Worshipers could go to an "Old Testament Theology Wall" that presented two texts and an extract from a scholarly commentary. Here, reading and reflecting was the mode of response; Perham and Gray-Reeves found it to be "serious Bible study." Another station featured a "travel journal" where worshipers could ponder Philippians 3:14–4:1 and write down their thoughts. For response to Luke 13:31-35 ("How often have I desired to gather your children together as a hen gathers her brood under her wings, and you were not willing!"), worshipers were invited to light a candle and place it upright in sand to use as a focus for meditation as they reflected on the text. Gray-Reeves and Perham describe this approach as "an individual movement towards what one is drawn to, without judgment of one's self or one another."[33]

As at the workshop I attended, individuals engaged the materials at each station and responded as they felt moved. While those who prepared the stations may have had an interpretive lens guiding their design, the worshipers' responses were unscripted. Unlike the workshop stations, the stations at Church of the Apostles focused on three specific readings and did not attempt to make connections between or among them, much less present the full narrative arc of Scripture. Though a very different form of response to the Word, these stations are in some ways parallel to a more conventional sermon in which one speaks and the other members of the assembly listen. The stations expect an active response; a sermon also ought to expect a response, to engage worshipers' hearts and minds. When worship is mission, the response to Scripture, whatever form it takes, enables the assembly to "understand and embrace" God's Word as it intersects with worshipers' lives.[34]

Some churches, particularly emerging churches that are actively experimenting with different forms of worship, blend the proclamation of Scripture with response. Rather than reading directly from a carefully selected translation of Scripture, these assemblies present Scripture by reading a paraphrase, showing a video clip, or enacting the story.[35] I was part of such an alternative form of worship in September 2013, when I participated in a service at Iona Abbey entitled "Boundary Crossing." When we entered the abbey church, we found an unhinged door propped up against a chair at the west end of the nave. After gathering with a spoken call-and-response and a song, the assembly was seated for what the service leaflet entitled "Engaging." A man moved from his place to stand next to the door. Six other people came from different places among the assembly — one in a hooded sweatshirt (hood up) wearing dark glasses, another in coveralls splattered with paint, another wearing an apron, another wearing a clerical collar, another with a baseball

---

33. Mary Gray-Reeves and Michael Perham, *The Hospitality of God: Emerging Worship for a Missional Church* (New York: Seabury Books; London: SPCK, 2011), pp. 51-52.

34. Schmit, *Sent and Gathered*, p. 181.

35. Gray-Reeves and Perham, *The Hospitality of God*, p. 48. See also Eddie Gibbs and Ryan K. Bolger, *Emerging Churches: Creating Christian Community in Postmodern Cultures* (Grand Rapids: Baker Academic, 2005), especially Chapter 8, "Participating as Producers."

cap, and one wearing a dark shirt. As they emerged from their places, they moved slowly toward the door, staring intently at it.

Once they had arrived at the door, the person standing next to it pushed it over so that it landed with a loud thud. He picked it up and dropped it again, then slowly moved up the aisle — continuing to drop and pick up the door — to the altar at the east end. The only sound we heard was the jarring banging of the door as it was moved end over end. The six others followed, still staring at the door. At the altar, the man with the door propped it up against the altar and left the worship space. The others slowly backed away to the west end, their eyes still fixed on the door.

Finally, the silence was broken. The first watcher came to a microphone and spoke words of accusation against Jesus because his actions had disrupted the social order and threatened imperial power. When she finished speaking, she strode to the door with a handful of four-inch spikes. As she walked, the assembly sang the repetitive chant "Miserere nobis, Domine" ("Lord, have mercy"). After placing the spikes near the door, she turned her back on the door and walked quickly away. The next speaker spoke her accusations, then came forward with a hammer, which she hung on the top of the door. Once again, the assembly sang "Miserere nobis, Domine." Next came a man with a rope coiled in a circle that looked something like a crown of thorns; he hung the rope on top of the door. Then, one after the other, two actors brought four-by-four beams, placing one upright and angling the other across the upright, using the coil of rope to support it. Each time an actor moved toward the door, the assembly sang the chant. Each actor turned away from the door and strode quickly away once he or she had set down an object. Finally, the last person placed a card inscribed "INRI" on the floor in front of the door.

Many of us were mystified as the scene began to unfold. The extended movement — the actors moving toward the door, then following the door end-over-end up the aisle, then backing away while gazing intently at the door — drew our attention, even though we didn't understand what was happening. Gradually, as actors spoke accusations against Jesus (never using his name, only "You") and set down their props, the meaning became evident. I thought about Jesus as the gate for the sheep (John 10:8-10), and Jesus' command to enter by the narrow door (Luke 13:23-25). I remembered the stained-glass window in the chapel where I worshiped as a child, depicting Jesus waiting at a door. The door in the window had no handle because, my mother explained, *we* had to open the door for Jesus (Rev. 3:19-21). I pondered what it means to cross a threshold. The extended dramatic presentation provided space for reflection, a response of sorts, as the scriptural story was being told. After the tableau was complete, the assembly joined the proclamation by singing "Look out, Jesus, beware."

Then the worship moved from "Engaging" to "Responding." One of the worship leaders talked about crossing boundaries, about how Jesus challenged the status quo and crossed lines, about the limits and boundaries we face. She called our attention to strips of yellow-and-black-striped caution tape on the floor, which created boundary lines. If we wished, she said, we could choose to go and stand at one of the lines and pray silently about boundaries that keep us from walking in newness of life with Christ. We could also choose to step over the line as a sign of commitment to follow Jesus, whose love crosses lines and exceeds limits that deny humanity fullness of life.

We stood to sing "Lord Jesus Christ, Shall I Stand Still?" The leader had said that during the final verse, we could move to make an act of commitment at one of the lines. When the song ended, the music continued for several minutes. I looked up from my own prayer and was deeply moved to see a number of people standing at different lines. Yet not everyone went to a line, and not everyone who did go to a line chose to step over it. Participating in the actions of standing at and stepping over a line was an individual decision, and the design of the worship made this physical response an invitation rather than an obligation.

Like the workshop "The Bible for Nones," the "Boundary Crossing" service invited worshipers to engage with Scripture. While the workshop presented the entire narrative arc and included both Old and New Testaments, the Iona service focused on Jesus' mission. Neither by itself would be sufficient to enable those unfamiliar with Scripture to learn the story. But each pointed to the possibility of creative proclamation and response to Scripture that intrigues and engages participants and thereby draws them into the story of salvation. As J. G. Davies points out, preaching is "an exposition of the written Word of God that it may become a living Word."[36] James

36. Davies, *Worship and Mission,* p. 132.

Smith underscores the relationship between the proclamation of Scripture and Christian discipleship: "The biblical story, situated in the context of the church's worship . . . , fills out and specifies what the kingdom *(telos)* of God's people looks like. . . . It shows us the kind of people we're called to be."[37] When worship is mission is worship . . . (as in our Möbius strip), the proclamation and response to the Word enable the assembly over time to learn the story of God's love for the world, from creation to consummation, and to find their place in that story.

Interpreting the Story

Scripture itself tells us of the importance of interpretation. On the road to Emmaus, after the resurrection, the risen Jesus encounters two dispirited disciples and interprets "the things about himself in all the scriptures" (Luke 24:27) — that is, in what Christians now call the Old Testament. Acts tells the story of Philip's encounter with an Ethiopian official who is reading Isaiah as he travels. When Philip asks him whether he understands what he is reading, the official replies, "How can I, unless someone guides me?" (Acts 8:31). So Philip joins the official in his chariot, "and starting with this scripture [Isaiah 53:7-8, which the official had been reading], he proclaimed to him the good news about Jesus" (Acts 8:35). In this story, the proclamation serves the mission of God. The official, upon hearing the good news, asks to be baptized, thus spreading the community of believers further, beyond Jerusalem and Judea.

Those who preach in the assembly participate in God's mission. "How are they to call on one in whom they have not believed? And how are they to believe in one of whom they have never heard? And how are they to hear without someone to proclaim him? And how are they to proclaim him unless they are sent?" (Rom. 10:14-15). Stephen Bevans and Roger Schroeder, drawing upon the work of Mortimer Arias, explain that proclamation communicates the gospel *about* Jesus, his life, ministry, death, and resurrection, as well as "the gospel *of* Jesus — how his parables called his disciples to be forgiving, how his miracles called them to be agents of healing and wholeness, how his

37. Smith, *Desiring the Kingdom*, p. 197.

exorcisms called them to be opposed absolutely to evil in every form, how his inclusive lifestyle called them to be inclusive." This is not just the story of what is past, but an invitation for "those who believe in the gospel of and about Jesus to join in making that gospel visible and audible in the world."[38]

Bevans and Schroeder are discussing proclamation in the world, outside of the assembly, but their remarks apply equally to preaching in the assembly. A sermon explores the gospel of and about Jesus and its claim on the assembly today, its significance for the world. More broadly, a sermon invites members of the assembly to make connections between their lives and the narrative arc of Scripture: the life and history of Israel; the life, death, and resurrection of Jesus; and the experiences of the early church. Nicholas Lash likens biblical texts to a script for the performance of a piece of music or drama: "The performance of Scripture *is* the life of the church."[39] Missional preaching helps worshipers imagine how they might perform Scripture in their daily lives. Gregory Augustine Pierce suggests that preachers prepare with the dismissal in mind, so that they connect the readings to mission.[40] The dynamic interplay of worship and mission is evident. In the performance of Scripture in worship, the assembly encounters the living God. God is at work, speaking anew and calling worshipers into new life. Worshipers are then sent forth to perform Scripture in the world, to participate in God's mission, to embody and enact the "liturgy after the liturgy."[41] Lash points out that "the *poles* of Christian interpretation are . . . patterns of human action: what was said and done and suffered, then by Jesus and his disciples, and what is said and done and suffered, now, by those who seek to share his obedience and his hope."[42] During worship, we give particular attention to what was said and done by Jesus and his disciples, and more broadly to God's action from creation to consummation. These texts shape us, disciplining and schooling us as followers of Christ who are called and sent to embody God's reconciling love.

38. Bevans and Schroeder, *Constants in Context*, pp. 357-58.

39. Nicholas Lash, *Theology on the Way to Emmaus* (London: SCM Press, 1986), p. 43.

40. Gregory F. Augustine Pierce, *The Mass Is Never Ended: Rediscovering Our Mission to Transform the World* (Notre Dame: Ave Maria Press, 2007), p. 49.

41. Ion Bria, *The Liturgy after the Liturgy: Mission and Witness from an Orthodox Perspective* (Geneva: WCC Publications, 1996), p. 21.

42. Lash, *Theology on the Way to Emmaus*, p. 42.

Missional preaching also gives the assembly new lenses, God-shaped lenses, with which to view the world. The task of missional preaching, says John Dally, "is to proclaim the reign of God in a way that listeners can grasp it and freely choose it as gift."[43] Drawing on the prophetic aspect of mission, preaching opens the eyes of the assembly to God at work in the world and to places in the world that are desperately in need of God's justice and righteousness. Dally argues that rather than informing the assembly of the correct interpretation of Scripture and attempting to convince them to respond, missional preaching proclaims the reign of God and invites members of the assembly to discern the significance of this proclamation.[44] Such preaching turns the assembly outward, toward the world, and issues an invitation — God's call — to participate in God's mission in the world, to engage in public service as ambassadors for reconciliation (2 Cor. 5:18-20) and as workers for justice, peace, and the integrity of creation.

Justice and Proclamation: Addressing Anti-Judaism

Missional preaching not only identifies injustice in the world and situations that are in need of God's healing and reconciling love. It is also mindful of the church's actions that are unjust and sinful. While not speaking specifically about preaching, Alan Kreider and Eleanor Kreider argue, "If we don't study our past, repent of it, and allow God to transform it, it will come back and haunt us. The repressed past impedes God's mission. . . . Some things we must recall with repentance and discard as 'baggage' that weighs us down."[45]

One important element of our past is the Christian accusation that Jews rejected Jesus and were responsible for his death. During the centuries of Christendom, Christians persecuted and murdered Jews in the name of Christianity. New Testament scholar Marilyn Salmon underscores how preaching often fomented violent responses. Christians, she writes, "were incited against Jews by the preaching of contempt they heard in their churches. Jews were charged with deicide, with rejecting God's Messiah, disobedience

43. Dally, *Choosing the Kingdom*, p. 105.
44. Dally, *Choosing the Kingdom*, pp. 107-21.
45. Kreider and Kreider, *Worship and Mission after Christendom*, p. 79.

against God for rejecting the truth of their own Scriptures. That was how the church interpreted its Scriptures."[46]

After the Holocaust, churches began to examine their teaching about Jews and Judaism and to repudiate anti-Jewish rhetoric and action. Many denominations issued official statements, and Christian scholars have sought to uncover and eradicate supersessionism, the idea that the church has replaced Israel as God's chosen people.[47]

Although some New Testament texts can be read as condemning Jewish practice and so providing a foundation for later Christian supersessionism, contemporary Christian and Jewish scholars point out that the original context for these texts is an argument within Judaism as Jews sought to understand the significance of Jesus. Jesus' followers, like other Jews in the first century, understood themselves in the context of their history. They drew upon their Scriptures, the Law and the prophets, to guide their lives and interpret their experiences, including their experiences of Jesus. Like believers today, Jews who lived in the first century, some of them disciples of Jesus, disagreed about the interpretation of Scripture, what Christians today call the Old Testament. Some of these disputes are evident in what Christians today call the New Testament. Eventually, these arguments led to divergent paths with different understandings of the community's identity and future with God.[48] Today, responsible and just Christian preaching in the assembly must be attentive to the possibility of anti-Jewish bias and guard against perpetuating anti-Jewish stereotypes. Polemical texts in the New Testament must be interpreted in their historical context, not applied to Jews of all times and places.

46. Marilyn J. Salmon, *Preaching without Contempt: Overcoming Unintended Anti-Judaism* (Minneapolis: Fortress Press, 2006), p. 10.

47. Daniel Joslyn-Siemiatkoski, "Moses Received the Torah at Sinai and Handed It On (Mishnah Avot 1:1): The Relevance of the Written and Oral Torah for Christians," *Anglican Theological Review* 91 (2009): 444-46.

48. Pontifical Biblical Commission, "The Jewish People and Their Sacred Scriptures in the Christian Bible" (2001; official English translation, 2002), available at http://www.vatican .va/roman_curia/congregations/cfaith/pcb_documents/rc_con_cfaith_doc_20020212_popolo -ebraico_en.html#1.%20Affirmation%20of%20a%20reciprocal%20relationship. See also Charles Miller, "Translation Errors in the Pontifical Biblical Commission's 'The Jewish People and Their Sacred Scriptures in the Christian Bible,'" *Biblical Theology Bulletin* 35, no. 1 (Spring 2005): 34-39. Miller argues that scholarly work on this document should rely on the original French text rather than the English translation.

The three-year lectionary has done a great service for Western Christianity by re-introducing the regular reading of Old Testament texts in Sunday worship, providing a much fuller presentation of the entire sweep of Scripture and its vision of God's mission. The lectionary that developed during the Middle Ages included only epistle and Gospel readings, and hence Christians who used this lectionary or some variant thereof rarely if ever heard Old Testament texts proclaimed in worship.[49] The common lectionary provides readings from the Old Testament for most of the liturgical year, including an option of semi-continuous readings during the season after Pentecost that provide even more of a narrative arc. However, for the season of Easter it appoints texts from Acts and the epistles rather than Old Testament passages. Historian Daniel Joslyn-Siemiatkoski criticizes this approach because "the implicit message is that the revelation of God to Israel . . . has no relevance as Christians celebrate the cornerstone of their faith, the resurrection of Jesus Christ from the dead."[50] Moreover, several of the readings appointed from Acts portray the Jewish authorities as responsible for the death of Jesus. For example, in Peter's sermon on Pentecost, appointed for the second Sunday of Easter in Year A, Peter tells the Israelites, "you crucified [Jesus] and killed [him] by the hands of those outside the law" (Acts 2:23).

Beyond giving attention to Old Testament narratives, missional preachers will also be sensitive to interpreting the New Testament in ways that do not denigrate Jewish people. In *Preaching the Gospels without Blaming the Jews*, Ronald Allen and Clark Williamson underscore the importance of eliminating anti-Judaism from preaching: "Anti-Judaism contradicts the good news which it is the preacher's task to re-present to the congregation.

---

49. The medieval missal appointed introit psalms for each Sunday or feast, but these were not part of the lectionary. From the late sixteenth century until at least the mid-nineteenth century, common practice in Anglican churches, both the Church of England and the Episcopal Church in the United States, was to celebrate both Morning Prayer and Holy Communion as a single Sunday service. These services would have included appointed readings from the Old and New Testaments as part of Morning Prayer and from an epistle and a Gospel for the communion service. For further discussion, see Byron D. Stuhlman, *Eucharistic Celebration: 1789-1979* (New York: Church Hymnal Corp., 1980), pp. 54-55, 96-98.

50. Daniel Joslyn-Siemiatkoski, "Anti-Judaism and the Liturgy: Theological Reflections on Covenant and Language," pp. 8-9 (unpublished paper presented to The Episcopal Church Standing Commission on Liturgy and Music, October 2010).

That good news is about the radical grace of God, God's unbounded love, the witness of God's mercy that is extended freely to absolutely everybody, *even* us. Anti-Judaism is an exclusivism, an us-them, insider-outsider point of view that makes being one of us the condition for gaining access to God's love and grace."[51] The subtitle of Marilyn Salmon's *Preaching without Contempt: Overcoming Unintended Anti-Judaism* suggests that anti-Jewish polemic may occur unwittingly rather than as a result of intentional ill will toward Jewish people. For example, she suggests that when preaching on the Gospel of John, preachers should "resist the temptation of using Jews or Jewish groups as a foil: the blind Pharisees, the Jewish authorities, the synagogue leaders, the Jews who question Jesus. A sermon might include at least a few sentences reminding us that all the people in the narrative were first-century Jews, that the Jews themselves were a minority and all were vulnerable to the imperial power of Rome, that the writer [of the Gospel] is not critical of all Jews and that he is disapproving of some believers."[52]

Missional preaching does not require that every sermon address directly the problem of Christian anti-Judaism. It does, however, require that preachers be aware of New Testament passages that can be interpreted as a blanket condemnation of Jewish people and guard against incorporating such perspectives into their sermons, and that those who listen to sermons ask themselves about the implications of Scripture for Christian relationships with Jewish people today. Missional preaching takes account of every aspect of mission, including interreligious dialogue,[53] and it invites and encourages the assembly to embody and enact the mission of God in the world.

Who Speaks?

The model of worship inherited from the medieval Western church gives authority to a single person, typically one who is ordained, to interpret the Word and preach in the assembly. In the sixteenth century, Protestant re-

---

51. Ronald J. Allen and Clark M. Williamson, *Preaching the Gospels without Blaming the Jews: A Lectionary Commentary* (London: SCM Press, 1989), p. 7.

52. Salmon, *Preaching without Contempt*, p. 121.

53. Bevans and Schroeder, *Constants in Context*, pp. 378-85.

formers urged that every Christian take an active role in the interpretation and practice of the faith, as Lutheran scholar Mary Jane Haemig explains: "The Lutheran reformers of the sixteenth century saw oversight of the teaching and practice of the Christian faith as the task of every Christian."[54] In most churches of the Reformation, however, this responsibility did not extend to preaching in worship.

Some of the more radical reformers argued that speaking in the assembly not be limited to the ordained leader. In 1547, Pilgram Marpeck, a leader in the Anabaptist movement, wrote, "We should . . . diligently discern what God the heavenly Father has conferred upon and given to each for the service of building up the body of Christ. The gifts of every single member must be heard and seen."[55] During the seventeenth century, English Baptist congregations introduced a practice of running exposition or commentary as Scripture was read in the assembly,[56] a practice that continued in some churches until the nineteenth century. The leader of worship would preach extemporaneously, followed by several others who would also preach extempore from the same texts.[57]

Although there is thus evidence that some churches extended the interpretation of Scripture during the assembly beyond preaching by a single ordained leader, to this day the response to the Word in many churches normally takes the form of a sermon that one person preaches. In some churches, particularly those in African-American traditions, the assembly responds audibly, but even in these churches the preacher has full responsibility for interpreting the Word for the assembly.

In 1966, J. G. Davies proposed that a dialogue of sorts replace the monologue sermon: "It should be possible to prepare the sermon by means of team work, so that through joint participation the concrete situations of

54. Mary Jane Haemig, "Laypeople as Overseers of the Faith: A Reformation Proposal," *Trinity Seminary Review* 27 (2006): 25.

55. Pilgram Marpeck, "Concerning the Lowliness of Christ (1547)," in *The Writings of Pilgram Marpeck*, ed. William Klaassen (Scottdale, Pa.: Herald Press, 1978), p. 442; cited by Kreider and Kreider in *Worship and Mission after Christendom*, p. 118.

56. Horton Davies, *The Worship of the English Puritans* (Westminster: Dacre Press, 1948), p. 95.

57. Christopher Ellis, *Gathering: A Theology and Spirituality of Worship in Free Church Tradition* (London: SCM Press, 2004), p. 128.

the contemporary world, known to the laity from within, may be taken into account." The purpose, Davies argued, was to advance God's mission. Citing Lesslie Newbigin, he insisted that a sermon must be more than a simple announcement of certain acts of God in history: "We have to show how 'God's unique and saving revelation of himself in Jesus Christ enables [people] to interpret what is happening to them and to respond to the calling of God in the midst of the life of the world.'"[58] Because of the complexity of contemporary society, Davies argued, preachers were no longer sufficiently familiar with the particular situations of their congregations to be able to help them connect Scripture with their daily lives.

Alan Kreider and Eleanor Kreider share Davies' concern that the sermon relate Scripture to the lives of the assembly and so foster the assembly's participation in God's mission. They call for multi-voiced worship — that is, worship in which many participants may speak. In the worship of the first-century Corinthian community, Kreider and Kreider argue, "each worshiper was able to make a contribution of some sort [1 Cor. 14:26]. They participated according to an etiquette of participation [1 Cor. 14:27-32], a kind of free liturgy, in which people took turns, in which members spoke freely, deferred to each other, and discerned what God had said; further, they brought hymns, teaching, and revelations."[59] In churches of various kinds today, they propose, it is possible for multi-voiced worship to complement the sermon.[60] They urge in particular the incorporation of testimony, a practice of Christians speaking about their experience of God in their lives. "Especially in Western cultures, in which we are surrounded by principled secularism and spiritual anorexia, testimony renews Christians in the belief that God is alive and that God's mission of comprehensive reconciliation is moving forward in surprising ways."[61]

Thomas Hoyt Jr., a New Testament scholar and bishop in the Christian Methodist Episcopal Church, discusses the practice of testimony in the black

58. Davies, *Worship and Mission*, p. 134, citing Lesslie Newbigin, *The Relevance of Trinitarian Doctrine for Today's Mission* (London: Edinburgh House Press for the World Council of Churches, 1963), p. 28.

59. Kreider and Kreider, *Worship and Mission after Christendom*, p. 107.

60. Kreider and Kreider, *Worship and Mission after Christendom*, pp. 121-29; quotation on p. 123.

61. Kreider and Kreider, *Worship and Mission after Christendom*, p. 130.

church. At Sunday morning worship and weeknight prayer meetings, people tell the truth of their lives; someone says, for example, "Thank you, God, for waking me up this morning; for putting shoes on my feet, clothes on my back, and food on my table. Thank you, God, for health and strength and the activities of my limbs. Thank you that I awoke this morning clothed in my right mind." Hoyt explains that such testimony is not just an individual act of speaking; rather, "that person's speech takes place within the context of other people's listening, expecting, and encouraging."[62] Moreover, testimony in the black church is rooted in biblical testimony, enabling African-Americans to recognize the activity of God in their own lives. Any vital Christian community can engage in the practice of testimony, Hoyt insists, since the key elements of Bible and Spirit are present in every Christian community. "Any time the gathered people 'project their humanity in the togetherness of the Spirit,' as James Cone puts it, they bear witness to God's transformative power in their midst."[63]

Hoyt includes preaching in his exploration of testimony. He explains, "The preacher is a witness who searches the Scriptures on behalf of the community and then returns to the community to speak what he or she has found." Preachers, Hoyt maintains, give testimony, a form of witness that requires a response from those who receive it. Thus preaching is a practice of the whole church, "one that makes compelling claims on both preacher and hearers."[64]

John Dally also calls for preaching to be a community activity. He maintains that "the missional sermon needs to become dialogical, either during the act of preaching itself or through opportunities following worship, in study and ministry group meetings, or in online parish blogs."[65] Such dialogue will invite members of the assembly to explore the implications of the reign of God and choose whether and how to live in accord with its precepts.

Dialogical preaching is a regular practice at St. Gregory of Nyssa Episcopal Church in San Francisco. Here, as in many assemblies, the proclamation of Scripture leads to a sermon. Then, as in very few assemblies, comes

---

62. Thomas Hoyt Jr., "Testimony," in *Practicing Our Faith: A Way of Life for a Searching People,* ed. Dorothy C. Bass, 2nd ed. (San Francisco: Jossey-Bass, 1997, 2010), p. 92.

63. Hoyt Jr., "Testimony," p. 95.

64. Hoyt Jr., "Testimony," p. 96.

65. Dally, *Choosing the Kingdom,* p. 120.

an invitation: the preacher invites members of the assembly to respond, encouraging people to listen to one another and to the silence, "since God is speaking in both."[66] Some people respond directly to the sermon; others speak about their experience of God in their lives or about their needs and concerns. The preacher facilitates the dialogue and draws it to a close. Such multi-voiced worship demonstrates that there is wisdom among the whole people of God, not just in the ordained leader of the assembly. Missional communities expect that God is at work in their midst, and they trust that the Spirit of God gives believers wisdom and understanding that will enable them to make connections between their experiences and the scriptural stories of God. In missional communities, authority for interpreting the Word is thus shared rather than limited to a credentialed leader.

Silence

A different way to share a response to the Word is through silence. When the assembly takes an extended time for silent reflection, whether after the proclamation of Scripture or after the sermon, there is an opportunity for the Spirit to speak to all. Quaker worship practice is founded on the principle of silence. Drawing on the work of Rudolf Otto, historian Horton Davies distinguishes "the numinous silence of sacrament" — that is, the experience of God's transcendence "in gracious, intimate presence"; "the silence of waiting," an inward detachment and concentration; and "the silence of union" — that is, the union of worshipers with one another and with God.[67] In silence, members of the assembly can listen for the still, small voice of God and be open to the movement of the Spirit in their midst.

Today, the practice of silence is countercultural. In the world around us, a soundtrack plays underneath most activities and in public places such as elevators and airports. Rarely do we experience true silence when we are with other people, and even when we are alone, many of us are tuned in to an iPod or similar device, or have a radio or a television playing. In a public meeting,

---

66. Paul Fromberg, e-mail message to the author, 20 November 2013.

67. Horton Davies, *Worship and Theology in England,* Book II, Volume III: *From Watts and Wesley to Maurice, 1690-1850* (Grand Rapids: Wm. B. Eerdmans, 1996), p. 119.

silence often leads participants to wonder what has gone wrong, or who has made a mistake. Yet some Christian assemblies intentionally incorporate silence in their worship, challenging the cultural norms.

A distinctive feature of worship in the Taizé community is an extended silence at each of the three daily services. After Scripture is proclaimed, the assembly sings a short chant, and then everyone falls silent for seven to ten minutes. Each week, the community welcomes hundreds of visitors, many between the ages of fifteen and twenty-nine. At the beginning of the week, many of the participants find that the silence seems endless, and the assembly is restless, worshipers shifting their bodies uncomfortably as they try to settle into unaccustomed stillness. But as the week progresses, worshipers become more and more at ease, and for many, the same period of silence begins to seem very brief. By the end of the week, the silence feels profound, as hundreds of people together wait on the Lord.[68]

In a study of the Taizé community, Jason Brian Santos explains, "For many [pilgrims to Taizé] . . . it's an opportunity to encounter God. Words and language always fall short in describing those transcendent moments we have with our Creator when we actually sit and listen. . . . [The brothers] have no expectation for what actually goes on during the silence. . . . At the core of it, the brothers hope that pilgrims experience freedom to encounter God or the Scripture in their own ways."[69] Silence in worship can thus be missional, as it creates space to tune the heart to God.

Creeds

Since the Middle Ages, a confession of faith has been one of the responses to the Word in many Western liturgies. When it was introduced in local churches during the fifth and sixth centuries, it served to affirm the assembly's orthodoxy in the midst of theological controversy. Only in 1014 did the church at Rome adopt the Nicene Creed at the mass and require its use

---

68. I am grateful to Brother John and Brother Jean-Marie for their willingness to talk with me about their worship practices when I visited the Taizé Community in October 2013.

69. Jason Brian Santos, *A Community Called Taizé: A Story of Prayer, Worship, and Reconciliation* (Downers Grove, Ill.: IVP Books, 2008), pp. 117-18.

throughout Western Europe. Thus, in its earliest use in the liturgy, the creed did not serve the purpose of mission but rather reinforced the conformity of belief that was characteristic of Christendom.

In 1966, J. G. Davies, on the basis of his historical analysis of the development and introduction of creeds into worship, concluded that the use of the Creed at the Eucharist "was inward-looking, being intended to safeguard the rigid orthodoxy of the worshiping community." Yet, rather than recommending that a creed not be used in worship, he proposed a missionary interpretation for its recitation. The Apostles' Creed, developed in the context of baptism, is "a recital, not of abstract truths, but of the mighty acts of God. . . . If employed in this way, the Church may be seen as called to be a mirror of that love and not a proselytizing body which purveys certain doctrines." Moreover, Davies argued, the confession of faith is a response to what God has said and "may be accepted as a summary of the Gospel and an indication of the meaning of the serving presence of the Church in mission."[70] James Smith also emphasizes the significance of the Creed: "The shared recitation of the Creed constitutes us as a *historical* people. We are heirs to a tradition, indebted to those who have handed on the faith across the generations. Like many of the practices of Christian worship, the Creed comes to us from an ancient world, and yet it is on our lips as a contemporary confession."[71] Smith helps us to see that the recitation of a creed in worship is transcultural, uniting us to Christians of many times and places. Gregory Augustine Pierce also points out the significance of the Creed as a transcultural affirmation: "We are assenting to being part of a two-thousand-year-old church that is still sending us on the same mission Jesus gave to his original disciples."[72]

Nonetheless, some Christians today experience a creed as more of a stumbling block than the foundation for a lively faith. In their study of emerging churches, Anglican bishops Michael Perham and Mary Gray-Reeves found that most did not include a creed in their worship. One community, Moot, founded in London in 2003, introduced a performance of the Apostles' Creed "with a marginally amended text, repeating it clause after clause after a leader, with a drum accompaniment, as a kind of rap." The

---

70. Davies, *Worship and Mission*, pp. 126-27.
71. Smith, *Desiring the Kingdom*, p. 191.
72. Pierce, *The Mass Is Never Ended*, p. 50.

priest-missioner, Ian Mobsby, explained, "Unchurched people found much Church of England traditional liturgy 'overly redemptive' in its language. Much of it [is] a strong reaction against a penal substitution doctrine of atonement." Even though Mobsby worked with the congregation for six years before introducing the Creed, he found that some people were still reluctant to say it.[73]

While some churches continue to include the Apostles' Creed or the Nicene Creed in worship, at least on some occasions, others are introducing alternative creedal statements. For example, *Voices United,* the hymn and worship book of the United Church of Canada, includes a "New Creed" that may be used at worship. This creed professes faith in the Triune God, "who has created and is creating, who has come in Jesus, the Word made flesh, to reconcile and make new, who works in us and others by the Spirit." This bare-bones confession of faith is followed by a statement of the community's participation in God's mission: "We are called to be the Church: to celebrate God's presence, to live with respect in Creation, to love and serve others, to seek justice and resist evil, to proclaim Jesus, crucified and risen, our judge and our hope." The creed concludes with a brief affirmation that God is with us "in life, in death, in life beyond death."[74]

The New Creed of the United Church of Canada uses contemporary idioms to express biblical faith and so may address the stumbling blocks that leaders like Mobsby encounter in their congregations. But an alternative wording, even one agreed on by a church body rather than a single local assembly, lacks the transcultural significance of the historic Nicene and Apostles' Creeds, which are important statements of ecumenical agreement through the ages. Missionally minded communities will listen carefully to those who find traditional creedal language perplexing or inauthentic. They will weigh these concerns along with the historic ecumenical significance of the Creeds when deciding whether to use a creed and, if so, which creed to use. In addition, missionally focused communities will consider how other elements of worship — for example, congregational songs or the

73. Gray-Reeves and Perham, *The Hospitality of God,* pp. 60-61. When I participated in a Sunday Eucharist with Moot in November 2013, a creed was not part of the service.

74. United Church of Canada, *Voices United* (Etobicoke, Ontario: United Church Publishing House, 1996), p. 918. The text is also available at United Church of Canada, "Beliefs: A New Creed," http://www.united-church.ca/beliefs/creed.

great thanksgiving prayer of the Eucharist — can also serve the purpose of a confession of faith that acknowledges God's call to participate in mission.

How the Assembly Proclaims and Responds to Scripture

The proclamation and response to Scripture is an embodied action, encompassing much more than the oral reading of words from a page. Jim Fodor explains the complex dynamic: "The entire 'liturgical scene' is significant: its aural peculiarities and unique architectural spaces, its rich auditory, olfactory, and visual elements, its ambiance, the gestures and movements of the worshipers, the prayers and acclamations, the sermon and the hymns."[75] Every act of worship, wherever it falls on the spectrum from highly ceremonial liturgy to largely unscripted free worship, involves a dynamic interplay of speech, song, and silence, of movement and objects within a worship space. To engage the assembly, missional worship must give attention to the full dynamics of the proclamation and response.

Attracting attention to the proclamation underscores its significance for the assembly. Different communities will accomplish this in their own way, drawing on customs particular to their worshiping tradition and utilizing the contours of their worship space. A shift in focus can occur in any assembly, whether, for example, the reader walks to a lectern where the book is already placed or the book is carried into the midst of the assembly in a formal procession accompanied by light (candles or tapers) and incense.

The book itself is significant because it contains the words of life. Some worshipers carry their own Bibles into worship and may follow along as Scripture is read aloud. In some churches, the book is given a prominent place on the lectern or on the altar/table, clearly visible to the assembly. It may be there from the beginning of worship, its size and elegance conveying its importance. Or, where there is a formal procession as part of the gathering, it may be carried into the worship space, held high for all to see, and solemnly placed where it can be seen by all. St. Gregory of Nyssa Episcopal Church in San Francisco uses a variation of this ritual. After the reading of the gospel and the sermon, a minister carries the book throughout the

75. Fodor, "Reading the Scriptures," p. 143.

assembly. Worshipers eagerly reach out to touch or kiss the book, or bow solemnly as it goes by, demonstrating deep reverence and respect not so much for the book itself as for the living Word it represents.

The structure of the proclamation of the Word depends in part on the number of readings. Whether one or several readings are used, each may be announced in a formal manner that not only identifies the book of the Bible being read and perhaps the chapter and verse as well, but also marks the beginning of this ritually significant event in the service. A formal conclusion such as "The Word of the Lord" or "Hear what the Spirit is saying to the church" underscores that God is speaking through the Scripture proclaimed. When more than one passage is read, the transition from one to the next may be marked with song and/or with movement. Many liturgical churches use the appointed psalm as a response to the first reading and sing an alleluia or a hymn in preparation for the Gospel. The proclamation of the Gospel may be given special prominence. It is usually last in the sequence of readings, and in some churches, only an ordained minister may read the Gospel. The entire assembly often stands while it is read as a sign of respect for Christ present in the reading of the Word. The assembly may respond to the announcement and/or conclusion of the Gospel reading with a brief acclamation such as "Glory to you, O Christ," a form dating back to the Middle Ages that acknowledges the living presence of Christ in the proclamation of the Gospel.

Regardless of the extent of the ceremony surrounding the proclamation, reading Scripture aloud in worship serves over time to inscribe the living Word of God on the hearts of worshipers. Clayton Schmit underscores the importance of preparation for the reading itself: "Bringing a written text to life in the hearing of an audience is an art that is related to oratory and drama. Oral interpretation calls on the reader to study a text, discern an adequate interpretation of it, and practice its oral presentation with an eye toward phrasing, use of pause, inflection, emphasis, tempo, tone, volume, eye contact, gesture, and diction."[76] Reading aloud is a physical activity that involves the bodies of both the reader and the listeners. Oral interpretation of Scripture, done well, enables the text to come alive in the assembly, to be an occasion of encounter with the God of Jesus Christ.

The response to the Word, whether sermon, testimony, silence, or creed,

---

76. Schmit, *Sent and Gathered*, p. 178.

enables the assembly to connect their experiences with the biblical narrative, what was said and done by Jesus and his disciples and, more broadly, God's action from creation to consummation. Together, the proclamation and response shape the people of God, disciplining and schooling us as followers of Christ who are called and sent in mission to embody God's reconciling love, sent out from worship as from a spinning top.

In hearing again the great story of salvation and remembering God's love and desire for all creation, the assembly also recognizes the many places and situations in need of God's healing and reconciling love. Mindful of the needs and concerns of the world, the assembly moves from proclamation and response to intercession, which I will explore in the next chapter.

CHAPTER 4

Praying for the World

Then we all rise together and pray.

Justin Martyr, mid–second century[1]

Lord, in your mercy, hear our prayer.

Having heard and reflected on the good news of God's love for the world, the assembly is reminded of the many places and situations in the world in need of God's justice and compassion. In its intercessory prayer, the assembly joins in the prayer of Christ for these needs and concerns and so participates in Christ's priestly ministry. Offering intercession for the needs of the world is thus a form of participation in God's mission, joining in God's desire for the well-being of the whole creation and expressing confidence in God's promise of a new creation. As in our Möbius strip, in the offering of intercessory prayer, worship is mission is worship . . .

---

1. Justin Martyr, *I Apology* 67, in *The Apostolic Fathers with Justin Martyr and Irenaeus*, Vol. 1 of *Ante-Nicene Fathers*, ed. Alexander Roberts and James Donaldson, Christian Classics Ethereal Library, available at http://www.ccel.org/ccel/schaff/anf01.viii.ii.lxvii.html.

A Poverty of Intercessory Prayer

During my sabbatical in 2008 and 2009, I took time away not only from teaching and other seminary responsibilities, but also from my parish, the community with whom I worshiped Sunday by Sunday. It was an opportunity for me to worship with many different communities and so to broaden my experience of worship in the United States today. As the year went on, I became increasingly aware of a poverty of intercessory prayer for the needs of the world.[2]

In one large congregation, well-known for its outreach in the African-American community, Sunday worship is a lively mix of song and sermon, celebration and community. As the service begins, a worship leader calls the people together with a prayer praising and thanking God for the new day; for God's presence and care sustaining each person, each hour of the day; for bringing this congregation together. After announcements, the choir — perhaps 200 strong — enters in procession and leads the assembly in an extended medley of praise. Afterwards, the pastor invites everyone to greet their neighbors nearby in the pews, and in the process, members of the congregation identify and welcome newcomers.

Eventually it comes time for prayer. The pastor invites worshipers who want prayer to come forward to the altar rail, and a number of people do so. At the direction of the pastor, worshipers who remain in their pews turn to their neighbors, forming groups of three or four, and in those groups, people speak their needs and hopes for God to work in their lives. Most of the groups join hands, and they pray for each person in turn. There is a strong sense of trust in God, a belief that God hears and answers prayer. There is a sincere expression of care for one another, even if people have just met in the context of this liturgy. The pastor concludes the prayers with an extemporaneous prayer focusing on the many needs of members of the assembly.

2. My experience in 2008 and 2009 contrasts with my experiences in England in the fall of 2013. Particularly during the daily prayer of Ripon College Cuddesdon, the theological college where I was staying, the scope of intercessory prayer was wide, although often the only voice heard was that of the officiant. In addition, my colleague John Kater, professor emeritus at Church Divinity School of the Pacific, described for me his experience in the Anglican Church in Hong Kong, where intercession was often offered spontaneously for pressing local situations, such as a dockworkers' strike, but rarely did worshipers mention particular individuals.

The sermon in this congregation is the centerpiece of worship, an event in classic African-American homiletical style. The pastor uses repetition and cadence to build a stirring proclamation, and the congregation responds vocally throughout. It is highly participatory and deeply engaging. There is a strong message of social justice, with the claim that God cares for the poor and oppressed and that God calls the assembly to action in response to the needs of the world. Yet, despite the very personal prayer for one another and the emphasis on justice in the sermon, during my two visits to this congregation I saw little or no intercession for the needs of the world at any time in over two hours of worship.

In another congregation, part of a church body with a historic commitment to peace, Sunday worship is equally lively. A small group of vocalists and instrumentalists leads the congregation in praise music. An exchange of the peace early in the liturgy builds a sense of community as people move freely through the worship space, longtime members taking care to welcome newcomers. Before the sermon, the children move out of the worship space to a Sunday-school room in a procession that weaves through the congregation as everyone sings.

This congregation has worked hard on its diversity. The worship space is wheelchair-accessible, and a number of people who use wheelchairs participate in worship. The assembly includes people of all ages. Although in the beginning this congregation was predominantly white, intentional anti-racism work over a decade has resulted in a more racially diverse assembly, and this growing diversity is reflected in the diverse genres of music in their worship.

Yet in this assembly too, the concern for others that is evident in the congregation's outreach is not manifest in intercession as an integral component of worship. A card for visitors outlines the structure of worship in this assembly — gathering, celebrating, equipping, and sharing — but does not mention prayer for the needs of the world. On my first visit, people offered a few short prayers here and there, none focused on intercession for the world. When I returned a few months later, worship included prayers for individual needs as part of the "gathering" at the beginning of the liturgy, but only a few brief intercessions for the church and the world later in this service.

No doubt my observations are influenced by my experience as an Episcopalian. I am accustomed to public worship that includes intercession. The

1979 *Book of Common Prayer* specifies the areas of concern — the universal church, its members, and its mission; the nation and all in authority; the welfare of the world; the concerns of the local community; those who suffer and those in any trouble; the departed — and the prayer book provides set forms that ensure that congregations cover all those areas.[3] So I come to worship with the expectation that we will be interceding for the world and the church.

Nevertheless, I think the Episcopal Church has its own poverty of intercessory prayer. Nearly twenty years ago, Daniel Stevick, professor emeritus of liturgy at Episcopal Divinity School, observed, "In some congregations, to be sure, the intercessions are prepared and led responsibly and caringly. Yet in many places they seem dull and habituated — seldom really slapdash, but evidencing little attention and imagination."[4] In my experience, little has changed since Stevick wrote his essay. In congregations that use the forms provided in the prayer book, the only concerns added are the most immediate ones for those individuals known personally to someone in the congregation — we pray for Aunt Susie who is having surgery, or someone's neighbor who is being treated for cancer, or a close friend who has died — and, perhaps, names from a list such as the Anglican Cycle of Prayer. When opportunity is given during worship for members of the assembly to voice their prayers, the most frequent — and often the only — prayers heard are for the sick and those who have died. Depending on the culture of the particular congregation, there may be no additions whatsoever from the assembly even when they are invited to add their concerns.

Prayer for the needs of the world is an important expression of our concern for the world and our hope for God's promised future. James K. A. Smith explains, "Because we are God's ambassadors and image bearers," we bring to God the needs and concerns of creation, "praying for each other, for the church, and for the world at large." Our prayer extends beyond ourselves and our immediate personal concerns to those outside our community of

3. *The Book of Common Prayer and Administration of the Sacraments and Other Rites and Ceremonies of the Church, Together with The Psalter or Psalms of David* (New York: Church Hymnal Corp., 1979), pp. 383-93.

4. Daniel B. Stevick, "'Let Us Pray for the Church and for the World,'" in *A Prayer Book for the 21st Century*, Liturgical Studies 3, ed. Ruth A. Meyers (New York: Church Hymnal Corp., 1996), p. 56.

faith.[5] When we pray for the world, we invite the Spirit to pray within us (Rom. 8:26-27), we express our hope for God's new creation, and we place our trust in God's infinite mercy and abundant love. In this way, we align ourselves with God's desires for the world, God's mission of reconciling love, and we participate in that mission.

Intercessory Prayer and Mission

My visits were not entirely random. In selecting congregations to visit, I sought communities of faith known for a lively engagement with the world, communities who seem to be participating intentionally in the mission of God. I wondered how these congregations' commitments were reflected in their worship, and how their worship formed them and shaped their commitments. I also wondered how worship in these congregations might be in itself an act of participation in God's mission.

Reflecting on the missional perspective in *Evangelical Lutheran Worship,* the 2006 worship book of the Evangelical Lutheran Church in America, Thomas Schattauer points out that worship is integrally related to the world: "In its worship, the Christian assembly enacts the truth about the world (e.g., life as God's gift, its brokenness through sin, the limit of death) and hope for the world in God's eschatological purpose (e.g., forgiveness, reconciliation, healing, justice, peace, salvation). Moreover, the world comes to worship in those who gather. Through language, music, art and architecture, ways of movement and gesture, the assembly in its worship embraces the world and turns it toward the purpose of God."[6] Of the many moments or aspects of liturgy that acknowledge the truth about the world and our hope for God's promised future, intercessory prayer is certainly one such moment, for in the intercessions, the assembly gives voice to its concerns and the needs of the world. *The Use of the Means of Grace,* the 1997 statement of the Evangelical Lutheran Church in America, explains, "On the grounds of the Word and

5. James K. A. Smith, *Desiring the Kingdom: Worship, Worldview, and Cultural Formation* (Grand Rapids: Baker Academic, 2009), pp. 193-94.

6. Thomas H. Schattauer, "The Missional Shape of Worship in *Evangelical Lutheran Worship,*" *Dialog* 47 (2008): 182.

promise of God the Church prays, in the power of the Spirit and in the name of Jesus Christ, for all the great needs of the world."[7]

The assembly's offering of intercessory prayer is part of its work on behalf of the world — that is, part of its liturgy, its public service. By praying in Christ, with Christ, and through Christ, the assembly expresses its confidence that God does love the world, that God is at work healing the broken-hearted and restoring all creation to wholeness. Prayer for the world is thus a form of participation in God's mission of reconciliation. Moreover, the intercessory prayer offered in the assembly is integrally related to mission in the world. *The Use of the Means of Grace* says that intercessory prayer "is also lived. Christians are called and empowered by the triune God to be a presence of faith, hope, and love in the midst of the needs of the community and the world."[8] As illustrated by our Möbius strip, worship and mission are in a dynamic relationship, our intercessions in the assembly are a missional offering on behalf of the whole world, and our actions in the world are embodying our prayer for all creation.

Patterns of Intercessory Prayer

Scripture offers us numerous examples of individuals who intercede with God for the needs of the world. Told of the impending destruction of the city of Sodom, Abraham pleads with God to spare the city for the sake of its righteous inhabitants. First extracting God's promise to save the city for the sake of fifty righteous people, Abraham proceeds to bargain, finally getting God to agree to spare Sodom if just ten righteous people can be found (Gen. 18:16-33). Generations later, as the people of Israel wander in the wilderness, often rebelling against God, Moses intercedes again and again, pleading with God to spare the people from threatened destruction (e.g., Exod. 17:1-7; Exod. 32:7-14; Num. 14:1-25; Num. 21:4-9; Deut. 9:8-21). Centuries later, when the Assyrians had come close to conquering the Is-

---

7. Evangelical Lutheran Church in America, *The Use of the Means of Grace: A Statement on the Practice of Word and Sacrament* (Minneapolis: Augsburg Fortress Press, 1997), Principle 53, p. 58.

8. *The Use of the Means of Grace*, Application 53A, p. 58.

raelites, Judith turns to God in prayer and begs God to deliver her people (Judith 9:1-14).

Underlying these pleas is an expectation that God will hear and respond. In her prayer, Judith spells out the qualities of God that form the basis of her confidence: "You are the God of the lowly, helper of the oppressed, upholder of the weak, protector of the forsaken, savior of those without hope" (Judith 9:11). God's steadfast love never ceases, the Scriptures tell us, and so we can plead with God to hear and have mercy.

The clearest scriptural command for Christians to intercede is in First Timothy: "I urge that supplications, prayers, intercessions, and thanksgivings should be made for everyone, for kings and all who are in high positions, so that we may lead a quiet and peaceable life in all godliness and dignity" (1 Tim. 2:1-2). Christians are to be concerned with the whole world, to pray "for everyone," because, as the letter-writer explains, God "desires everyone to be saved" (1 Tim. 2:4).

Clement, bishop of Rome in the late first century, gives the content of one such prayer:

> Save the afflicted among us, have mercy on the lowly.
> Raise up the fallen, show yourself to those in need.
> Heal the sick, and bring back those who have strayed.
> Fill the hungry, give freedom to our prisoners.
> Raise up the weak, console the fainthearted.[9]

In contrast to the exhortation in First Timothy to pray for rulers and civil authorities, Clement's prayer shows particular concern for those who are poor or weak or in need.

Writing at the end of the second century, Tertullian explains the distinctiveness of Christian prayer: "In days gone by, withal prayer used to call down plagues, scatter the armies of foes, withhold the wholesome influences of the showers. Now, however, the prayer of righteousness averts all God's anger,

---

9. *Springtime of the Liturgy: Liturgical Texts of the First Four Centuries,* by Lucien Deiss, trans. Matthew J. O'Connell (Collegeville, Minn.: Liturgical Press, 1979), pp. 82-85, cited by Ruth C. Duck in *Finding Words for Worship: A Guide for Leaders* (Louisville: Westminster John Knox Press, 1995), p. 77.

keeps bivouac on behalf of personal enemies, makes supplication on behalf of persecutors." Continuing, Tertullian underscores the breadth of concerns that Christian prayer addresses:

> It knows nothing save how to recall the souls of the departed from the very path of death, to transform the weak, to restore the sick, to purge the possessed, to open prison bars, to loose the bonds of the innocent. Likewise it washes away faults, repels temptations, extinguishes persecutions, consoles the faint-spirited, cheers the high-spirited, escorts travelers, appeases waves, makes robbers stand aghast, nourishes the poor, governs the rich, upraises the fallen, arrests the falling, confirms the standing.[10]

The earliest reference to intercession in the liturgy dates to the mid–second century, in the First Apology of Justin Martyr. Describing the baptismal Eucharist, Justin explains that the newly baptized join the assembly "in order that we may offer hearty prayers in common for ourselves and for the baptized [illuminated] person, and for all others in every place."[11] Following these prayers, the assembly exchanges the kiss of peace, then proceeds to the liturgy of the table. Justin goes on to describe the weekly Sunday assembly, at which "all rise together and pray" immediately following the reading of Scripture and a sermon.[12] Intercession, according to Justin, was a regular part of the weekly assembly of the Christians in Rome.

Justin offers no rationale or theological reflection for this sequence, and other patristic sources tell us virtually nothing else about the intercessions as part of the liturgy of the Word. We don't actually know how Christians came to put their liturgy together in this way. Yet this is the sequence adopted in most contemporary Western liturgical revisions. The *Constitution on the Sacred Liturgy* of the Second Vatican Council called for the restoration of the intercessory prayers, after centuries during which intercession was not

10. Tertullian, *On Prayer* 29, trans. S. Thelwall, in *Latin Christianity: Its Founder, Tertullian,* Vol. 3 of *Ante-Nicene Fathers,* ed. Allan Menzies, Christian Classics Ethereal Library, available at http://www.ccel.org/ccel/schaff/anf03.vi.iv.xxix.html.

11. Justin Martyr, *I Apology* 65, in *The Apostolic Fathers with Justin Martyr and Irenaeus,* Vol. 1 of *Ante-Nicene Fathers,* ed. Alexander Roberts and James Donaldson, Christian Classics Ethereal Library, available at http://www.ccel.org/ccel/schaff/anf01.viii.ii.lxv.html.

12. Justin, *I Apology* 67.

part of the official liturgy for the Eucharist outside of the Eucharistic prayer: "Especially on Sundays and feasts of obligation there is to be restored, after the Gospel and the homily, 'the common prayer' or 'the prayer of the faithful.' By this prayer, in which the people are to take part, intercession will be made for holy Church, for the civil authorities, for those oppressed by various needs, for all [humankind], and for the salvation of the entire world."[13] The most recent worship books of other Western churches locate intercessions in the same place — that is, after the Gospel and the homily.

The inner logic of this sequence suggests that our prayers for the world are another aspect of our response to the proclamation of the Word. Having heard anew the story of God's love for the world — or, more accurately, a portion of that story — and having considered the meaning of this proclamation in the sermon, the assembly then speaks its yearning for God's continuing action in the world today. We remember what God has done, the mission of God revealed especially in sending Jesus and sending the Spirit, and we remember God's promises of justice, peace, forgiveness, reconciliation, and mercy. In light of this good news of salvation for us and for the whole world, we can see more clearly the broken and hurting places in our world, the sin that separates us from God and from one another, the evil powers that corrupt and destroy God's creation. And so we move from proclamation and response to intercession, speaking aloud before God the truth about our world and our hope for God's promised new creation. In so doing, we join God's mission of reconciling love for the world.

While prayers of the faithful are now commonly part of the liturgy of the Word, for centuries the Western Eucharistic liturgy contained only vestiges of these prayers — in the use of the *Kyrie* ("Lord, have mercy") as part of the entrance rite and the presider's "Let us pray" at the start of the offertory. Instead, it was the canon (the Eucharistic prayer), like most Eastern Eucharistic prayers, that included intercession. In the Western canon and in Egyptian Eucharistic prayers, the intercessions came at the beginning, before the institution narrative, while in other Eastern Eucharistic prayers, the intercessions were found at the end of the prayer. The Western prayers

---

13. *Constitution on the Sacred Liturgy (Sacrosanctum Concilium),* par. 53 (4 December 1963), available at http://www.vatican.va/archive/hist_councils/ii_vatican_council/documents/vat-ii_const_19631204_sacrosanctum-concilium_en.html.

were rather succinct, a paragraph of prayer for the living, followed by another paragraph of prayer for the dead. In Eastern prayers, by contrast, the intercessions could be quite extensive. Diptychs — slate tablets listing specific persons to be remembered in the assembly's prayer — were held up for the presider to read during the Eucharistic prayer.

It is possible that these intercessions are an expansion of the epiclesis, the invocation of the Spirit over the congregation, thus extending the assembly's concern to encompass the whole world.[14] Certainly the inclusion of intercessions in the Eucharistic prayer places the assembly's concerns and hopes in direct proximity to the Eucharistic sacrifice and so makes an implicit connection to Christ's self-offering for the sake of the world.

United Methodist scholar Don Saliers cautions against making too much of the inclusion of intercessions in the Eucharistic prayer: "The more important point is that the Eucharistic assembly enters into a comprehensive prayer for the world and all that dwell therein. . . . Even when intercessions occur at the end of the liturgy of the Word, the point is that they flow from the heart of the community. The very reason for the gathering is to receive the gifts of God and to join Christ's ongoing liturgy in the midst of the world."[15] In other words, in its intercessory prayer, whether that prayer is a response to the proclamation of the Word or part of the Eucharistic prayer, the assembly participates in Christ's liturgy, Christ's self-offering for the sake of the world.

Prayer as a Priestly Offering

The assembly's ministry of intercession is rooted in Christ, and more precisely, in Christ's priestly ministry. The book of Hebrews depicts Christ as the great high priest who mediates a new and eternal covenant. Because he is a high priest who sympathizes with our weaknesses, we can approach him and "receive mercy and find grace to help in time of need" (Heb. 4:16).

---

14. Leonel L. Mitchell, *Praying Shapes Believing: A Theological Commentary on The Book of Common Prayer* (Minneapolis: Winston Press, 1985), p. 171.

15. Don E. Saliers, *Worship as Theology: Foretaste of Glory Divine* (Nashville: Abingdon Press, 1994), pp. 129-30.

It is not just our own needs, however, that are presented at the throne of grace. In early Jewish tradition, while many types of individuals might intercede with God, the work of intercession was entrusted to priests.[16] The book of Exodus directs that "Aaron shall bear the names of the sons of Israel in the breast-piece of judgment on his heart when he goes into the holy place, for a continual remembrance before the Lord" (Exod. 28:29). The high priest literally carried the names of the twelve patriarchs on his garments, symbolically representing the whole people of Israel, as a sign of his intercession for them. For Christians, this work of intercession is taken up in perpetuity by Christ, who "always lives to make intercession for them" (Heb. 7:25).[17] Christians thus came to understand that their prayers, intercessions as well as praise and thanksgiving, are offered through Christ and with Christ and in Christ.

While Christ's priesthood is unique, Christians through baptism are associated with that priesthood. Peter told early believers, "You are a chosen race, a royal priesthood, a holy nation, God's own people" (1 Peter 2:9). Centuries later, reacting to the entrenched ecclesiastical hierarchy of the Late Middle Ages, Martin Luther gave new emphasis to the concept of a priesthood of believers, constituted through baptism: "As for the unction by a pope or a bishop, tonsure, ordination, consecration, and clothes differing from those of [laypeople] — all this may make a hypocrite or an anointed puppet, but never a Christian or a spiritual [person]. Thus we are all consecrated as priests by baptism, as St. Peter says: 'Ye are a royal priesthood, a holy nation' (1 Pet. 2:9); and in the book of Revelation: 'and hast made us unto our God (by thy blood) kings and priests' (Rev. 5:10)."[18]

So, even as we proclaim that Christ in heaven continuously intercedes for us and for the whole world, all Christians, joined in Christ's heavenly priesthood through baptism, are called into the work of intercession. Liturgical scholar Paul Bradshaw describes this as the ecclesiological dimension of Christian prayer: "If . . . worship is to be true to the priestly character of

---

16. Harold W. Attridge, *Hebrews: A Commentary on the Epistle to the Hebrews,* ed. Helmut Koester (Philadelphia: Fortress Press, 1989), p. 211.

17. J. G. Davies, *Worship and Mission* (London: SCM Press, 1966; New York: Association Press, 1967), pp. 121-25.

18. Martin Luther, "Address to the Christian Nobility of the German Nation," in *Readings in European History,* ed. J. H. Robinson (Boston: Ginn, 1906), Hanover Historical Texts Project, ed. Monica Banas (1996), available at http://history.hanover.edu/texts/luthad.html.

the Christian life and its participation in the priesthood of Christ, it should, therefore, have at its heart the offering of praise and of intercessory prayer."[19] While Bradshaw is speaking specifically of daily prayer, his remarks apply equally to Sunday worship, whether or not it includes a celebration of communion. Intercession is, or ought to be, a central component of the weekly Christian assembly.

The significance of intercession as a priestly ministry may help explain why Justin, along with other patristic sources, reports that the newly baptized joined the community for intercessory prayer for the first time on the occasion of their baptism.[20] Interceding for the needs of the world was both a privilege and a responsibility of the body of Christ, the priesthood constituted through baptism.

Participating in the priestly ministry of intercession is one important way in which the liturgical assembly enacts the mission of God. This mission is a mission of reconciling love, restoring all people to unity with God and one another in Christ. Moreover, God's mission extends to all creation, as the apostle Paul suggests in Romans: "The whole creation has been groaning in labor pains," awaiting redemption (Rom. 8:22). Our intercession is thus intercession for the whole created order. Tertullian proposes that creation itself prays: "Every creature prays; cattle and wild beasts pray and bend their knees; and when they issue from their layers and lairs, they look up heavenward with no idle mouth, making their breath vibrate after their own manner. Nay, the birds too, rising out of the nest, upraise themselves heavenward, and, instead of hands, expand the cross of their wings, and say somewhat to seem like prayer."[21]

The breadth of God's steadfast love, extending to the whole world, means that the scope of our intercession must be wide. In 1966, J. G. Davies criticized worship that does not look beyond itself. A priesthood, Davies argued, "is never established for itself, so for the royal priesthood to celebrate its own *cultus* for its own needs is to deny its very *raison d'être;* it would cease in fact to function as a priesthood. An introverted *cultus* performed by the covenant people is therefore a contradiction of their office, a rejection of their commis-

---

19. Paul F. Bradshaw, *Two Ways of Praying* (Nashville: Abingdon Press, 1995), p. 63.
20. Justin, *I Apology* 65.
21. Tertullian, *On Prayer* 29.

sion, and a failure to participate in the *missio Dei*. It makes nonsense of the whole idea of covenant and priesthood."[22] Davies helps us see that our baptismal priesthood is integrally related to mission. As a priestly people, we are ministers of God's reconciling love in the world. When we gather for worship, it is not primarily for our own needs but rather for the needs of the world.

Other scholars writing more recently also urge that the assembly's intercession attend to the needs of the whole world. James Smith maintains that in intercessory prayer, we are reminded that we are called to be God's people for the sake of the world. "As a congregation, while we pray for one another, we also pray for those outside our community of faith: for our neighborhoods; for municipal government leaders; for the poor and those in prison; for those suffering persecution, exploitation, or the effects of natural disaster; even for our enemies."[23] Lutheran liturgical scholar Gordon Lathrop locates the ministry of intercession in the assembly's participation in Christ's priesthood: "The Christian community, when it is faithful in worship, genuinely stands before God as priests for the world, crying out to God for all those throughout the world and in our neighborhood." Lathrop is careful to say "when [the assembly] is faithful in worship," implying that the assembly may not always be faithful and suggesting the need for ongoing reform. "Worship renewal," continues Lathrop, "must always be about the recovery of the seriousness and importance of this intercessory prayer. The temptations to pray only for ourselves, for our congregation, even only for our own sick must be resisted."[24] Eleanor Kreider and Alan Kreider emphasize the missional dimension of intercessory prayer as they imagine how visitors to missional congregations will experience their prayer:

> The outsiders observe that the worshiping community has a particular concern for reconciliation. They may not initially understand that this grows out of the worshipers' understanding of God's mission, which is to reconcile all things and all people in and to God in Christ. But they note the worshipers' concern for peace in the world; peace permeates their

22. J. G. Davies, *Worship and Mission*, p. 95.

23. Smith, *Desiring the Kingdom*, pp. 193-94.

24. Gordon W. Lathrop, "Liturgy and Mission in the North American Context," in *Inside Out: Worship in an Age of Mission*, ed. Thomas H. Schattauer (Minneapolis: Fortress Press, 1999), p. 210.

prayers. . . . The prayers of the community are wide-ranging and passionate. They bring the broken world, with its wars, hunger, injustice, and persecution, before God with trusting concentration; and they cry out to God that God will bring his kingdom of justice, peace, and joy.[25]

In our contemporary North American consumer culture, intercessory prayer has a countercultural dimension. As followers of Christ who share in his eternal priesthood, we are called to resist the forces of individualism and consumerism, and maintain an outward focus in our worship. Underscoring the importance of this approach, Davies insists that only worship "which is outward-looking and related to the world can be regarded as an authentic act of Christian worship. If it is not worldly, in this sense, then Christians are not exercising their baptismal priesthood."[26] Davies is speaking here of the entirety of worship, not just the intercessions. But the intercessions are certainly part of worship, and Davies makes clear that the proper exercise of our baptismal priesthood requires that the horizon of our intercessions extend far beyond prayer for those we know and love, beyond prayer for our local community, to encompass all of creation and our enemies.

The Effects of Our Prayer

But what precisely are we doing when we pray for the world? Do we really think that God is unaware of the needs of the world? And how are we to understand the reality that our prayers are not always answered as we wish them to be?

Saint Augustine, writing to a woman named Proba who had asked him about prayer, cites numerous Gospel passages that encourage steadfast prayer, saying, "[God] who knows before we ask Him what things we need has nevertheless given us exhortation to prayer." Augustine goes on to explain the effect of our prayer: "When the . . . apostle [Paul] says, 'Let your requests be made known unto God' [Phil. 4:6], this is not to be understood as if

---

25. Alan Kreider and Eleanor Kreider, *Worship and Mission after Christendom* (Scottdale, Pa., and Waterloo, Ontario: Herald Press, 2011), pp. 235-36.

26. J. G. Davies, *Worship and Mission,* p. 95.

thereby they become known to God, who certainly knew them before they were uttered, but in this sense, that they are to be made known to ourselves in the presence of God by patient waiting upon [God]."[27] Through the discipline of intercessory prayer, we give voice to the needs of the world and so come to new or deeper awareness of those needs and greater understanding of our call to respond not only with intercession but also with action in the world, our worship and mission flowing into and out of each other, as they do in our Möbius strip.

It may be that we literally become aware of things of which we had not been conscious. After all, Paul tells us, "We do not know how to pray as we ought, but that very Spirit intercedes with sighs too deep for words. And God, who searches the heart, knows what is the mind of the Spirit, because the Spirit intercedes for the saints according to the will of God" (Rom. 8:26). Through our prayer, God may open our eyes and our hearts in new ways to the needs of the world.

Even when we bring into our prayers individuals and situations that are well-known to us, naming them in prayer reminds us that they are within the sphere of God's merciful and steadfast love. Naming them in prayer also reminds us of our responsibility to them and may even spur us to action. Consider the story of Spring Garden Baptist Church in Toronto when they found their neighborhood plunged into chaos by a teachers' strike. Recognizing the impact not only on teachers and other school employees but also on children and youth and on working parents, the congregation began to pray, as is their custom when they become aware of crises:

> As they prayed, they began to reason that if they were praying for the schools and the teachers and the students and their families, and if the God they were praying to was a real and living presence, then of course they must act in line with that confidence. Quickly, with primary initiatives from high school students and teachers within the congregation, they organized a Teachers' Strike Day School for as many children as they could accommodate. High schoolers became tutors to younger children, working parents were helped in the care of their out-of-school children — and

27. Augustine, *Letter 130*, pars. 15, 18, New Advent: The Fathers of the Church, available at http://www.newadvent.org/fathers/1102130.htm.

the local news camera crew came to get some footage! The spontaneous initiative became a political act, born of their simple responsiveness to things they knew God cared about.[28]

For the people of Spring Garden Baptist Church, not only was intercession itself an act of participation in God's mission, but intercession also drew them more deeply into that mission as they responded to the needs of their neighborhood. The energy of the intercession that was part of their worship moved from the core of worship into action, into mission in the world, like a spinning top. Whether our prayers are for the needs of our own neighborhoods or of sisters and brothers halfway around the world, intercession may transform us, leading us to acts of compassion and service.

Moreover, if our intercession impels us to renewed engagement with the mission of God in the world, our interactions with our neighbors (nearby or far away) propel us back to intercessory prayer, just as the energy of a spinning top flows in and out of the core. Our experiences in the world inform our intercession, and our intercession schools us in compassion and turns our hearts once again to the world, like our Möbius strip, in which worship is mission is worship. . . . In this interplay of prayer and action, action and prayer, we identify more and more with Christ, as Don Saliers explains: "Christ's own life is one of active prayer and prayerful action. . . . In exploring what Christ's life-liturgy signifies, we ponder afresh the necessity of prayer and action in mutuality. These are what humanity needs to be whole, and the tension required by living particular moments of the liturgy — now beholding God, now making one's prayer a concrete act of mercy — is necessary to growing up into the 'measure of the full stature of Christ' (Ephesians 4:13b)."[29]

Through our intercession and through our action, we put on Christ. When we offer our prayer through Christ and with Christ and in Christ, Christ prays for us and with us and in us.[30] Our intercession is thus an exercise of our baptismal priesthood, in which we share in Christ's continuing priestly ministry and so participate in the mission of God.

---

28. Lois Y. Barrett et al., *Treasure in Clay Jars: Patterns in Missional Faithfulness* (Grand Rapids: Wm. B. Eerdmans, 2004), p. 114.

29. Saliers, *Worship as Theology*, p. 135.

30. Bradshaw, *Two Ways of Praying*, p. 64.

While intercessory prayer can thus have a salutary effect on us, its effect on God is a more vexing theological question. Scriptural stories of God hearing and answering prayer and the teaching of Jesus encourage us to persevere in prayer. Sometimes our prayer results in a miraculous healing, but often it does not. God's ways are mysterious, beyond our knowing, and our prayers may not be answered as we wish. Yet we nonetheless offer our prayer with confidence that God is at work in our midst. Reflecting on contemporary challenges to praying, Eleanor Kreider and Alan Kreider express the importance of confidence that God is present and at work among us: "Congolese, Haitian, and Zimbabwean Christians who face desperate crises; Christians in the West who face inner-city gang wars, familial crises, and financial reverses; all of us who face ecological degradation, climate change, and nuclear proliferation — all of us know that we can survive only if God is real and intervenes to liberate us and others against powers that conspire to squash shalom."[31]

The proclamation of Scripture includes both memory and hope. It not only tells us how God has acted in the past but also gives us a glimpse of the eschatological horizon, the promised new heaven and new earth, where "death will be no more; mourning and crying and pain will be no more, for the first things have passed away" (Rev. 21:4). So we offer our intercession, trusting in God's steadfast love and abiding mercy.

How the Assembly Prays for the World and the Church

Given the importance of intercession, how might communities of faith develop robust practices of intercessory prayer in their worship? How might their prayer propel them into mission in the world, and their mission in the world inform their prayer? What steps can we take to alleviate the poverty of intercessory prayer in our churches?

First, and perhaps most obvious, we can recognize that intercession for the needs of the world is a vital component when Christians assemble for worship. The official contemporary worship books of mainline Protestant churches, along with the current Roman Catholic missal, all include inter-

31. Kreider and Kreider, *Worship and Mission after Christendom*, p. 170.

cession in the recommended or required sequence of the Sunday assembly, and most place these intercessions as a response to the proclamation of the Word.[32] Yet this is not universally practiced, as I discovered in my congregational visits. In the congregation in which small groups prayed for one another's needs, there was a strong sense of compassion for the other, although this concern for the other did not extend beyond members of the assembly, at least in the form of intercession. Such absence of intentional intercession for the needs of the world, whether this happens occasionally or is the routine practice, diminishes the enactment of the assembly's baptismal priesthood. The same is also true for churches whose intercessory prayer has become a perfunctory recitation of a prescribed form or is focused primarily on local needs and loved ones of members of the community.

The scope of the intercessions must be broad. *Evangelical Lutheran Worship,* the 2006 worship book of the Evangelical Lutheran Church in America, calls for prayers that reflect "the wideness of God's mercy for the whole world."[33] Rather than providing set forms, the book lists the general areas to be included in the prayers. It is the work of the local community to give substance to those areas, to enflesh the outline with the specific needs of the world. A Roman Catholic congregation, the St. Giles Family Mass Community in Oak Park, Illinois, has an "open mike" Prayers of the Faithful. Sometimes the prayers are about sick relatives and other individuals personally known to members of the assembly. But other intercessions have a broader scope. For example, someone prays not only for a sister who has cancer but also for all other people throughout the world who are struggling with the disease. Some members of the assembly approach the mike with particular prayers for social issues.[34]

Several years ago, Franklin Reformed Church in Nutley, New Jersey, began to give particular attention to intercession for their local community. The pastor explained that they had become known in their town as "the church that prays." For several years, the pastor has been teaching members

32. The United Methodist *Book of Worship* allows intercessions to be an expanded form of opening prayers as an alternative to being a response to the Word. See *The United Methodist Book of Worship* (Nashville: United Methodist Publishing House, 1992), p. 25.

33. *Evangelical Lutheran Worship: Pew Edition* (Minneapolis: Augsburg Fortress Press, 2006), pp. 105, 127, 218.

34. Stephen Bevans, e-mail message to the author, 29 November 2013.

of the congregation to ask people, "Can I pray about that for you?" Gradually, people who are not members of the congregation — and, in some cases, not Christian — have begun to call and ask for prayer. Those names and concerns are put on the congregation's prayer list, which appears as an insert in the Sunday bulletin — an extensive list, far longer than that of most congregations several times the size of this one. During worship, when it comes time for intercession, people in the pews raise their hands to be recognized. As each person speaks aloud his or her concern, the pastor repeats the need so that all can hear, typically broadening the prayer for a specific person, so that, for example, a prayer for a particular seventh-grader struggling in school becomes intercession for the needs of all schoolchildren in the community. The prayers then conclude with an extensive pastoral prayer.

In this situation, the pastor's leadership is key. When she is away, a lay minister leads worship, and one of them explained to me that they were learning to repeat and extend the intercessions that members of the assembly named. Especially notable in this example is that this practice of intentional prayer for the local community is turning the hearts of members of that congregation outward, to the needs of the world. They are learning to listen with the ears of Christ.

This assembly averages forty to fifty people on a Sunday morning. Their denomination does not have a strong liturgical tradition, and an informal style of worship works well in this assembly. Other assemblies, of larger size or in contexts accustomed to more formal or scripted liturgy, require a different approach.

In the Episcopal Church, the 1979 *Book of Common Prayer* gives communities wide latitude in offering intercession. In some congregations, the prayers are written each week, or seasonally. A priest told me of working with his congregation to distribute authority and responsibility for the prayers of the people. He began by putting sermons and articles in the parish newsletter and teaching about the theology of intercession, inviting people to participate in a five-week course of study that would equip them to compose and lead the intercessions. He extended personal invitations to several people he thought would be especially likely candidates for this ministry. Others came forward on their own initiative. The course of study was far more than teaching about the technical details of crafting intercessory prayer. The heart of the course was theological reflection on prayer, particularly liturgical prayer, and working together to develop a statement about prayer. By the end of the five weeks, participants had some practice in composing prayers, and they were ready to write intercessions for the congregation's worship. Response to this process was overwhelmingly positive. Participants in the course, including the priest who led the course, reported a deepened understanding of intercessory prayer. Moreover, members of the congregation who didn't participate in the program also found their prayer enriched, and some were deeply moved as they were invited to pray in new ways.[35]

These are two different experiences of intercessory prayer, in two very different contexts. In both congregations, there was a process of education and formation, calling attention to the theology of intercessory prayer and encouraging the entire congregation to engage this baptismal ministry in new and deeper ways. In both congregations, purposeful attention to intercessory prayer stirred the assembly to look outward, beyond their immediate needs and concerns.

Fostering more dynamic practices of intercession in Christian worship is essential to the church's engagement in the mission of God. Baptized into Christ, sharing in Christ's eternal priesthood, we are to be concerned for the welfare of the whole world. The assembly's intercession speaks the truth about the world, with confidence that God hears our cries. Our prayers then become acts of mercy in the world, and our experiences in the world inform our prayer, in an ongoing cycle of adoration and action, the spinning top that is mission. Through it all, through prayerful action and active prayer, we participate in Christ's liturgy, offered for the life of the world.

In the structure of contemporary Western liturgies, intercessory prayer yields to the great prayer of thanksgiving that is central to the celebration of the Eucharistic meal. But first, I will consider practices of reconciliation in the assembly's worship.

35. Randal Gardner, "The Prayers of the People: A Congregational Exercise in Christian Formation and Lay Liturgical Leadership as a Sign of the Ministry of the Baptized," D.Min. thesis, Virginia Theological Seminary, April 2005; see especially Chapter 6.

CHAPTER 5

Enacting Reconciliation

Having ended the prayers, we salute one another with a kiss.

Justin Martyr, mid–second century[1]

God is forgiveness. Dare to forgive and God will be with you.
God is forgiveness. Love and do not fear.

Songs from Taizé[2]

In this chapter, I consider how worship enacts reconciliation. In the classical Anglican structure of Holy Communion, a confession of sin and absolution followed the intercession and led into the liturgy of the table. Many churches today place a penitential rite at the beginning of worship, while others do not include a confession of sin in worship or omit it on occasion.

Whether or not worship includes an explicit confession of sin, worship is always an act of reconciliation, restoring the assembly to right relationship with God, with one another, and with all creation. I begin this chapter with a discussion of God's mission of reconciliation. Then, in addition to

1. Justin Martyr, *I Apology 67*, in *The Apostolic Fathers with Justin Martyr and Irenaeus*, Vol. 1 of *Ante-Nicene Fathers*, ed. Alexander Roberts and James Donaldson, Christian Classics Ethereal Library, available at http://www.ccel.org/ccel/schaff/anf01.viii.ii.lxvii.html.

2. *Songs from Taizé, 2013-2014* (Taizé, France: Ateliers et Presses de Taizé, 2013), #113.

considering the confession of sin, I also explore the exchange of the peace as a practice of reconciliation.

Mission as Reconciliation

Scripture tells the story of God's desire and God's mission to restore humankind to right relationships. All that God does, from creation to the promised new creation, manifests divine love for the world. In Jesus, God's own self entered human history. Theologian Catherine LaCugna explains the significance of Jesus' ministry: "Jesus preached the reign of God . . . [and] revealed the order of a new household . . . a new dwelling place where the Samaritan woman, the tax collector, and the leper are equally at home."[3] Jesus thus shows us God's wide embrace, drawing in those at the margins, building a new community of reconciliation. Moreover, through Christ and through the Spirit, God calls and sends us to participate in this mission of reconciling love. "In Christ," the apostle Paul writes, "God was reconciling the world to himself, not counting their trespasses against them, and entrusting the message of reconciliation to us" (2 Cor. 5:19).

While Christians through the ages have been called into God's mission of reconciliation, Stephen Bevans and Roger Schroeder argue that mission in the church today must give particular attention to the work of reconciliation. What marks this time, they say, "is the phenomenon of globalization, which . . . has connected the peoples in the world as never before in history and . . . also threatens, perhaps as never before, to exclude whole peoples from economic and political participation and to extinguish traditional languages and cultures."[4] The need for reconciliation is evident in the litany of places that experienced violence and devastation at the end of the twentieth century and the beginning of the twenty-first: Bosnia-Herzegovina, Rwanda, Burundi, Congo, Sudan, Afghanistan, Iraq, Syria, Israel, and Palestine — and the list could go on. In addition, "indigenous peoples in every part of the world . . .

3. Catherine Mowry LaCugna, *God for Us: The Trinity and Christian Life* (San Francisco: HarperSanFrancisco, 1991), p. 378.

4. Stephen B. Bevans and Roger P. Schroeder, *Constants in Context: A Theology of Mission for Today* (Maryknoll, N.Y.: Orbis Books, 2004), p. 390.

are demanding recognition of and compensation for the damage done by majority populations to their traditional ways of life and their cultures."[5] In this context, say Bevans and Schroeder, the church preaches and bears witness to "the 'already' but 'not yet' reign of the triune God. . . . In the midst of unspeakable violence, unbearable pain, and indelible scars on people's memory, the church as God's minister of reconciliation proclaims that in Christ and in his community, healing is possible."[6]

By proclaiming reconciliation, Bevans and Schroeder maintain, the church "offers a powerful view of *salvation* as breaking in upon human beings, offering healing and wholeness, offering a new vision of what the world can be, offering forgiveness without denying the importance of consequences."[7] David Bosch also understands mission as salvation, which he views as a present reality as well as God's promised future for humankind. Salvation is the experience of God's healing, justice, and mercy. On the one hand, says Bosch, through Christ's incarnation, life, death, and resurrection, salvation is already a reality, and Christians are called to mediate that reality, to respond to the needs of the world and work for change. On the other hand, final salvation will come not through human action but only through God and only in God's time. Nonetheless, Bosch insists, "Mission means being involved in the ongoing dialogue between God, who offers . . . salvation, and the world, which . . . craves that salvation."[8] Christians do not themselves effect reconciliation; rather, they offer God's reconciling love and thereby participate in God's mission.

The authors of *Missional Church* argue that reconciliation "is not an individual and private matter, but an ecclesial practice that fosters, shapes, and sustains missional communities."[9] The practice of reconciliation has been the distinctive charism of the community of Taizé since its beginnings during World War II. In 1940, as the war began, Roger Schutz-Marsauche, the Swiss founder of the community, decided to seek a place in France to create a house of refuge and of prayer. "I found myself as if impelled to do everything I could to build a

---

5. Bevans and Schroeder, *Constants in Context,* p. 390.

6. Bevans and Schroeder, *Constants in Context,* pp. 390-91.

7. Bevans and Schroeder, *Constants in Context,* pp. 393-94; emphasis in the original.

8. David J. Bosch, *Transforming Mission: Paradigm Shifts in Theology of Mission* (Maryknoll, N.Y.: Orbis Books, 1991), p. 400.

9. *Missional Church: A Vision for the Sending of the Church in North America,* ed. Darrell L. Guder (Grand Rapids: Wm. B. Eerdmans, 1998), p. 166.

community life in which reconciliation would be realized, made concrete, day by day."[10] After locating a house in the village of Taizé, France, Roger began offering refuge to Jews and others fleeing from the Nazis. Late in 1942, while in Switzerland to raise funds for his work, Roger was betrayed to the Gestapo and so remained in Switzerland until the liberation of France in the fall of 1944.

When Roger returned to France, three prospective brothers accompanied him, and they asked themselves who "would be the most bereft in the human desert where they were to settle."[11] The answer presented itself when the Allied forces opened camps for German prisoners of war in some villages near Taizé. The nascent community shared what little food they had, and each week they welcomed the prisoners of war to their home for a meal and prayer. A 1986 biography of Brother Roger explains the impact of these early ministries in Taizé: "To have known the two situations, that of the political refugees, those who were hiding, those who were seeking refuge, and then very shortly afterwards that of the German prisoners of war who were 'just as innocent as the first,' remains for Brother Roger a powerful experience."[12]

In 1949, seven men took monastic vows of poverty, celibacy, and obedience, marking the formal organization of the Taizé community. During the 1950s, a growing number of pilgrims from France, Switzerland, Germany, England, and the Netherlands journeyed to Taizé for Sunday services. The community, whose members at that time were Protestants, had obtained permission to worship in the Roman Catholic church building in the village of Taizé. By the late 1950s, however, the tiny building was no longer adequate for the community and its pilgrims. The solution to this problem brought with it an echo of the brothers' ministry with German prisoners of war: the newly founded German organization *Aktion Sühnezeichen* ("Action Reconciliation") approached the Taizé community with an offer to raise the funds and provide a workforce to construct a new church building.[13]

Aktion Sühnezeichen had begun in 1958 at a synod of the *evangelische Kirche,* the Evangelical Church in Germany. A statement read aloud at the synod acknowledged German guilt for Nazi crimes and complicity in those

10. Brother Roger, cited by Kathryn Spink in *A Universal Heart: The Life and Vision of Brother Roger of Taizé,* 2nd ed. (London: SPCK, 2005), p. 28.

11. Spink, *A Universal Heart,* p. 49.

12. Spink, *A Universal Heart,* p. 50.

13. Spink, *A Universal Heart,* pp. 57-60, 76-77.

crimes. Two-thirds of the members of the synod signed the statement. The founders of *Aktion Sühnezeichen* believed that reconciliation required the perpetrators of the crimes and their descendants to take the first step toward reconciliation by rebuilding places destroyed in the war and through other construction projects.[14]

The inauguration of the Taizé community's Church of Reconciliation on August 6, 1962, the feast of the Transfiguration of Christ, was itself a sign of reconciliation, this time reconciliation among churches. From the very beginnings of the community, Brother Roger, a pastor in the Swiss Reformed tradition, had been in dialogue with leaders of the Roman Catholic Church, including Popes Pius XII and John XXIII. The inauguration of the Church of Reconciliation brought together members of the Central Committee of the World Council of Churches, the president of the Federation of Protestant Churches in France, the president of the German Evangelical Church, the Roman Catholic bishop of Rouen, a representative of the Patriarch of Constantinople, and a special envoy from the Archbishop of Canterbury.[15] Today, the membership of the Taizé community stands as a continuing witness to reconciliation among churches, as the community has about one hundred brothers from the Reformed, Lutheran, Anglican, and Roman Catholic traditions who worship together and welcome pilgrims from many different Christian traditions.

After the church building was opened in 1962, an ever-growing number of pilgrims, especially young people, visited the community. For many years, most were from Roman Catholic or Protestant traditions. But as Communism began to fall in 1989, travel from East to West became possible for the first time in many years, and immediately pilgrims from Eastern Orthodox traditions flocked to Taizé. As a sign of their welcome of these Christians from Eastern Europe, the brothers erected several onion-shaped domes on the roof of the Church of Reconciliation.[16]

For the Taizé community, reconciliation among churches is integrally related to reconciliation in the world. From the beginning of the Taizé community, Brother Roger wanted it to embody reconciliation. "He had always thought

14. "History of ARSP in Germany," Action Reconciliation Service for Peace, available at https://www.asf-ev.de/en/about-us/history.html.

15. Spink, *A Universal Heart*, pp. 78-79.

16. Jason Brian Santos, *A Community Called Taizé: A Story of Prayer, Worship, and Reconciliation* (Downers Grove, Ill.: IVP Books, 2008), p. 74.

that Christians would be reconciled by broadening their horizons, by going out to those who differed from themselves, by being open to non-believers, by carrying the preoccupations of those who were in difficulty, and by being attentive to the poorest of the poor. It was the vision of the reconciliation of the whole of humanity which made the effort of striving for reconciliation between Christians worthwhile."[17] On August 9, 2012, in a celebration commemorating the fiftieth anniversary of the opening of the church building, Brother Alois, now the prior of the community, recalled the words of Brother Roger fifty years earlier: "After being here in this Church of Reconciliation, rather than taking away the memory of the walls [of this building], may [pilgrims] remember the call for reconciliation and make it the daily bread of their life."[18]

The Taizé community stands as a powerful witness to God's gift of reconciliation. Yet every Christian is called to participate in God's mission of reconciliation. Bevans and Schroeder point out the need for reconciliation in several different contexts. Those who have experienced violence or devastating loss need reconciliation on a personal level, and Christians are called to offer healing both to those within the Christian community and to those who are not part of the church. Cultural reconciliation involves ministry with "women and men of cultural groups whose cultural identity has been ignored, disparaged, or stolen from them altogether." Political reconciliation addresses the need for restoration after politically motivated violence, such as the work carried out by the Truth and Reconciliation Commission in South Africa. Finally, Bevans and Schroeder call for reconciliation within the church. As Roman Catholics, they speak only of their own church, recognizing that church's role in wounding women, gays and lesbians, divorced people, cultural groups, and victims of clergy sexual abuse.[19] Certainly the need for reconciliation among churches is also pressing. Reconciliation with creation is yet another dimension, particularly in light of contemporary ecological crises, including global warming, the extinction of species, and the depletion of natural resources.[20]

17. Spink, *A Universal Heart*, p. 134.

18. Cited by Brother Alois, "The Church of Reconciliation at 50" (9 August 2012) at http://www.taize.fr/en_article14240.html.

19. Bevans and Schroeder, *Constants in Context*, pp. 391-92.

20. Bevans and Schroeder understand work for the integrity of creation to be an element of mission as prophetic dialogue, although they do not call this "reconciliation." See *Constants in Context*, pp. 375-78.

As the writers of *Missional Church* point out, the ministry of reconciliation, whatever the context, is a practice of the church, one that is an "antidote to competitive, alienating individualism in North American culture."[21] This ministry is dialogical: we ourselves are reconciled to God through Christ and so are drawn into the work of reconciliation. The ongoing dialogue of worship and mission, evident in our Möbius strip, is at work here: reconciled with God and with one another in the assembly for worship, we go forth as ministers of God's reconciliation in the world. We gather again in the assembly, drawn into the center of the spinning top, bringing with us our experiences of reconciliation in the world, our awareness of places where reconciliation is still elusive, and our sorrow at our own sinful behavior. In his remarks on the fiftieth anniversary of the Church of Reconciliation, Brother Alois of Taizé pointed out that the pilgrims experienced reconciliation through prayer and worship: "We welcome the reconciliation of Christ in many ways: in the Eucharist, in praying the Our Father, and even by simply saying from the bottom of our heart this age-old prayer: 'Jesus Christ, Son of God, come and help me.'"[22]

Repentance and Confession of Sin

Reconciliation begins with repentance and conversion, recognizing our sin and brokenness and desiring transformation. The prophets of Israel again and again called the community to amendment of life. Worship practices alone were insufficient. "I [the Lord] hate, I despise your festivals, and I take no delight in your solemn assemblies," proclaims the prophet Amos, "but let justice roll down like waters, and righteousness like an ever-flowing stream" (Amos 5:21, 24). The prophet Micah asks, "With what shall I come before the LORD, and bow myself before God on high?" The response comes, "He has told you, O mortal, what is good; and what does the LORD require of you but to do justice, and to love kindness, and to walk humbly with your God?" (Micah 6:6, 8).

The call to repentance is integral to Jesus' ministry. Like the prophets of Israel, John the Baptist proclaimed a baptism of repentance, leading to a

21. *Missional Church,* ed. Guder, p. 166.

22. Brother Alois, "The Church of Reconciliation at 50" (9 August 2012), available at http://www.taize.fr/en_article14240.html.

change in behavior (Luke 3:3-14). Jesus then began his ministry with a call to repentance: "The time is fulfilled, and the kingdom of God has come near; repent, and believe in the good news" (Mark 1:15). On the day of Pentecost, those who heard Peter's sermon were "cut to the heart" and asked, "What should we do?" Peter replied, "Repent, and be baptized every one of you in the name of Jesus Christ so that your sins may be forgiven; and you will receive the gift of the Holy Spirit" (Acts 2:37-38).

The fundamental Christian expression of repentance and new life is baptism. "We have been buried with [Christ] by baptism into death, so that, just as Christ was raised from the dead by the glory of the Father, so we too might walk in newness of life," the apostle Paul proclaims, continuing, "We know that our old self was crucified with him so that the body of sin might be destroyed, and we might no longer be enslaved to sin. For whoever has died is freed from sin" (Rom. 6:4, 6). Some fourth-century baptismal liturgies vividly enacted this death to sin and resurrection to new life, as Cyril, bishop of Jerusalem in the mid–fourth century, explained in an address to the newly baptized: "First, ye entered into the outer hall of the baptistery, and there facing towards the West ye heard the command to stretch forth your hand, and as in the presence of Satan ye renounced him. . . . What then did each of you standing up say? 'I renounce thee, Satan, thou wicked and most cruel tyrant!'"[23] Renunciations such as this continue to be part of baptism in many churches today, as, for example, these renunciations in the 1979 *Book of Common Prayer:*

> Do you renounce Satan and all the spiritual forces of wickedness that rebel against God?
> *I renounce them.*
> Do you renounce the evil powers of this world which corrupt and destroy the creatures of God?
> *I renounce them.*
> Do you renounce all sinful desires that draw you from the love of God?
> *I renounce them.*[24]

---

23. Cyril of Jerusalem, *Mystagogical Catechesis* I.2, 4, in *Sacraments and Worship: The Sources of Christian Theology,* ed. Maxwell E. Johnson (Louisville: Westminster John Knox Press, 2012), p. 121.

24. *The Book of Common Prayer and Administration of the Sacraments and Other Rites*

Reformed theologian James K. A. Smith explains that the baptismal renunciations "are rejecting not temporal material existence per se, nor cultural life as such, but rather the perversions and distortions of both that characterize fallen humanity."[25]

After renouncing sin and evil, candidates for baptism turn to Christ. In the 1979 *Book of Common Prayer,* three questions follow the renunciations:

Do you turn to Jesus Christ and accept him as your Savior?
I do.
Do you put your whole trust in his grace and love?
I do.
Do you promise to follow and obey him as your Lord?
I do.[26]

To convert is to turn, to change one's life by embracing a new reality. In some ancient baptismal rites, candidates enacted their conversion by turning their bodies from the West, the place of the devil, to the East, the place of the rising sun, alluding to the prophecy of Malachi: "the sun of righteousness shall rise, with healing in its wings" (Mal. 4:2). Having turned to Christ, the candidates were then plunged into the waters of baptism, as Cyril reminded the newly baptized: "Ye were led to the holy pool of divine baptism. . . . And each of you was asked, whether [you] believed in the name of the Father, and of the Son, and of the Holy Ghost, and ye made that saving confession, and descended three times into the water, and ascended again, here . . . covertly pointing by a figure at the three days of burial of Christ."[27] Immersed in the waters of baptism and so buried with Christ in death, the newly baptized came up from the font to new life in Christ.

In this new life of baptism, God sends us in mission, to be Christ's people in the world, to embody his message of forgiveness and new life. The renunciations, however, are not to be forgotten. Rather, they are, as Smith

---

and Ceremonies of the Church, Together with The Psalter or Psalms of David (New York: Church Hymnal Corp., 1979), p. 302.

25. James K. A. Smith, *Desiring the Kingdom: Worship, Worldview, and Cultural Formation* (Grand Rapids: Baker Academic, 2009), p. 189.

26. *The Book of Common Prayer* 1979, pp. 302-3.

27. Cyril, *Mystagogical Catechesis* II.4, in *Sacraments and Worship,* pp. 121-22.

asserts, "ongoing renunciations that characterize life as a new creature. . . . Our baptism signals that we are new creatures, with new desires, a new passion for a very different kingdom; thus we renounce (and keep renouncing) our former desires."[28]

In the "already" but "not yet" of the reign of God, Christians walk in newness of life yet also await the fullness of God's new creation. While baptism signifies repentance and new life, Christians sometimes fall short in the ongoing work of renunciation, as the Baptismal Covenant in the 1979 *Book of Common Prayer* acknowledges with this question: "Will you persevere in resisting evil, and, whenever you fall into sin, repent and return to the Lord?"[29]

Gradually, over the course of Christian history, churches developed penitential practices to address the reality of postbaptismal sin. For several centuries, serious postbaptismal sin required public confession, accompanied by fasting, prayer, and the wearing of sackcloth and ashes, and some people postponed baptism until they were near death rather than risk falling into sin after their baptism. In the sixth century a system of individual, private, "tariff penance" (so called because a specific act of penance was prescribed as a kind of tariff for each particular sin) began to replace the practice of public penance. By the thirteenth century, penance was considered a sacrament in the Western church, and the Fourth Lateran Council in 1215 required Christians to make an annual private confession to a priest in order to receive absolution.[30]

Both public penance and tariff penance dealt with individual sin, and the rites focused on penitence. In the Western mass, penitential prayers of preparation at the beginning of the mass began to appear as early as the ninth century. Within a few centuries, the prayers took shape as a mutual confession of sin between the priest and other ministers serving in the liturgy.[31]

28. Smith, *Desiring the Kingdom,* pp. 187, 189.

29. *The Book of Common Prayer* 1979, p. 304.

30. Although a decree of the Fourth Lateran Council made an annual confession compulsory for every Christian, it was commonly understood to be required only for those conscious of mortal sin. See J. Dallen, "Penance, Sacrament of," in *New Catholic Encyclopedia,* 2nd ed., vol. 11 (Detroit: Gale, 2003), pp. 66-72, available online at Gale Virtual Reference Library.

31. John Baldovin, "The Introductory Rites: History of the Latin Text and Rite," in *A Commentary on the Order of Mass of The Roman Missal: A New English Translation, developed*

The assembly, however, was not part of this confession. A communal general confession of sin as part of Sunday worship first developed during the sixteenth-century Reformation as Protestant reformers rejected the medieval sacrament of penance. This practice of general confession continues to this day in many Protestant churches, and the 1969 Roman missal replaced the private prayers of the priest and other ministers with a communal penitential rite at the beginning of the mass.[32]

A confession of sin during worship acknowledges that we have been alienated from God, from one another, and from creation through our action and our inaction. Clayton Schmit points out, "The honest confession of sins either privately or corporately is an essential spiritual practice for faithful disciples. If done corporately in worship, it signals a strong Protestant impulse that private confession before a priest is not a requirement for faith."[33]

Our confession admits not only our personal transgressions; it also, James Smith asserts, "owns up to our complicity with all sorts of evil that disorders the world and corrupts creation."[34] In one confession of sin used in the Episcopal Church, worshipers "repent of the evil that enslaves us, the evil we have done, and the evil done on our behalf."[35] This confession recognizes forces of evil that exist beyond human control, sometimes referred to as powers and principalities (Eph. 6:12). Bevans and Schroeder summarize Walter Wink's description of these powers "as not so much spiritual demons but as the intangible power, often a mixture of good and bad, of global corporations, national governments, various ideological expressions like capitalism or socialism, or sociological trends like globalization."[36] Though human be-

---

under the auspices of the Catholic Academy of Liturgy, ed. Edward Foley et al. (Collegeville, Minn.: Liturgical Press, 2011), p. 121.

32. Dominic E. Serra, "The Introductory Rites: Theology of the Latin Text and Rite," in *Commentary on the Order of Mass,* ed. Foley et al., p. 129.

33. Clayton J. Schmit, *Sent and Gathered: A Worship Manual for the Missional Church* (Grand Rapids: Baker Academic, 2009), p. 170.

34. Smith, *Desiring the Kingdom,* p. 178.

35. Episcopal Church, *Enriching Our Worship 1: Morning and Evening Prayer, The Great Litany, The Holy Eucharist,* Supplemental Liturgical Materials Prepared by the Standing Liturgical Commission, 1997 (New York: Church Publishing, 1998), p. 19.

36. Walter Wink, *Naming the Powers: The Language of Power in the New Testament* (Minneapolis: Fortress Press, 1984); Wink, *Unmasking the Powers: The Invisible Forces that Determine Human Existence* (Minneapolis: Fortress Press, 1986); Wink, *Engaging the Powers: Discernment*

ings are called, as Smith says, "to be God's image bearers to and for the world," because of sin and evil "we create institutions and systems that are unjust, not only because of individual bad choices but also because the very structures and systems of these institutions are wrongly ordered, fostering systemic racism or patriarchy or exploitation of the poor."[37] A confession of sin from the Presbyterian Church in Canada acknowledges the effects of systemic evil not only on human relationships but also on the whole created order: "We confess our sin and the sin of this world . . . we are a people divided against ourselves as we cling to the values of a broken world. The profit and pleasures we pursue lay waste the land and pollute the sea. The fears and jealousies that we harbor set neighbor against neighbor and nation against nation."[38]

By confessing our sin, Christians acknowledge our desire to be conformed to Christ, to live as Christ's people in the world. The practice of confession, whether public communal confession or individual private confession, thus restores us to our baptismal union with God, through Christ, and so enables us to participate as redeemed sinners in God's mission of reconciliation.

Forgiveness

When we confess our sins, we are seeking God's forgiveness. The gift of God's forgiveness is integrally related to our forgiveness of one another. "Forgive us our sins, as we forgive those who sin against us," we pray in the Lord's Prayer. As we accept God's forgiveness and as we forgive others, we participate in God's mission of reconciliation. "Forgiveness begins with God's love," writes United Methodist minister L. Gregory Jones, "as that love works toward reconciliation amid the sin and evil that mar God's good creation. Forgiveness aims to restore us to communion with God, with one another, and with the whole creation. . . . The healing that comes with God's forgiveness strengthens us to be involved in other practices that are witness to God's forgiving,

---

and Resistance in a World of Domination (Minneapolis: Fortress Press, 1986); cited by Bevans and Schroeder, *Constants in Context,* p. 371.

37. Smith, *Desiring the Kingdom,* p. 178.

38. *The Book of Common Worship* (Presbyterian Church in Canada, 1991), 28, alt.; cited by Smith, *Desiring the Kingdom,* pp. 178-79.

re-creating activity for the world."[39] Lutheran pastor Richard Rouse explains this dual process of forgiving and being forgiven: "Forgiveness is being able to let go of remembered hurt and pain, looking toward the future, rather than dwelling on the past. . . . The road to forgiveness also requires that we both acknowledge our own need for pardon and embrace for ourselves the fullness of God's gift of grace offered to us and to all people."[40]

Rouse knows well the cost and the blessings of the spiritual discipline of forgiveness. On August 9, 1992, the church building of Trinity Lutheran Church in Lynnwood, Washington, where Rouse was serving as pastor, burned to the ground, the work of an arsonist. For the congregation, this was an especially devastating loss. A remodeling of the building had been nearing completion. Instead of planning for its dedication, members of the congregation assembled in the church parking lot on Sunday morning a few hours after the fire began, the charred embers of the church building still smoldering behind them. In his sermon that morning, Rouse assured the assembly, "There will be new life coming out of this death and destruction. Like the phoenix rising out of the ashes, Trinity will rise again!" During the prayers, a young woman pleaded, "Hear our prayers, Lord, for the troubled soul who did this tragic thing."[41]

The fire at Trinity was one of the first in a series of arson fires in the greater Seattle area. Businesses, churches, and homes were all targeted, and by early October that year, nearly fifty fires were determined to be arson-related. On Monday, February 8, 1993, six months after the fire at Trinity Church, Rouse opened his morning paper and learned that the arsonist had been apprehended. Rouse was stunned. A few months before the fire, he had met with the same man, Paul Keller, an advertising salesman who had been assisting in the preparation of a mailing for Trinity. At that meeting, Rouse and Keller discussed not only advertising strategy but also theology, faith, and ministry. Rouse describes his thoughts as he drove to work that morning. "I resolved to go and see Paul in jail. I had to know why he had done this. And despite my hurt and anger, part of my heart softened. I knew Paul must

---

39. L. Gregory Jones, "Forgiveness," in *Practicing Our Faith: A Way of Life for a Searching People,* ed. Dorothy C. Bass, 2nd ed. (San Francisco: Jossey-Bass, 1997, 2010), p. 138.

40. Richard W. Rouse, *Fire of Grace: The Healing Power of Forgiveness* (Minneapolis: Augsburg Press, 2005), p. xv.

41. Rouse, *Fire of Grace,* pp. 4-14; quotations on p. 11.

be hurting too — and feeling scared. He was a brother in Christ, and I felt obligated to visit him. I recalled Jesus' admonition to visit those who were sick or in prison [Matthew 25]."[42]

A few days later, Rouse met with Keller at the jail. Keller acknowledged that his life had been a shambles: his marriage had ended in divorce, he was in the midst of bankruptcy proceedings, and he had begun to drink heavily. Keller insisted that he had not intended to hurt anyone, yet he also accepted responsibility and expressed a willingness to go to prison. In response, Rouse assured Keller, "Remember that no matter what you've done, you are still a baptized child of God. He may not like what you've done, but he still loves you. And God forgives you." Rouse continued, "I can't speak for the congregation, but I forgive you."[43]

The following Sunday, the Gospel appointed in the lectionary came from Jesus' Sermon on the Mount: "Love your enemies and pray for those who persecute you" (Matt. 5:44). Rouse decided to tell the congregation about his visit with Keller. In his sermon, Rouse explained, "[Forgiving Paul] was Christ speaking through me. . . . I don't think I could have done it by myself. I believe in that moment I was God's instrument of healing love." Rouse encouraged his congregation to "be a community of grace . . . a place where others experience the love and forgiveness of Christ."[44]

Rouse continued to visit Keller in jail, and a few weeks later, a letter from Keller arrived, addressed to the congregation. It began, "I want each one of you to know how deeply sorrowful I am for the fire that burned your church." Keller went on to say that though he was a Christian, he had let God down. He continued, "I humbly ask you for your forgiveness."[45]

One month after his arrest, Keller pleaded guilty to thirty-two arsons. While he was awaiting sentencing, the leadership of Trinity Church sent a letter of forgiveness to Keller. "Jesus told us that we must forgive those who sin against us not seven times, but seventy-seven times [Matt. 18:22] . . . That is the hard part because it is not in human nature to forgive," the letter read. "But because we are Christians and have accepted Jesus as Lord, then

42. Rouse, *Fire of Grace,* p. 33.
43. Rouse, *Fire of Grace,* p. 37.
44. Rouse, *Fire of Grace,* pp. 39-40.
45. Rouse, *Fire of Grace,* p. 43.

the easy part is actually forgiving someone for sinning against us. . . . [We] want to extend to you . . . not only our forgiveness, bur also our love and our prayers."[46] This letter from the leadership council makes clear that forgiveness and reconciliation become possible only through the grace of Christ. L. Gregory Jones points out that the requirement to forgive "seventy-seven times" also means that our forgiveness needs to become habitual.[47]

Bevans and Schroeder emphasize that the ministry of reconciliation is "without a doubt a ministry of prophetic dialogue." They continue, "The witness and proclamation to victims of injustice and violence that reconciliation is a possibility and that it is thoroughly God's work are actions that take real courage. Reconciliation is undoubtedly a countercultural movement, a call to envision not a repaired world but a new creation."[48] As the experience of Trinity Church shows, offering forgiveness to the perpetrator of violence is also an act of courage for victims, a countercultural act that envisions a new creation where the "wolf shall live with the lamb" (Isa. 11:6), and "God will wipe away every tear" (Rev. 21:4).

In this situation, much of the work of forgiveness occurred outside worship, through the relationship that formed between Keller and Rouse. Yet there is a close connection between the mission of reconciliation in the world and the mission of reconciliation in worship. At Trinity Lutheran Church, the practices wove in and out of each other, as in our spinning top. The prayer for the arsonist offered on the day of the fire, while not a prayer of forgiveness, acknowledged the arsonist's humanity, identifying him as a "troubled soul." Rouse's sermons proclaimed the good news of forgiveness, the truth that no one is beyond God's reconciling love, and he invited the assembly to share in offering forgiveness. Several worship services marked the path from destruction to new life, linking forgiveness and reconciliation with healing. One of them, a service of remembrance held just after a crew had demolished the charred remains of the church and removed the rubble, acknowledged the congregation's grief and celebrated the promise of new life with a baptism. Signs of new life were also evident at a celebration to break ground. At the laying of the cornerstone, two years after the fire, Keller contributed a taped

46. Rouse, *Fire of Grace*, p. 63.

47. Jones, "Forgiveness," p. 142.

48. Bevans and Schroeder, *Constants in Context*, p. 393.

message from his prison cell. "I'm constantly reminded . . . that God's love is never out of reach. His forgiveness and his grace are always available for the asking," Keller said to the assembly. He went on, "I want each of you to know that I have felt your prayers and have wept time and again over the precious forgiveness that many have offered in letter and in the spoken word."[49]

While Rouse and others forgave Keller, it was not a matter of "forgive and forget." At a community service of healing, held one month after Keller was sentenced to life in prison, Rouse said to the assembly, "There's been a lot of hurt and pain that has surfaced because of the fires. We need to now put that behind us and move toward healing and wholeness."[50] Rouse was calling the people of his community not to forget, but to relinquish hurt and bitterness and choose instead a path of healing and hope. Bevans and Schroeder explain that reconciliation "remembers and still rages, laments, and grieves. But it does so with the grace of wholeness."[51]

The willingness to acknowledge Paul Keller's humanity and view him with the eyes of Christ characterizes the work of forgiveness at Trinity. That same spirit of forgiveness was evident in the Taizé community after the violent death of their founder, Brother Roger. On August 16, 2005, a thirty-six-year-old Romanian woman, known to the community and known to be mentally disturbed, stabbed Brother Roger in the Church of Reconciliation. He died within minutes. At the funeral one week later, the new prior, Brother Alois, offered this prayer: "God of goodness, we entrust to your forgiveness Luminita Solcan, who, in a deranged act, put an end to the life of our brother Roger. With Christ on the cross we say to you: Father, forgive her, she does not know what she did. Holy Spirit, we pray to you for the people of Romania and for the young Romanians who are so loved in Taizé."[52]

Because we know God's forgiveness, we are able to offer forgiveness to others, recognizing that they too are within the reach of God's saving em-

---

49. Rouse, *Fire of Grace*, p. 107.

50. Rouse, *Fire of Grace*, pp. 72-73.

51. Bevans and Schroeder, *Constants in Context*, p. 394.

52. *Dieu de bonté, nous confions à ton pardon Luminita Solcan qui, dans un acte maladif, a mis fin à la vie de notre frère Roger. Avec le Christ sur la croix nous te disons : Père, pardonne-lui, elle ne sait pas ce qu'elle a fait. Esprit Saint, nous te prions pour le peuple de Roumanie et pour les jeunes Roumains tellement aimés à Taizé.* Brother John of Taizé, e-mail message to the author, 9 November 2013; translation provided by Brother John.

brace.[53] Through forgiveness, we become able to embrace new life in Christ and live in the power of the Spirit. L. Gregory Jones explains, "The Christian practice of forgiveness involves us in a whole way of life, a way that is shaped by an ever-deepening friendship with God and with other people."[54]

In worship, a formal confession of sin is usually followed by a declaration of pardon or an absolution, assuring members of the assembly that God forgives them. James Smith underscores that God's forgiveness "comes as a gift, the overflowing of Christ's work on the cross." He continues, "God's forgiveness [does not] stem from simply dismissing the demands of justice or ignoring the brokenness of creation; rather, God himself takes on our sin and its effects in the Son, on the cross, who also triumphs over them in the resurrection. Our brokenness and violence are met by the grace of God, who suffered violence for our sake and in turn graces and empowers us . . . to be his image bearers to and for the world."[55]

The liturgical act of confession and absolution is thus integrally related to participation in God's mission of reconciliation in the world, like our Möbius strip, in which worship is mission is worship. . . . J. G. Davies emphasizes, "The liturgical absolution has no meaning or efficacy apart from forgiveness actualized in everyday life. . . . Forgiveness by God becomes a reality for us only insofar as, in response to it, we also forgive. . . . We may say that the sign and seal of our pardon is engagement in Christ's service; our forgiveness is a committal to service and mission."[56] Through our forgiveness of others, we participate in the mission of God, seeking reconciliation with God and with one another.

The Peace of Christ

According to the Gospel of John, after his resurrection Jesus appeared to his disciples as they cowered behind locked doors. His greeting, "Peace be with you" (John 20:19), offered God's *shalom* — that is, well-being, healing, and

---

53. Prayer for Mission, *The Book of Common Prayer* 1979, p. 101.

54. Jones, "Forgiveness," p. 132.

55. Smith, *Desiring the Kingdom*, pp. 179-80.

56. J. G. Davies, *Worship and Mission* (London: SCM Press, 1966; New York: Association Press, 1967), pp. 128-29.

wholeness. After the traumatic events of Jesus' arrest and crucifixion, it was surely a comfort for the disciples to be greeted with the peace of God. Moreover, Jesus' greeting of peace was an act of reconciliation with the disciples who had deserted him when he was arrested.

In early Christian communities, a greeting of peace became part of the baptismal rite, welcoming the newly baptized into the assembly. "Having ended the prayers, we salute one another with a kiss," Justin Martyr explains in his description of baptism.[57] From immersion in the watery grave of the font, the newly baptized ascended to new life in Christ, to participate in the reconciling mission of God. The exchange of the peace signified their membership in the new community that is the body of Christ.

Reconciliation with one's sisters and brothers in Christ was considered essential for worship. In his Sermon on the Mount, Jesus said, "When you are offering your gift at the altar, if you remember that your brother or sister has something against you, leave your gift there before the altar and go; first be reconciled to your brother or sister, and then come and offer your gift" (Matt. 5:23-24). Alan Kreider and Eleanor Kreider emphasize that making peace was and is a prerequisite for worship. Citing Cyprian of Carthage and the third-century Syrian church order *Didascalia Apostolorum*, Kreider and Kreider conclude, "True prayer was possible only where there was peace between Christian brothers and sisters."[58]

In addition to the baptismal greeting of peace, an exchange of Christ's peace was part of the regular celebration of the Eucharist. Writing at the beginning of the third century, Tertullian describes the kiss of peace as the "seal of prayer."[59] In most churches, both East and West, the peace was exchanged after the intercessions and before the Eucharistic prayer, expressing the union of Christians with one another as they came to offer the great prayer of thanksgiving. By the fifth century, however, the peace took place

57. Justin Martyr, *I Apology* 65, in *The Apostolic Fathers with Justin Martyr and Irenaeus,* Vol. 1 of *Ante-Nicene Fathers,* ed. Alexander Roberts and James Donaldson, Christian Classics Ethereal Library, available at http://www.ccel.org/ccel/schaff/anf01.viii.ii.lxv.html.

58. Alan Kreider and Eleanor Kreider, *Worship and Mission after Christendom* (Scottdale, Pa., and Waterloo, Ontario: Herald Press, 2011), p. 168.

59. Tertullian, *On Prayer* 18, trans. S. Thelwall, in *Latin Christianity: Its Founder, Tertullian,* Vol. 3 of *Ante-Nicene Fathers,* ed. Allan Menzies, Christian Classics Ethereal Library, available at http://www.ccel.org/ccel/schaff/anf03.vi.iv.xviii.html.

in the Roman rite just before the breaking of the bread and the distribution of communion.[60] Later in the Middle Ages, rather than offering a kiss of peace to one another, members of the assembly would kiss a "peace-board," a piece of wood, ivory, or metal decorated with a cross or some other religious symbol.[61] This liturgical practice of exchanging peace no longer reflected the work of making peace with one's brothers and sisters. The link between worship and mission, between reconciliation in the world and reconciliation in the assembly, had disappeared.

Alan Kreider and Eleanor Kreider urge that the peace "regain the significance it had in pre-Christendom . . . [as] an opportunity to repent and restore relationships."[62] Beginning with the liturgy of the Church of South India in 1950, the exchange of the peace has re-emerged in many contemporary assemblies. In the Church of South India, the practice is highly stylized. The presider first offers peace to assisting ministers through a double handclasp, two hands extended to two hands, coming together and gently releasing. As the presider and the assistants then make their way through the assembly, they clasp hands with the person at the end of each row, and the peace then moves along each row, from one person to another. When I first experienced this, I had been accustomed to the much freer movement as the peace is exchanged in many Western churches, and I was startled, then chagrined to realize that I had not been attentive to the local custom. However the peace is offered, in a missional congregation its exchange in the assembly will reflect the congregation's concern for peacemaking in the world and its participation in God's mission of reconciliation, in a continuity suggested by our Möbius strip.

How the Assembly Enacts Reconciliation

Because God's reconciling love is at the heart of mission, we can view the entire act of worship as an expression of reconciliation, a form of participation in God's mission, in which worshipers receive God's gracious love.

60. Graham Woolfenden, "'Let Us Offer Each Other the Sign of Peace' — An Enquiry," *Worship* 67 (1993): 242-46.

61. "Kiss of Peace," *New Catholic Encyclopedia*, 2nd ed., vol. 8 (Detroit: Gale, 2003), p. 18, available online at Gale Virtual Reference Library.

62. Kreider and Kreider, *Worship and Mission after Christendom*, p. 169.

L. Gregory Jones explains, "Worship and prayer prepare us to reclaim and imagine the gift and the task of practicing forgiveness. They remind us of God's redemptive activity, stimulate our imagination, and call us forth to a renewed commitment to embody God's forgiveness throughout our lives."[63] Within the worship service, the assembly may engage in specific acts of penitence and repentance, of forgiveness and reconciliation, and these may occur at several places in the order of service.

When the assembly participates in a penitential rite as it gathers, the people acknowledge that we approach God with a need for restoration and a recognition that we fall short of God's desires for us. Gregory Augustine Pierce emphasizes that the primary thing we have failed to do "is to bring about that kingdom of God we were sent forth to help inaugurate." Yet, says Pierce, "We don't beat ourselves up about it. Instead, we ask for forgiveness — from God, from one another, from ourselves. . . . And then, surprisingly, we are forgiven."[64] This rite of penitence may take the form of a series of biddings, to which the assembly responds, "Lord, have mercy," or it may be a formal prayer of confession.

As an alternative to a penitential rite during the gathering, a confession of sin might take place after the proclamation and response to the Word. In hearing and responding to the Word, members of the assembly remember God's love and desire for all creation and their call to participate in God's mission of reconciling love. They may also recognize how they have fallen short in responding to their call to enact God's mission in the world. As James Smith explains, we fail "to be God's image bearers to and for the world."[65] By confessing our sin, we own up to our responsibility and seek God's forgiveness. The confession may be a specific prayer that follows the intercessions, or penitential petitions may be included in the intercessory prayers.

Smith explains the salutary effect of the confession: "Having been formed largely in churches that did not include confession as a regular part of worship, I now find that the liturgical act of confession, while it makes me uncomfortable, also gives honest voice to what I know about myself. . . .

---

63. Jones, "Forgiveness," p. 145.

64. Gregory F. Augustine Pierce, *The Mass Is Never Ended: Rediscovering Our Mission to Transform the World* (Notre Dame: Ave Maria Press, 2007), pp. 43-44.

65. Smith, *Desiring the Kingdom*, p. 178.

While on one level I would rather not be reminded of all my failures and sins and violations, on another level I never escape the knowledge of them, and the rite of confession makes room for honesty about that."[66] By honestly acknowledging their own shortcomings as well as their complicity in systemic sins, Christians repent, turning once again to God, trusting in God's steadfast and abundant mercy. Through such repentance, Christians are restored to their baptismal union with God in Christ.

Repentance can be expressed through more than words. During the 1990s, Holy Family Episcopal Church in Half Moon Bay, California, introduced a practice of "confession stones." Each worshiper received a stone, and the presider invited the assembly to call to mind their sins, things done and left undone, and imagine placing those sins on the stones. After the presider led a short, responsive prayer of confession, children collected the stones and brought them to the presider, who poured water over them as the assembly sang a song based on the words of the prophet Ezekiel: "I [God] will sprinkle clean water upon you. . . . A new heart I will give you, and a new spirit I will put within you; and I will remove from your body the heart of stone and give you a heart of flesh" (Ezek. 36:25-26).[67] This ritual became a regular practice at Holy Family Church for several years because it was such a vivid expression of repentance, one that was easy for worshipers of all ages to comprehend.

A liturgical confession of sin is usually followed by an absolution or declaration of pardon. This assurance of God's forgiveness offers hope to the assembly, reminding them that through Christ they walk in newness of life.

In their study of emerging churches, Mary Gray-Reeves and Michael Perham found a wide range of penitential practices. In some, there was no explicit element of penitence, while in others a leader said prayers of confession. In a few of these churches, words of absolution or pardon followed the confession, but several did not include any formal declaration. Gray-Reeves and Perham explain this as "an understanding in some of the emergent churches that absolution comes in the very act of confessing and that a formal priestly absolution has no function."[68] Perhaps this decision also

66. Smith, *Desiring the Kingdom,* p. 180.

67. Caroline S. Fairless, *Children at Worship: Congregations in Bloom* (New York: Church Publishing, 2000), pp. 87-91.

68. Mary Gray-Reeves and Michael Perham, *The Hospitality of God: Emerging Worship for a Missional Church* (New York: Seabury Books; London: SPCK, 2011), p. 87.

reflects a rejection of hierarchy and an insistence on shared ministry that characterizes many emerging churches. Yet, while not every assembly included a formal absolution after confession of sin, Gray-Reeves and Perham concluded that "the theological message of emergent churches was above all else of a loving and forgiving God, known in Jesus Christ, who very much wants a connection with individuals."[69] Clayton Schmit shows a similar concern for this theological message of God's reconciling love in his insistence that a form of absolution or pardon is essential: "Words of absolution are among the most powerful and meaningful spoken in worship. They indicate the good news of the gospel in concrete and immediate terms."[70]

In addition to a formal statement of penitence, the assembly may enact reconciliation by offering Christ's peace to one another. Emphasizing the missional significance of the peace, J. G. Davies insisted that "it can . . . never be reduced to a simple formula: it has to be found and worked out in actual situations. The goal toward which God is working, i.e., the ultimate end of mission, is the establishment of *shalom,* and this involves the realization of the full potentialities of all creation and its ultimate reconciliation and unity in Christ."[71] The peace we offer one another in the assembly is an expression of our reconciled relationships with one another and with God. "When we embrace one another in peace," Thomas Hoyt says, "we testify to the reconciliation God intends for all people."[72] The peace we receive in the assembly is the peace we carry into the world in mission. Here, as with other elements of worship, mission and worship flow into one another, as they do in our Möbius strip and our spinning top.

In many traditions, the exchange of the peace leads immediately to the celebration of the communion meal. Just as the peace enacts God's reconciliation, so too the Eucharist is itself an embodiment of reconciliation, a feast that offers forgiveness of sins and union with Christ. In the next chapter, I consider how the Eucharistic meal expresses and shapes the assembly's participation in God's mission of reconciliation.

---

69. Gray-Reeves and Perham, *The Hospitality of God,* p. 87.
70. Schmit, *Sent and Gathered,* p. 170.
71. Davies, *Worship and Mission,* p. 130.
72. Thomas Hoyt Jr., "Testimony," in *Practicing Our Faith,* ed. Bass, p. 99.

CHAPTER 6

Celebrating the Communion Meal

Bread and wine and water are brought, and the president in like man-
ner offers prayers and thanksgivings, according to his ability, and the
people assent, saying Amen; and there is a distribution to each, and
a participation of that over which thanks have been given.

Justin Martyr, mid–second century[1]

The table of bread and wine is now to be made ready.
It is the table of company with Jesus, and all who love him.
It is the table of sharing with the poor of the world, with whom
      Jesus identified himself.
It is the table of communion with the earth, in which Christ became
      incarnate.
So come to this table,
you who have much faith and you who would like to have more;
you who have been here often and you who have not been for a long
      time;
you who have tried to follow Jesus, and you who have failed;

---

1. Justin, *I Apology* 67, in *The Apostolic Fathers with Justin Martyr and Irenaeus*, Vol. 1 of *Ante-Nicene Fathers*, ed. Alexander Roberts and James Donaldson, Christian Classics Ethereal Library, available at http://www.ccel.org/ccel/schaff/anf01.viii.ii.lxvii.html.

Come.

It is Christ who invites us to meet him here.

Iona Abbey Worship Book[2]

Having feasted on the Word, offered intercession for the needs of the world, and enacted reconciliation with one another and with God, the assembly may turn to the celebration of the communion meal. Not every congregation includes the Lord's Supper in their Sunday worship every week, while some celebrate the Eucharist several times a week, or even daily. Yet regardless of the frequency of celebration, Holy Communion is central to Christian faith and practice.[3] Some contemporary scholars assert that the Eucharist makes or manifests the church, the body of Christ.[4]

In this chapter I consider missional aspects of the celebration of communion, what is sometimes called the liturgy of the table. By participating in the communion meal, the assembly is united with Christ, with one another, and with creation. As members of the body of Christ, the assembly experiences God's reconciling love and is drawn into God's mission to restore humankind to right relationship with all creation and with God. *Baptism, Eucharist, and Ministry,* the 1982 ecumenical statement of the World Council of Churches, underscores the missional character of the Eucharist and the connection between the liturgical celebration and mission in the world: "The very celebration of the eucharist is an instance of the Church's participation

2. "Extra Resources for the Sunday Morning Communion," *Iona Abbey Worship Book* (Glasgow: Wild Goose Publications, 2001), p. 53.

3. "Eucharist," par. 1, *Baptism, Eucharist, and Ministry,* Faith and Order Paper No. 111 (Geneva: World Council of Churches, 1982), available at http://www.oikoumene.org/en/resources/documents/wcc-commissions/faith-and-order-commission/i-unity-the-church-and-its-mission/baptism-eucharist-and-ministry-faith-and-order-paper-no-111-the-lima-text?set_language=en.

4. Peter Cruchley-Jones cites several contemporary sources that underscore the significance of the Eucharist for the church's identity. Although criticizing what he terms "ecclesiocentricity" — that is, the church's efforts to contain the power of the Eucharist — he also emphasizes the significance of the Eucharist as God's engagement with the world. See Peter Cruchley-Jones, "A Eucharistic Understanding of Mission — A Missiological Understanding of Eucharist," in *Mission Matters,* ed. Lynne Price, Juan Sepúlveda, and Graeme Smith, Studies in the Intercultural History of Christianity, 103 (Frankfurt: Peter Lang, 1997), pp. 109-19.

in God's mission in the world. This participation takes everyday form in the proclamation of the Gospel, service of the neighbor, and faithful presence in the world. . . . The eucharist brings into the present age a new reality which transforms Christians into the image of Christ and therefore makes them his effective witnesses."[5]

Eating in the Company of Jesus

Christian scholars today locate the origins of the Eucharist not only in Jesus' last supper with his disciples but also in the wider context of his table fellowship during his ministry and after his resurrection. The Gospels report that Jesus ate and drank with tax collectors and sinners — such as Matthew (Matt. 9:9-13) and Zacchaeus (Luke 19:1-7) — behavior that some considered scandalous. Liturgical scholar Paul Bradshaw explains that some more pious Jews at the time of Jesus "were very careful about not only *what* they ate (so as to observe the dietary laws prescribed in the Old Testament) but also *with whom* they shared a meal, since eating with those they regarded as impure would compromise their own ritual purity."[6] By eating both with those considered unclean and with the more pious Pharisees (Luke 7:36), Jesus embodied God's gracious and boundless love and so enacted God's mission.

Jesus did more than dine with those on the margins of society. He also called them to new life, to repent and be reconciled with God. When criticized for dining with tax collectors and other sinners, Jesus replied, "Those who are well have no need of a physician, but those who are sick; I have come to call not the righteous but sinners to repentance" (Luke 5:31-32). Zacchaeus took this call to heart, promising to give half his possessions to the poor and to repay fourfold those whom he had defrauded. In response, Jesus assured Zacchaeus, "Today salvation has come to this house" (Luke 19:9).

Jesus' boundary-breaking practice of table fellowship was thus an enacted parable, a proclamation that the reign of God had come near. He also used the image of a banquet in his teaching about the reign of God. The

---

5. "Eucharist," par. 25-26, *Baptism, Eucharist, and Ministry.*

6. Paul F. Bradshaw, *Early Christian Worship: A Basic Introduction to Ideas and Practice* (Collegeville, Minn.: Liturgical Press, 2010), p. 42.

Jewish community of his time would have been familiar with the vision of the eschatological banquet. The prophet Isaiah had announced, "On this mountain the LORD of hosts will make for all peoples a feast of rich food, a feast of well-aged wines, of rich food filled with marrow, of well-aged wines strained clear" (Isa. 25:6); Isaiah had promised that God's salvation would come, that God would wipe away the tears from every face. Jesus taught that those gathered at the banquet would come from all directions: "I tell you, many will come from east and west and will eat with Abraham and Isaac and Jacob in the kingdom of heaven" (Matt. 8:11). Filipino theologian Antonio Pernia comments, "The primary image Jesus used for the kingdom was table fellowship, the subject of many of his parables and the object of many meals he shared with outcasts and sinners. Through this image Jesus announced that God . . . was inviting everyone — everyone without exception — to communion with him."[7] From this eschatological perspective we can understand Jesus' feeding of the multitudes as an anticipation of the messianic banquet where all are satisfied.

Among the first followers of Jesus, meals eaten in the name of Jesus also had eschatological significance. Writing to the church in Corinth, the apostle Paul reminds them of the significance of Jesus' last supper with the disciples: "For as often as you eat this bread and drink the cup, you proclaim the Lord's death until he comes" (1 Cor. 11:26).

Meals eaten in memory of Jesus did more than proclaim his death in anticipation of his second coming. In their table fellowship, the followers of the Crucified and Risen One experienced him as present in their midst. On the evening of the day of resurrection, two disciples walking from Jerusalem to Emmaus encountered a stranger who interpreted the events of Jesus' life, death, and resurrection in light of the Hebrew Scriptures. Only after he sat at table with them, blessing and breaking bread, did they recognize Jesus. Returning to the disciples still in Jerusalem, the two men reported "how [Jesus] had been made known to them in the breaking of the bread" (Luke 24:35).

The accounts of Jesus' last supper with his disciples are even more explicit about Jesus' presence in the breaking of the bread. Jesus says, "This is

---

7. Antonio Pernia et al., *The Eucharist and Our Mission, Following the Word* 7 (Rome: SVD Publications, 1996), p. 38, cited by Stephan B. Bevans and Roger P. Schroeder, *Prophetic Dialogue: Reflections on Christian Mission Today* (Maryknoll, N.Y.: Orbis Books, 2011), p. 103.

my body. . . . This is my blood" (Mark 14:22, 24; Matt. 26:26, 28).[8] As we discussed in Chapter 2, meals shared in memory of Jesus eventually became the
sharing of a fragment of bread and a sip of wine, more like the celebration of
the Eucharist we know today. Theologians identified the bread and wine with
Jesus' flesh and blood. "There is one flesh of our Lord Jesus Christ, and one
cup to [show forth] the unity of his blood," wrote Ignatius, bishop of Antioch
at the end of the first century.[9] Justin Martyr also understood the Eucharistic
bread and wine as Jesus' body and blood: "The food which is blessed by the
prayer of His word, and from which our blood and flesh by transmutation
are nourished, is the flesh and blood of that Jesus who was made flesh."[10] For
Justin, "the bread and cup become the flesh and blood of the incarnate Jesus
in order to feed and transform the flesh and blood of believers — his life
enables their new life," explains Paul Bradshaw.[11] Augustine, bishop of Hippo
at the end of the fourth century, expressed a similar understanding: "If you
then are the body and members of Christ, your mystery is laid on the table
of the Lord, your mystery you receive."[12]

    In the communion meal, Christians partake of the body and blood of
Christ. Theologian Catherine LaCugna comments, "Through the eucharist
we participate explicitly in the triune life of God. . . . By receiving communion we take Christ into our bodies; we now exist in a new way. . . . Renewed
as Christ, we take the liturgy . . . into the world."[13] In our communion with
Christ, we become one with Christ, just as in baptism we put on Christ (Gal.
3:26-27). Having received Christ, members of the assembly go forth to be
Christ in the world, to enact God's mission of reconciliation, and they then

---

8. The narrative as given in Luke and in 1 Corinthians reads instead, "This cup is the new
covenant in my blood" (Luke 22:20; 1 Cor. 11:25).

9. Ignatius, Epistle to the Philadelphians 4, available at http://www.ccel.org/ccel/schaff/
anf01.v.vi.iv.html.

10. Justin Martyr, *I Apology* 66, in *The Apostolic Fathers with Justin Martyr and Irenaeus,*
Vol. 1 of *Ante-Nicene Fathers,* ed. Alexander Roberts and James Donaldson, Christian Classics
Ethereal Library, available at http://www.ccel.org/ccel/schaff/anf01.viii.ii.lxvi.html.

11. Paul F. Bradshaw, *Eucharistic Origins* (New York and Oxford: Oxford University Press,
2004), p. 89.

12. Augustine of Hippo, Sermon 272, in *Sacraments and Worship: The Sources of Christian
Theology,* ed. Maxwell E. Johnson (Louisville: Westminster John Knox Press, 2012), p. 210.

13. Catherine Mowry LaCugna, *God for Us: The Trinity and Christian Life* (San Francisco:
HarperSanFrancisco, 1991), p. 406.

return to receive Christ once again. "When we eat the flesh and blood of Jesus," Roman Catholic writer Gregory Augustine Pierce explains, "we *become* the body and blood of Christ to the world. We are going out into the world to continue *his* mission to inaugurate the kingdom of God."[14] Worship in the assembly flows into mission in the world, which flows into worship, as in our Möbius strip or in our spinning top.

Reciting the words of Jesus over the bread and the cup is a common practice in most churches today, whether those words are part of a full Eucharistic prayer or read as a scriptural warrant preceding communion. The ecumenical document *Baptism, Eucharist, and Ministry* affirms that "the eucharistic meal is the sacrament of the body and blood of Christ, the sacrament of his real presence."[15] While thus affirming the presence of Christ in the Eucharist, the document also acknowledges differences between churches about the nature of that presence: "Many churches believe that by the words of Jesus and by the power of the Holy Spirit, the bread and wine of the eucharist become, in a real though mysterious manner, the body and blood of the risen Christ, i.e., of the living Christ present in all his fullness. . . . Some other churches, while affirming a real presence of Christ at the eucharist, do not link that presence so definitively with the signs of bread and wine."[16] Baptist theologian Christopher Ellis, noting different theological understandings of the Lord's Supper, points out, "Whatever the theological understanding of . . . the sacramental nature of the Supper, we may see in it the church gathered around the paschal mystery of Christ crucified, raised, and ascended." Most Baptists, Ellis continues, "have resisted identifying the presence of Christ with the bread and wine and have preferred to locate the divine presence among those gathered around the table, both collectively and individually. . . . For the church, this is a rite which represents to its members the costliness of their salvation and invites them to respond in heartfelt gratitude and love."[17]

Differences among Christians in their understandings of Eucharistic presence have been heated and divisive at various times in Christian his-

14. Gregory F. Augustine Pierce, *The Mass Is Never Ended: Rediscovering Our Mission to Transform the World* (Notre Dame: Ave Maria Press, 2007), p. 60.

15. "Eucharist," par. 13, *Baptism, Eucharist, and Ministry*.

16. "Eucharist," commentary on par. 13, *Baptism, Eucharist, and Ministry*.

17. Christopher J. Ellis, *Gathering: A Theology and Spirituality of Worship in Free Church Tradition* (London: SCM Press, 2004), p. 194.

tory. Our collective failure to agree on this and other matters has resulted in separate communion tables and thereby diminished the church's witness in the world, as the ecumenical statement *Baptism, Eucharist, and Ministry* recognizes: "Insofar as Christians cannot unite in full fellowship around the same table to eat the same loaf and drink from the same cup, their missionary witness is weakened at both the individual and the corporate levels."[18]

I became acutely aware of the painful cost of our differences when I served as a representative of the Episcopal Church on the Anglican-Roman Catholic Consultation in the United States. At our meetings, we would gather for celebrations of the Eucharist, sometimes with a Roman Catholic presider and at other times an Episcopalian. We could proclaim and respond to the Word as one body; together we could reply "Lord, have mercy" to intercessory petitions; together we could confess our sins and receive absolution; we could exchange Christ's peace with one another. But when it came time for communion, not everyone could partake. Roman Catholics and Anglicans do not officially share communion; despite nearly five decades of dialogue, we have not yet reached that level of agreement. Each time we gathered to celebrate the Eucharist, I was vividly reminded of the scandal of our division.

Yet the hope of full communion remains. The celebration of the Eucharist both remembers Jesus' self-giving love and anticipates the fullness of that love, as United Methodist scholar Don Saliers writes: "The gifts given in the . . . holy meal obliterate the conditions that keep us separated and alienated. We are reconciled to God and to neighbor. The communion is a foretaste of glory divine and a foreshadowing of the new Jerusalem." Saliers explains that not only do we remember Christ's self-offering, but we also implore *God* to remember. "We are appealing to God in the very act of the common meal to remember what God has promised in the law and the prophets, fulfilled in Jesus Christ. . . . The living memory *(anamnesis)* of all God has accomplished in Christ is dependent upon calling upon God's Holy Spirit bringing the assembly to life in the signs and the prayers."[19] The Eucharist is a meal of both memory and hope, uniting us with Christ and giving us a foretaste of the reign of God.

18. "Eucharist," par. 26, *Baptism, Eucharist, and Ministry.*
19. Don E. Saliers, *Worship as Theology: Foretaste of Glory Divine* (Nashville: Abingdon Press, 1994), pp. 60-61.

Communion and Hospitality with the Peoples of the World

The Eucharist unites us not only with Christ but also with one another as members of the body of Christ. "The cup of blessing that we bless, is it not a sharing in the blood of Christ? The bread that we break, is it not a sharing in the body of Christ?" the apostle Paul writes to the church at Corinth, continuing, "Because there is one bread, we who are many are one body, for we all partake of the one bread" (1 Cor. 10:16-17).

We know from Paul's letter that the Corinthian church was divided, disagreeing over matters such as sexual morality and dietary regulations. Paul was especially perturbed about their meal practices. Alan Kreider and Eleanor Kreider elaborate: "The problem lay in the Corinthians' behavior, which uncritically conformed to Greco-Roman patterns of social stratification and exacerbated divisions within the community. Instead of bonding all members together, the Corinthians' way of eating divided members along class and economic lines which, Paul contended, expressed 'contempt for the church of God.'"[20] The Corinthian church had contextualized their table fellowship by adopting customs of a Greco-Roman banquet, but they had been insufficiently critical of those aspects of the local culture that ran counter to the gospel.[21] People were eating as soon as they arrived for the meal, with the result that wealthier members of the assembly were eating too much and getting drunk, while poorer members who arrived later, perhaps after work, went hungry.

To remedy the problem, Paul directed the Corinthians to wait until everyone arrived before beginning the meal. Those who were hungry could eat at home before joining the community to share the common bread and cup. Reminding them that they were sharing in the body and blood of Christ, Paul warned them to eat and drink in a manner befitting their membership in Christ: "Whoever, therefore, eats the bread or drinks the cup of the Lord in an unworthy manner will be answerable for the body and blood of the Lord . . . all who eat and drink without discerning the body, eat and drink judgment against themselves" (1 Cor. 11:27-29). Among various possible interpretations

---

20. Alan Kreider and Eleanor Kreider, *Worship and Mission after Christendom* (Scottdale, Pa., and Waterloo, Ontario: Herald Press, 2011), p. 98.

21. Kreider and Kreider, *Worship and Mission after Christendom*, pp. 94-96.

of Paul's urging to "discern the body," a key understanding is that the "body" is the body of Christ. Eleanor Kreider and Alan Kreider explain: "This community — this body — included members who were poor as well as rich, slave as well as free, women as well as men. . . . The meal could not be the Lord's Supper unless the body of Christ that participated in it was Christ-like, with a life that manifested equality and justice before the God they worshiped."[22]

We who take Christ into our bodies at communion and so are restored to our baptismal union with Christ must also *be* Christ, not only in the world but also with one another, and so participate in God's mission in the assembly as well as in the world. In the body of Christ, "There is no longer Jew or Greek, there is no longer slave or free, there is no longer male and female" (Gal. 3:28). "At the common table of bread and wine," Catherine LaCugna writes, "prejudice, intolerance, and alienation are to pass away."[23] Our practices in the assembly shape us as a new community, one in which divisions of class, race, ethnicity, gender, sexuality, and any other human category are overcome through God's reconciling love.

In addition to community meals in memory of Jesus — that is, the Lord's Supper — table fellowship and hospitality were key in the growth of the first-century community, notably in the pivotal event of Peter's baptism of Cornelius, the first recorded conversion of a Gentile, as Stephen Bevans and Roger Schroeder point out.[24] In chapter 10 of Acts, Peter has a vision in which something like a large sheet comes down from heaven, filled with animals, reptiles, and birds. A voice tells Peter, "Get up, Peter; kill and eat," to which Peter responds, "By no means, Lord; for I have never eaten anything that is profane or unclean." The voice then chastises Peter: "What God has made clean, you must not call profane" (Acts 10:13-15). This occurs three times, and though Peter does not immediately understand, messengers soon arrive to summon Peter, saying, "Cornelius, a centurion, an upright and God-fearing man, who is well spoken of by the whole Jewish nation, was directed by a holy angel to send for you to come to his house and to hear what you have to say" (Acts 10:22).

---

22. Kreider and Kreider, *Worship and Mission after Christendom*, pp. 98-99.

23. LaCugna, *God for Us*, p. 406.

24. Bevans and Schroeder, *Prophetic Dialogue*, pp. 105-6. The exegesis of Acts 10–11 in this and the following paragraphs is based largely on the work of Bevans and Schroeder.

When Peter arrives at Cornelius's house, he declares, "You yourselves know that it is unlawful for a Jew to associate with or to visit a Gentile; but God has shown me that I should not call anyone profane or unclean" (Acts 10:28). After Cornelius explains that God had directed him in a vision to send for Peter, Peter acknowledges a dramatic change in his understanding of God: "I truly understand that God shows no partiality" (Acts 10:34). As Peter preaches, the Holy Spirit descends on those who hear the word, giving them the gift of tongues. Peter then decides to baptize Cornelius and his household: "Can anyone withhold the water for baptizing these people who have received the Holy Spirit just as we have?" (Acts 10:47).

According to the narrative in Acts, Peter breaks multiple religious and cultural boundaries. Righteous Jews did not associate with or visit Gentiles, yet Peter welcomes the messengers to spend the night with him and travels with them on an overnight journey to the home of Cornelius. In the extended time they spent together, it is possible that they shared meals together.[25] After baptizing Cornelius, Peter remains with him for several days, again in all likelihood eating meals with Gentiles. And, most significantly, by baptizing Cornelius and his household, Peter breaks boundaries that had defined the first followers of Jesus as observant Jews.

Peter's willingness to associate with Gentiles suggests that the boundary-breaking characteristic of life in Christ extends beyond the radical equality of believers to a care for all the peoples of the world. "All kinds of injustice, racism, separation, and lack of freedom are radically challenged when we share in the body and blood of Christ," declares *Baptism, Eucharist, and Ministry.*[26] When we participate in communion, we experience God's reconciling mercy and hospitality, and we realize that God's love extends to all, that Christ died for all. The words over the cup in some contemporary worship books emphasize that Jesus' self-sacrifice was offered for the sake of the whole world: "This is my Blood of the new Covenant, which is poured out for you and *for all* for the forgiveness of sins."[27] Knowing ourselves to be forgiven and freed

25. Bevans and Schroeder, *Prophetic Dialogue,* pp. 105-6.

26. "Eucharist," par. 20, *Baptism, Eucharist, and Ministry.*

27. Episcopal Church, *Enriching Our Worship 1: Morning and Evening Prayer, The Great Litany, The Holy Eucharist,* Supplemental Liturgical Materials Prepared by the Standing Liturgical Commission, 1997 (New York: Church Publishing, 1998), pp. 59, 61, 64, 66, 68. The first English translation of the post–Vatican II revision of The Roman Missal translated the Latin

sinners, we are called to enact that gracious mercy, boundless compassion, and hospitality in our everyday lives, worship becoming mission.

At the Open Door Community in Atlanta, a residential community in the Catholic Worker tradition, practices of Eucharist and hospitality are intertwined. In this community, "Hosts make room for those with no place, sharing themselves and their lives rather than only their skills. They offer hospitality in response to the people and needs they have encountered — needs for nourishment, place, safety, justice, friendship, and the knowledge of God's love and grace. But they also offer welcome as a way of responding to the gospel."[28] Several times each week, this community serves meals, provides showers and changes of clothes for those who are homeless, and staffs free medical clinics. Volunteers from neighboring congregations, and some who are not members of any congregation, support the work of the residential community.[29] On Sunday afternoons, the dining room is transformed from a place of eating to a place of worship. "Here homeless people, pastors, students, professors, children, and teens join together with community members around the welcome table." Singing and preaching lead into the Eucharistic meal, and then the communion table once again becomes a dining table as worship flows into the evening meal.[30]

Theologian Christine Pohl reflects on the relationship between the communion meal and daily meals in this and other communities: "A certain kind of worship — the Eucharist — and a certain kind of activity — the shared daily meal — combine to form the heart of the Christian practice of hospitality at the Open Door and other Christian communities that excel in this

---

pro multis in the narrative as "for all," but the 2010 translation reads "for many," a change that a number of English-speaking Roman Catholics disagree with. See, for example, Tom Elich, "Eucharistic Prayer II: The ICEL 2010 Translation," in *A Commentary on the Order of Mass of The Roman Missal: A New English Translation, developed under the auspices of the Catholic Academy of Liturgy,* ed. Edward Foley et al. (Collegeville, Minn.: Liturgical Press, 2011), pp. 330-31; Anscar Chupungco, "Eucharistic Prayers for Reconciliation: EP RI: The ICEL 2010 Translation," in *A Commentary on the Order of Mass of The Roman Missal,* ed. Foley et al., pp. 480-81.

28. Christine D. Pohl, "A Community's Practice of Hospitality," in *Practicing Theology: Beliefs and Practices in Christian Life,* ed. Miroslav Volf and Dorothy C. Bass (Grand Rapids: Wm. B. Eerdmans, 2002), p. 125.

29. "Hospitality and Resistance in Metro Atlanta," The Open Door Community, available at http://opendoorcommunity.org/.

30. Pohl, "A Community's Practice of Hospitality," p. 128.

practice. In the Eucharist, Jesus' sacrificial welcome is continually re-enacted; in the daily meal, practitioners remember and recognize God's generous and gracious provision, as they enjoy one another's company and feed one another's bodies."[31] Craig Dykstra and Dorothy Bass underscore these connections: "We begin to understand that the family table, the table provided for the destitute, the table of holy communion, and the eschatological table where all people will feast in the fullness of God are not isolated from one another, but are part of a coherent whole constituted by the encompassing, unifying reality of God's active presence for the life of the world."[32] In a way suggested by our Möbius strip and our spinning top, celebrating the communion meal is integrally connected to Christian practices in the world, to participation in God's mission today.

Communion with the Earth

God's concern for the life of the world is a concern not only for all the peoples of the earth but also for all of creation. Liturgical scholar Mary McGann emphasizes the connection between the table we share with all the peoples of the earth and the table of communion with the earth: "Jesus' example of inviting all to the table of life, to the feast of God's prodigious abundance, of making a place for the little ones who hunger and thirst yet are denied a place at life's banquet, calls worshiping communities to embody this gospel vision: to spread a table that is as wide as God's mercy and compassion for all earth's peoples and creatures."[33]

Our concern for all earth's creatures — indeed, for all creation — arises from our understanding of God, who as creator of heaven and earth brought all things into being. "Theologically," McGann explains, "each creature in the web of life is a symbol of God's presence; each is intrinsically good, embraced by God and called into God's redemptive future."[34] The bread and wine of the

---

31. Pohl, "A Community's Practice of Hospitality," p. 135.

32. Craig Dykstra and Dorothy C. Bass, "A Theological Understanding of Christian Practices," in *Practicing Theology,* ed. Volf and Bass, p. 29.

33. Mary E. McGann, "Making Vital Connections: Developing Creational Consciousness in Life and Worship," *Liturgy* 27, no. 2 (2012): 52-53.

34. McGann, "Making Vital Connections," p. 52.

Eucharist, fruits of creation, the stuff of everyday life, disclose the goodness of God's creative work.[35] Moreover, they are "expressions of God's generous goodness and ever-abundant love" for us and for all creation.[36] In our use of bread and wine for communion, we recognize the goodness of God in creation and the interrelatedness of all life.[37]

Yet even as we rejoice in God's presence in creation, we also yearn for new creation. The apostle Paul writes to the church at Rome, "We know that the whole creation has been groaning in labor pains until now; and not only the creation, but we ourselves, who have the first fruits of the Spirit, groan inwardly while we wait for adoption, the redemption of our bodies" (Rom. 8:22-23). God promises a new heaven and a new earth (Rev. 21:1), a new creation. Our feast of bread and wine, a foretaste of the heavenly banquet, gives us a glimpse of "Jesus as Lord of heaven and earth, ruling his creation in love. . . . Through bread and wine we see the hope of a world transfigured, renewed, and restored."[38]

In our anticipation of God's promised new creation, we do not wait passively. Participation in God's mission of reconciliation requires us to engage in work for the integrity of creation, as Stephen Bevans and Roger Schroeder explain: "Mission witnesses to, proclaims, celebrates and works for a new way of thinking about and seeing human beings, earth's creatures, and the created universe itself."[39] Although recognition of the holiness of creation is not a new theological understanding, work for the preservation of creation is especially pressing today. McGann says bluntly, "The earth is in crisis," and continues, "Even a cursory assessment of its health reveals that forests are in decline, soil and water supplies are being depleted far beyond their ability

35. Robert Webber, *Ancient-Future Worship: Proclaiming and Enacting God's Narrative* (Grand Rapids: Baker Books, 2008), p. 141; James K. A. Smith, *Desiring the Kingdom: Worship, Worldview, and Cultural Formation* (Grand Rapids: Baker Academic, 2009), p. 199.

36. Paul J. Wadell, "Sharing Peace: Discipline and Trust," in *The Blackwell Companion to Christian Ethics*, ed. Stanley Hauerwas and Samuel Wells (Oxford and Malden, Mass.: Blackwell Publishing, 2004), p. 295.

37. *Missional Church: A Vision for the Sending of the Church in North America*, ed. Darrell L. Guder (Grand Rapids: Wm. B. Eerdmans, 1998), p. 165.

38. Webber, *Ancient-Future Worship*, p. 144.

39. Stephen B. Bevans and Roger P. Schroeder, *Constants in Context: A Theology of Mission for Today* (Maryknoll, N.Y.: Orbis Books, 2004), pp. 375-76.

to be replenished, and species of living creatures are being destroyed at an alarming rate." She concludes, "The only hope of stemming the tide of these cumulative factors, which jeopardize life on our planet, lies in a fundamental shift in how human communities see themselves as part of the planetary community of life."[40]

Missional response to the earth's crisis includes both worship and prophetic dialogue in the world, like our spinning top and our Möbius strip. Recognizing human responsibility for and complicity in the alarming depletion of the earth's resources and destruction of life of all kinds, our worship must include lament, to "give voice to the victims so that their cries reach our ears and hearts," and confession, so that we "acknowledge our collusion and inaction in the face of their [victims'] anguish."[41] For example, a Eucharistic prayer of the Episcopal Church connects human failure to care for creation and mistreatment of one another: "You gave the world into our care, that we might be your faithful stewards and show forth your bountiful grace. But we failed to honor your image in one another and in ourselves; we would not see your goodness in the world around us; and so we violated your creation, abused one another, and rejected your love."[42] In addition to confession and lament, our practices of eating and drinking at the Lord's table, says McGann, "must engage us sensibly in that deep, revelatory pleasure that discloses the delightfulness of God at the heart of creation's gifts."[43]

In worship, we both revel in God's bounty and God's love, and lament and confess our failure to care for God's gifts responsibly and adequately. From worship, we go forth to embody God's mission in the world, to enact our care for the earth with renewed commitment. Salvation, we must realize, includes "not only *human* well-being, but the well-being of all of creation as well."[44] McGann calls us to "embrace Christianity's ancient sacramental cosmology, which perceived the entire cosmic community of living beings as grounded in divine life, guided by divine wisdom, redeemed by Christ, and intrinsically related by God's design. From this vision flows the moral imperative: to heal and restore the world through an ethic of love, care, and

40. McGann, "Making Vital Connections," p. 54.
41. McGann, "Making Vital Connections," p. 55.
42. Eucharistic Prayer 1, *Enriching Our Worship 1*, p. 58.
43. McGann, "Making Vital Connections," p. 58.
44. Bevans and Schroeder, *Constants in Context*, p. 377.

responsibility, to recognize the earth as a sacramental commons intended for all to reverence and share, and to re-imagine the common good as the good of the entire earth community."[45]

Offering

The bread and wine for communion represent not only God's generosity and love in creation but also the offering of human labor. J. G. Davies reminds us, "We do not present just grain and grapes, but bread and wine which are a microcosm of our present industrial system." Continuing, he points out the complex human endeavor behind the seemingly simple gifts of bread and wine:

> The [wheat] and the grapes have been farmed or harvested in diverse quarters of the globe with implements that have been forged of metals mined in many different areas and powered by all kinds of fuel. They have been transported by a vast system of shipping, imported by means of an elaborate method of international exchange under the scrutiny of customs and excise organizations; they have been processed by a multitude of related trades and finally distributed by another network of transport and retailing. Each loaf, each cup of wine, represents the unity of industrial and economic effort; the differentiation, which is characteristic of modern secularized society, finds its unity in a single loaf of bread and a cup of wine.[46]

Even if a congregation decides to make its own bread and wine for communion, human labor is involved not only in kneading bread and crushing grapes but also in the implements used to grow and process the grain and the grapes. When we pause to reflect, we can see that the bread and wine of our communion meal represent the interconnection of life.

Some congregations make the offering of bread and wine explicit in a prayer said after preparing the table: "Blessed are you, Lord God of all cre-

---

45. McGann, "Making Vital Connections," p. 57.

46. J. G. Davies, *Worship and Mission* (London: SCM Press, 1966; New York: Association Press, 1967), p. 100.

ation: for through your goodness we have received the bread we offer you: fruit of the earth and work of human hands, it will become for us the bread of life. . . . Blessed are you, Lord God of all creation: for through your goodness we have received the wine we offer you: fruit of the vine and work of human hands, it will become our spiritual drink."[47] Whether or not there are explicit prayers such as these offering the bread and wine, we can understand the gifts as representative not only of human labor but also of our self-offering to God. In the Eucharistic liturgy, a work for the common good, we receive gratefully what God has given us and offer ourselves as participants in God's mission for the life of the world. Though our offering — the work we have done since we were last sent forth — is imperfect, says Gregory Augustine Pierce, our gift is found acceptable.[48]

Moreover, we offer ourselves in union with Christ, the Word made flesh who lived among us, the Crucified and Risen One who calls us into new life. Christians understand Christ's sacrifice and its relation to the Eucharist and to our self-offering in different ways. Robert Webber, an evangelical Anglican, explains, "[Jesus'] blood, which is the life of the flesh, grants us a new life, a new beginning, and it makes us new creatures refashioned after his image. We are nourished by the image of Jesus' sacrifice, for it manifests to us our union with him in his sufferings. His life of sacrifice is to become our life of self-giving, for we abide in him and he in us."[49] Baptist theologian Christopher Ellis points to the connection between the meal and holy living: "At the communal meal with its emphasis on the redemptive work of Christ . . . we find the call to holy living as well as the devotional offering of the heart — and both are in response to the cross."[50] United Methodist scholar Don Saliers views Jesus' life and death as an expression of God's self-giving: "God's self-giving and the worshipers' symbolic self-giving at the table of the eucharist embrace as the mystery at the heart of the eucharistic action. . . . Christ is both the celebrant and the one given and received. What he embodies is God's eternal self-giving to the world."[51] Roman Catholic liturgical

---

47. "The Preparation of the Gifts: The English Text," in *A Commentary on the Order of Mass of The Roman Missal,* ed. Foley et al., p. 197.

48. Pierce, *The Mass Is Never Ended,* pp. 55-56.

49. Webber, *Ancient-Future Worship,* p. 143.

50. Ellis, *Gathering,* p. 195.

51. Saliers, *Worship as Theology,* p. 96.

scholar Mary McGann underscores the relation between the transformation of the gifts and our transformation: "Our eucharistic offering must gather up the fruitfulness of God's good and holy creation, actively inviting the Creator Spirit to transform us as these gifts are transformed, so that all creation might rightly give God praise through Christ our Lord."[52]

In the celebration of the Eucharist, the assembly is drawn into God's mission of reconciling love, manifest most especially in the life, death, and resurrection of Jesus. At the communion table, we remember God's self-giving, and we offer ourselves as participants in that sacrifice. The ecumenical statement *Baptism, Eucharist, and Ministry* stresses the connection between our Eucharistic offering and the sacrificial offering of our lives: "In Christ we offer ourselves as a living and holy sacrifice in our daily lives (Romans 12:1; 1 Peter 2:5); this spiritual worship, acceptable to God, is nourished in the Eucharist, in which we are sanctified and reconciled in love, in order to be servants of reconciliation in the world."[53] Worship and mission thus flow into and out of one another (as they do in our Möbius strip and in our spinning top), as we receive the gift of God's self-offering and offer ourselves in union with Christ both at the communion table and in the world.

Thanksgiving

Our offering at the Eucharist is also an offering of the sacrifice of praise, an offering closely related to our daily self-offering. "Through [Christ], then, let us continually offer a sacrifice of praise to God, that is, the fruit of lips that confess his name. Do not neglect to do good and to share what you have, for such sacrifices are pleasing to God" (Heb. 13:15-16). Moreover, our praise flows into thanksgiving. For example, the anaphora (Eucharistic prayer) of St. John Chrysostom, regularly used today in the Byzantine rite, begins, "It is fitting and right to hymn you, to bless you, to praise you, to give you thanks, to worship you in all places of your dominion. For you are God, ineffable, inconceivable, invisible, incomprehensible, existing always and in the same way, you and your only-begotten Son and your Holy Spirit. You brought us out of non-existence

---

52. McGann, "Making Vital Connections," p. 57.
53. "Eucharist," par. 10, *Baptism, Eucharist, and Ministry.*

into existence; and when we had fallen you raised us up again, and did not cease to do everything until you had brought us up to heaven, and granted us the kingdom that is to come."[54] In this prayer, the assembly worships God, responding with thanks to the awesome, transcendent one who is worthy of praise and acknowledging God's work in creation and in redemption.

The prayer at the Eucharist, known in some traditions as the "great thanksgiving," is a proclamation of God's love for the world, revealed in the incarnation, life, death, and resurrection of Jesus. Many contemporary Eucharistic prayers have a wide scope, giving thanks for God's work in creation and the calling of the people of Israel, for the life and ministry of Jesus as well as his death and resurrection, and for the calling together of a new community to witness to the good news. Just as the assembly is drawn into the stream of salvation history through the proclamation and response to the Word, so too in the thankful remembering of the Eucharistic prayer the assembly is drawn into God's mission of reconciling love. Catherine LaCugna describes this as a participation in the Triune life of God: "We offer praise and thanksgiving to God, who is the fountain of all holiness; we join our prayer to that of the high priest Jesus, who presents our prayers and petitions to God; we call upon the Holy Spirit to create a holy body of Christ."[55]

Our remembering is thus far more than recalling events that are long past. "The act of gratitude makes the founding events present and the future as well," writes Don Saliers.[56] Describing the Baptist practice of the recitation of the words of institution, Christopher Ellis argues that these words "enable the congregation to participate in the drama of the upper room as well as participate in the drama of salvation in Christ."[57] By remembering the words of Jesus and offering a prayer of thanksgiving, the assembly understands itself to be integrally connected with the "primitive community" and the "eschatological community."[58] Ellis recalls the words of C. H. Dodd: "At each eucharist, we are *there* — we are in the night in which he was betrayed, at Golgotha, before the empty tomb on Easter day, and in the upper room before he appeared; *and* we are at the moment of his coming, with angels

---

54. The Anaphora of St. John Chrysostom, in *Sacraments and Worship*, ed. Johnson, p. 199.
55. LaCugna, *God for Us*, p. 406.
56. Saliers, *Worship as Theology*, p. 96.
57. Ellis, *Gathering*, p. 192.
58. Ellis, *Gathering*, p. 193.

and archangels and all the company of heaven, in the twinkling of an eye at the last trump."[59] Robert Webber links this remembering, which includes both memory and hope, with the communion bread and wine: "At bread and wine we see creation, fall, incarnation, death, resurrection, ascension, church, the kingdom, and the promises of the new heavens and new earth and our own transfiguration accomplished through God's union with us established through Jesus by the Spirit."[60]

Recognizing what God has done and is doing in the world, members of the assembly acknowledge their dependence on God. "This dependence refers to the whole of life, and so thanksgiving embraces sacrificial participation in mission in dependence upon God, for it is an offering of the whole self through service in obedience to him from whom we have received everything."[61] Our thanksgiving does not deny the suffering and struggles of the world, but rather locates them in the larger horizon of the arc of salvation history. Christian thanksgiving has an eschatological thrust, celebrating the inauguration of the reign of God in the life, death, and resurrection of Jesus even as it yearns for the fullness of the reign that is yet to come.

In Eucharistic prayers, thankful remembering yields to hope-filled supplication. Don Saliers asserts that "the power of God's Holy Spirit . . . animates both the calling upon God and the efficacy of the church's prayer."[62] The Spirit, in other words, prays through us, interceding "with sighs too deep for words" (Rom. 8:26), and the Spirit assures us that God hears and answers our prayers. We call upon the Holy Spirit, LaCugna reminds us, asking God to draw us together as one body, the body of Christ. But the horizon of prayer is even wider, for our prayer is offered on behalf of the whole world, on behalf of all creation. The Eucharist is not just for us, for one particular assembly now gathered. "The God whom we love and adore," LaCugna asserts, "is in communion with everything and everyone."[63] So our Eucharistic prayer remembers the in-breaking of the reign of God through the life, death, and resurrection of Jesus, and it anticipates the fulfillment of God's promises,

59. C. H. Dodd, *The Apostolic Preaching and Its Developments* (London: Hodder & Stoughton, 1944), p. 94, cited by Ellis, *Gathering,* p. 193.

60. Webber, *Ancient-Future Worship,* p. 141.

61. Davies, *Worship and Mission,* p. 121.

62. Saliers, *Worship as Theology,* p. 110.

63. LaCugna, *God for Us,* p. 406.

the new creation in which all are reconciled to God and to one another. The assembly thus offers its Eucharistic prayer, through Christ and in the power of the Spirit, for the life of the world, and so the assembly bears witness to and participates in God's mission.

Invitation to the Table

As we discussed in Chapter 2, missional churches will welcome all to worship, without distinction, and so enact God's all-embracing love. Should this welcome include an invitation for those who are not baptized to receive communion?

Churches in Western societies today are encountering a new context, one that is bringing to the fore the question of who may come to the table. In a Christendom world, almost everyone was baptized, and those who were not (for example, Jews) would not have readily entered a Christian assembly for worship. In our post-Christendom world, it is increasingly likely that our assemblies will include people of other faiths and people with no religious background or commitments. A 2008 Gallup poll found that 77 percent of Americans claimed to identify with some form of Christian religion, a drop of 14 percent from 1948, the first year that Gallup began measuring religious affiliation in the United States.[64] A study from the Pew Research Forum released in 2012 showed that 78.4 percent of all adults identify themselves as part of a Christian tradition, while 16.1 percent claim no religious affiliation. Moreover, the Pew study reported, "More than one-quarter of American adults (28 percent) have left the faith in which they were raised in favor of another religion — or no religion at all. If change in affiliation from one type of Protestantism to another is included, 44 percent of adults have either switched religious affiliation, moved from being unaffiliated with any religion to being affiliated with a particular faith, or dropped any connection to a specific religious tradition."[65] The significant amount of move-

---

64. Frank Newport, "This Easter, Smaller Percentage of Americans Are Christian," *Gallup*, 10 April 2009, available at http://www.gallup.com/poll/117409/easter-smaller-percentage-americans-christian.aspx.

65. "Summary of Key Findings," Pew Forum on Religion and Public Life, *Religious Landscape Survey*, available at http://religions.pewforum.org/reports#.

ment, whether between religious faiths or from no affiliation to participation, means that a Sunday assembly is likely to include newcomers, some of whom have not been baptized, especially if that community is intentional about its witness in the world.

Recognizing the breadth of God's love for the world, some churches today are extending expansive invitations to receive communion. The Iona Abbey community recognizes the complexity of the life of faith, both our subjective experience of having faith and our failures and successes in following Jesus, by their invitation to "come to this table, you who have much faith and you who would like to have more; you who have been here often and you who have not been for a long time; you who have tried to follow Jesus, and you who have failed."[66] Some assemblies extend an even wider invitation, explicitly inviting everyone present to receive communion whether or not they have been baptized.

The impulse toward an open table stems from a value of radical hospitality that is rooted in the memory of Jesus as one who embodied unconditional love and so broke boundaries and dined with sinners and tax collectors. Our invitation to the Lord's Supper, proponents of an open table argue, must reflect Christ's boundless love. The table, they point out, is Christ's table. "It is Christ who invites us to meet him here," says the invitation at Iona Abbey.[67]

Those who argue against opening the table to unbaptized persons do so on the basis of strong historical precedent as well as the sacramental logic of baptism and communion. The *Didache*, a church order usually dated to the late first or early second century, sets a clear demarcation: "But let no one eat or drink of your Eucharist, unless they have been baptized into the name of the Lord; for concerning this also the Lord has said, 'Give not that which is holy to the dogs.'"[68] However, such proscriptions are often better evidence of what they purport to forbid than the practice they require.[69] The

---

66. "Extra Resources for the Sunday Morning Communion," *Iona Abbey Worship Book*, p. 53.

67. "Extra Resources for the Sunday Morning Communion," *Iona Abbey Worship Book*, p. 53.

68. *Didache* 9, trans. Alexander Roberts and James Donaldson, in *Early Christian Writings*, ed. Peter Kirby (2001), available at http://www.earlychristianwritings.com/text/didache-roberts .html.

69. Paul Bradshaw urges a hermeneutics of suspicion when interpreting ancient liturgical

statement in the *Didache* suggests that some first-century communities were giving communion to those who were not yet baptized. If that were not so, the author would have no reason to make such a strong statement forbidding the practice. Thus it is possible that in the first century some entered the community by joining in their ritual meals and subsequently being baptized. However, scholars generally agree that by the second century, only those who had been baptized were admitted to communion, as Justin Martyr writes in his First Apology: "And this food is called among us *eucharistia* [*thanksgiving*], of which no one is allowed to partake but [the one] who believes that the things which we teach are true, and who has been washed with the washing that is for the remission of sins, and unto regeneration."[70] The intent of an "apology" is to explain a practice to outsiders, not to regulate a community's behavior, so we may conclude that Justin describes what by his time was the normative practice in his community, a norm that became embedded in Christian tradition handed down through the centuries.

Those who favor maintaining the historical precedent of baptism leading to communion also point to the sacramental logic of baptism and communion. In his 1966 study of worship and mission, J. G. Davies argued that baptism and Eucharist "are only to be understood fully in their interdependence. Unless they are integrated, their meaning may become distorted." Furthermore, Davies asserted, the interdependence of the sacraments is significant for our understanding of mission: "Baptism is to be understood as ordination to the royal priesthood, which is to be exercised in mission for the whole world, and . . . it effects inclusion within the covenant, which is itself a commission. In the eucharist the baptismal ordination and inclusion within the covenant are reaffirmed."[71] Lutheran liturgical scholar Mark Bangert, writing in 1999, also emphasized the missional significance of the Eucharist: "The meal is not an end in itself but is always an icon through which one is drawn into the pervasive mission of the church, that is, to faithful living

---

documents, including liturgical legislation. See Paul F. Bradshaw, *The Search for the Origins of Christian Worship*, 2nd ed. (New York: Oxford University Press, 2002), pp. 14-20.

70. Justin Martyr, *I Apology* 66, in *The Apostolic Fathers with Justin Martyr and Irenaeus*, Vol. 1 of *Ante-Nicene Fathers*, ed. Alexander Roberts and James Donaldson, Christian Classics Ethereal Library, available at http://www.ccel.org/ccel/schaff/anf01.viii.ii.lxvi.html.

71. Davies, *Worship and Mission*, pp. 92-93.

as part of the body of Christ in the world."[72] Hospitality at the communion table is not sufficient; the meal also draws its participants into mission and so calls for commitment to Jesus, a commitment that is rooted in baptism.

In an effort to understand and assess this emerging practice, Episcopal priest and historical scholar Stephen Edmondson studied four congregations in the Episcopal Church that give an open invitation to communion, gathering members of these congregations for theological reflection on their practice. In his conversations, Edmondson found a rich theological understanding of God's grace freely offered, coupled with the necessity of response to that grace as a way of participating in God's mission. Rejecting the establishment of clear boundaries defining access to communion, members of these congregations recognized the need to extend their welcome to those who have been denied access on the basis of race, sexual orientation, or social status, and to seek out those who had been excluded from the table and even from the church building. In one parish, "the practice of the open table was bound closely to their outreach to the homeless in downtown Washington. Their 8 a.m. service combines a breakfast for those who otherwise might go without material sustenance with a eucharist to provide all — the cooks and the diners — their needed spiritual sustenance. Inviting folks in this context to one table, while excluding them from the other, makes little sense in light of the gathered congregation."[73]

Edmondson also points out that the invitation to the table must be viewed in the wider context of a congregation's ministry of welcome and hospitality. The question is not just who may come to the table, but how we invite and welcome strangers into our midst to share the fullness of life in Christ. "We have not been truly hospitable to our guests," Edmondson writes, "unless we tell them the stories and share with them the deep learnings of our lives so that they may join us in the journey of the Christian family."[74] He concludes that we practice true hospitality when the community as a whole extends an expansive welcome: "When we greet those who have joined us at the table with the question 'Have you come here to stay?' or when we orient

72. Mark P. Bangert, "Holy Communion: Taste and See," in *Inside Out: Worship in an Age of Mission,* ed. Thomas H. Schattauer (Minneapolis: Fortress Press, 1999), p. 82.

73. Stephen Edmondson, "Opening the Table: The Body of Christ and God's Prodigal Grace," *Anglican Theological Review* 91 (2009): 222.

74. Edmondson, "Opening the Table," p. 233.

them to our community with the expectation that they will want to stay, then we have recognized that the fullness of what we have to offer lies not in the simple reception of the eucharist, but in the embrace of the Christian community and the gospel way of life to which it is called."[75]

Edmondson helps us see that the invitation to communion is only one aspect of a community's welcome. How do we invite people not only to be fed with the body and blood of Christ, but also to be washed with the waters of baptism, to die with Christ and be raised to new life? Edmondson emphasizes the importance of being drawn into the paschal mystery of Jesus' dying and rising: "Only through the continual baptismal immersion of the Christian community in Christ's story can it be transformed into a paschal community that reflects the true image of Christ's love."[76]

Missional communities will consider their practices of baptism and Eucharist in the context of their entire community life, not just their worship life. Both baptism and communion express God's abundant grace, freely offered, manifest in Jesus' boundary-breaking ministry with religious leaders and with sinners on the margins or outside of the community. Both baptism and communion also anticipate a response to God's grace, joining in Christ's servant ministry, participating in God's mission of reconciliation. Lutheran liturgical scholar Thomas Schattauer proposes, "Our practice needs to uphold baptism as God's open welcome to life in Christ for all rather than to make it a sign of exclusion. Our practice of communion needs to uphold the connection to a baptized assembly and to the baptismal implication for the individual, realized or not."[77]

When considering their invitation to communion, missional communities will reflect deeply on the totality of their practices of baptism and communion along with their practices of welcome and incorporation into the life of faith. Too rigid a requirement of baptism before communion can make it a barrier rather than a generous, grace-filled invitation to share in abundant life in Christ. Too free a welcome to communion without baptism can make it a form of cheap grace rather a welcome to share in Christ's service in the

75. Edmondson, "Opening the Table," p. 234.

76. Edmondson, "Opening the Table," p. 233.

77. Thomas H. Schattauer, "Some Thoughts on the Invitation to Communion in the ELCA," unpublished paper, December 2012, p. 2.

world. Some churches may emphasize the priority of baptism before coming to communion, while others may offer an expansive invitation to communion while also encouraging those who are not yet Christian to come to the font. In any community of faith, baptism need not be presented as a barrier preventing access to God's mercy and grace. Rather, a generous invitation to baptism will emphasize that Christ seeks out the lost and welcomes sinners, calling all to repentance and new life, and a generous invitation to communion will acknowledge the implications of communion for participation in God's mission of reconciliation in the world.

How the Assembly Celebrates the Communion Meal

Like the proclamation of Scripture in the Sunday assembly, the celebration of the Eucharist is transcultural, transcending particular cultural expressions and so uniting believers across time, space, culture, and confession. Specific patterns and practices of communion, however, vary from church to church, and Christian traditions differ from one another in their theological interpretations of the communion meal. The ecumenical document *Baptism, Eucharist, and Ministry* does not attempt to offer a single, uniform model for celebrating communion but rather acknowledges and affirms diversity: "The liturgical reform movement has brought the churches closer together in the manner of celebrating the Lord's Supper. However, a certain liturgical diversity compatible with our common eucharistic faith is recognized as a healthy and enriching fact. The affirmation of a common eucharistic faith does not imply uniformity in either liturgy or practice."[78]

In *The Shape of the Liturgy*, first published in 1945, Anglican Benedictine monk Gregory Dix argued that the Eucharistic rite, from very early in Christian history, invariably included four primary actions based on Jesus' actions at the Last Supper: bread and wine are taken and placed on the table, a prayer of thanksgiving is said over the bread and the wine together, the bread is broken, and the bread and the wine are distributed to the assembly. Although subsequent scholarship has nuanced Dix's work,[79] the fourfold

78. "Eucharist," par. 28, *Baptism, Eucharist, and Ministry.*
79. See, for example, Kenneth W. Stevenson, *Gregory Dix — Twenty-five Years On*, Grove

pattern he identified has had an enormous influence on contemporary liturgical practice and the revision of worship books.

Taking the bread and the wine. Whether the action of taking bread and wine for communion is a simple, functional action of setting the table for the celebration of communion or a highly ritualized offertory, the primary purpose of the action is preparatory. The term "offertory," used in many churches, implies that the Eucharistic offering is made at this point. However, in churches that include a full Eucharistic prayer, an offering usually takes place in the course of the prayer, as the assembly in prayer remembers Jesus' command to "do this" in memory of him and so "presents" or "offers" the bread and the wine to God. In Eastern liturgical traditions, the action of offering is understood to take place entirely within the prayer and not with the bringing of the gifts.[80]

The connection between taking bread and wine and offering them is emphasized in the practice of many congregations of taking up the collection at this point in the liturgy. Money and other gifts, along with bread and wine, are then presented as a minister prepares the table. (We will consider the collection in the next chapter of this book.)

Missional communities will recognize the bread and the wine as the fruit of the earth and the work of human hands, whether or not an offertory prayer makes this explicit. Moreover, those in missional communities will understand that they offer their whole selves, uniting with Christ in his sacrifice of love. Many Eucharistic prayers acknowledge the self-offering of members of the assembly, in union with Christ's self-offering.

Blessing the bread and the wine: Eucharistic prayer. In a Eucharistic prayer, the assembly gives thanks over the bread and the wine, remembering God's work in creation and in salvation history. As we remember God's mission of reconciliation from creation to new creation, we locate ourselves in the arc of salvation history and so come to understand ourselves as participants in God's mission.

For centuries, many Eucharistic prayers focused primarily or even ex-

---

Liturgical Study 10 (Bramcote, Nottingham: Grove Books, 1977); Paul F. Bradshaw and Maxwell E. Johnson, *The Eucharistic Liturgies: Their Evolution and Interpretation,* Alcuin Club Collections 87 (London: SPCK; Collegeville, Minn.: Liturgical Press, 2012), pp. 20-21, 111-15.

80. Graham Woolfenden, " 'Let Us Offer Each Other the Sign of Peace' — An Inquiry," *Worship* 67 (1993): 243.

clusively on God's work in redemption and not on God's work in creation. Mary McGann urges, "A contemporary creational consciousness calls us to redress the historical imbalance that has focused worship primarily on redemption with little emphasis on creation and to restore the reciprocity of these profoundly connected acts of God. . . . The language of our rites must come alive with images of the vastness and magnificence of creation that can awaken our religious imagination to God's work in the universe."[81] As our prayer stirs us to celebrate the splendor of creation, we also recognize God's call to us to care for creation as one aspect of our participation in God's mission.

For centuries, Western Eucharistic theology has given particular attention to the narrative of Jesus' institution of the supper, and in some traditions these words were considered to be *the* moment of consecration, underscored by the presider's elevation of the bread and the cup at this point in the prayer. In traditions that view the Eucharist as an ordinance done in response to Jesus' command rather than as a sacrament, the narrative also has a central role as the scriptural warrant for the community's practice.

Many contemporary Western texts of the Eucharistic prayer have complemented this emphasis on the institution narrative with an invocation of the Holy Spirit upon the assembly and its offering of bread and wine. *Baptism, Eucharist, and Ministry* explains, "The Spirit makes the crucified and risen Christ really present to us in the eucharistic meal, fulfilling the promise contained in the words of institution."[82]

The Eucharistic prayer is not just words, however. As the prayer of the community, the assembly's thanksgiving for God's gifts in creation and redemption, it must be enacted in a manner that engages the full assembly. Mary Gray-Reeves and Michael Perham describe two such celebrations:

> [At The Crossing in Boston], when [the presider] improvised the eucharistic prayer, there were no words spoken by the community gathered in a circle around the altar; instead we were engaged by gesture, everyone with arms uplifted throughout, apart from during the prayer for the Holy Spirit to work upon the gifts, when everyone extended their hands towards the

---

81. McGann, "Making Vital Connections," p. 57.
82. "Eucharist," par. 14, *Baptism, Eucharist, and Ministry.*

bread and the wine. . . . At Moot [in London] two weeks later the community gathered around the altar in the same way, and everyone hummed (it was a hum, rather than a drone) through the eucharistic prayer while [the presider] sang the words. That had something of the same effect [as the shared gesture at The Crossing] and was followed by the Lord's Prayer, in which all stood with hands held out in prayer.[83]

In richly embodied celebrations such as these, the assembly is drawn into the Eucharistic offering of thanks and praise, celebrating their reconciliation with God through Christ and expressing their hope for the fullness of this reconciliation to be realized for the whole created order.

Breaking the bread. Like taking the bread and the wine, this action is first of all functional: bread is broken in order to be shared. But the action readily lends itself to theological interpretation, as a metaphor for unity and diversity in Christ. "The bread that we break, is it not a sharing in the body of Christ?" writes Paul to the Corinthians, in words that some churches use today at the breaking of the bread. "Because there is one bread, we who are many are one body, for we all partake of the one bread" (1 Cor. 10:16-17). The church order *Didache,* from the late first or early second century, uses the metaphor of broken bread to express hope for eschatological union with God: "Even as this broken bread was scattered over the hills, and was gathered together and became one, so let Thy Church be gathered together from the ends of the earth into Thy kingdom." This text is the basis for a contemporary hymn.[84]

A metaphorical interpretation of broken bread will be more apparent when the bread used for communion is bread that can actually be broken, more substantial than the wafers that some churches use for the sake of convenience. Though a fragment of bread and a sip of wine only hint at a full meal, these primary signs can evoke layers of meaning — for example, meals shared at family tables, the bread Abraham served his three visitors near Mamre (Gen. 18:1-8), Jesus' meals with outcasts and sinners, the dis-

---

83. Mary Gray-Reeves and Michael Perham, *The Hospitality of God: Emerging Worship for a Missional Church* (New York: Seabury Books; London: SPCK, 2011), p. 100.

84. "Father, We Thank Thee," *The Hymnal 1982* (New York: Church Hymnal Corp., 1985), #302.

ciples' recognition of the Crucified and Risen One in the breaking of the bread (Luke 24:30-35), and the eschatological banquet foretold by Isaiah (Isa. 25:6-9).

Sharing a common cup can also be a potent symbol. "The cup of blessing that we bless, is it not a sharing in the blood of Christ?" asks the apostle Paul (1 Cor. 10:16). Churches that use individual communion cups would do well to consider the symbolic value of their practice and ask themselves whether it enables the assembly to understand itself as sharing in the blood of Christ.

Clayton Schmit points out, "Through understanding the symbolic nature of the signs in worship, we are able to draw on the shared conventions of interpretation that make our central symbols and actions meaningful for us as worshipers."[85] Ensuring that the primary symbols of bread and wine communicate clearly what we want them to communicate will enable worship to express vividly the connection of the assembly's action to the mission of God.

Sharing the bread and the wine. In the Eucharistic action, thankful remembrance leads to communion, eating and drinking in the company of Jesus. *Baptism, Eucharist, and Ministry* emphasizes the significance of this action: "The sharing in one bread and the common cup in a given place demonstrates and effects the oneness of the sharers with Christ and with their fellow sharers in all times and places." But this sharing extends beyond the body of Christ to "embrace all aspects of life."[86] Sharing communion expresses and enacts God's reconciling love.

A vivid portrayal of reconciliation through communion is enacted in the 1984 movie *Places in the Heart*. Set in the southern United States during the 1930s, the movie tells the story of Edna, a white woman who is forced to take over her debt-ridden cotton farm after her husband, the town sheriff, is accidentally killed by a drunken African-American gunman. She takes in a blind boarder named Mr. Will and an African-American hobo named Moze, who assist her as she tries to bring in her cotton crop in the face of nearly insurmountable odds. As the plot develops, racial conflict is underscored in a confrontation with the Ku Klux Klan. The final scene of the film, set in a church service, begins with the minister proclaiming a text from 1 Corinthi-

---

85. Clayton J. Schmit, *Sent and Gathered: A Worship Manual for the Missional Church* (Grand Rapids: Baker Academic, 2009), p. 117.

86. "Eucharist," pars. 19-20, *Baptism, Eucharist, and Ministry.*

ans: "If I speak in the tongues of mortals and of angels, but do not have love, I am a noisy gong or a clanging cymbal" (1 Cor. 13:1). As the reading ends, the choir stands and begins to sing "I Come to the Garden Alone." Ushers begin to pass bread and wine along the pews, and as the trays move from one person to another, the minister proclaims the words of institution. The minister concludes, "This is my blood that was shed for you," and the camera focuses on the tray of communion cups passed from person to person. We see each of the characters from the film; as they pass the tray of wine, some say to the next person, "The peace of God." When the trays reach the pew where the main characters are seated, first Moze, then Mr. Will, then Edna's two young children and Edna herself receive the wine. As Edna hands the wine to the person sitting next to her, we see that it is her dead husband, Royce. Royce receives the wine, and then, saying "The peace of God," he hands it on to the next person: the gunman who killed him. The gunman receives the wine, turns to face Royce, and replies, "The peace of God."

The communion scene in this film shows an assembly sharing bread and wine solemnly and with deep reverence. Mary McGann writes, "Eating and drinking at the Lord's table must engage us sensibly in that deep, revelatory pleasure that discloses the delightfulness of God at the heart of creation's gifts."[87] We participate in communion through the gracious mercy of God, and our celebrations ought to reflect our deep gratitude for God's abundant grace as well as our joy at sharing the feast with one another and with Christ.

In his research on vital and faithful churches, Thomas Long found that they "move to a joyous festival experience toward the end of the worship service." When celebrating the Lord's Supper, these congregations incorporate "quiet and reflective moments and themes" but also "employ the language and mood of joy to emphasize that the eucharist is a thankful heavenly banquet." Most of the congregations he studied included communion as a regular part of their Sunday worship, but those that did not still moved to a joyous festival experience near the end of the worship service. In some, this occurred through preaching, which "gradually built toward an emotional climax that led hearers nearer to the place of festival." Others included joyful elements such as music, dance, and testimony in the latter part of worship. Long explains the reason for this celebration: "Because the good news has

87. McGann, "Making Vital Connections," p. 58.

been proclaimed, the dead have come to life, the lost have been found, and, as the father of the prodigal son put it, 'We had to celebrate and rejoice.'"[88]

In missional worship, the assembly encounters the living God, the source of life who drew near to us in Christ. Engaged once again in the story of God's love for the world from creation to new creation, and knowing themselves to be reconciled to God, to one another, and to all creation, the assembly rejoices and gives thanks. As *Places in the Heart* shows, communion gives us a foretaste of the eschatological banquet, reconciling us with Christ and with one another. By sharing communion, having offered thankful remembrance and hope-filled supplication,[89] the assembly enacts and participates in the mission of God.

In the next chapter we will explore the final movement of worship: going forth in mission in the name of Christ.

---

88. Thomas C. Long, *Beyond the Worship Wars: Building Vital and Faithful Worship* (Herndon, Va.: Alban Institute, 2001), p. 94.

89. Thomas H. Schattauer, "Liturgical Assembly as Locus of Mission," in *Inside Out,* ed. Schattauer, p. 10.

CHAPTER 7

Going Forth in the Name of Christ

To those who are absent a portion is sent by the deacons. And they who are well to do, and willing, give what each thinks fit; and what is collected is deposited with the president, who succours the orphans and widows and those who, through sickness or any other cause, are in want, and those who are in bonds and the strangers sojourning among us, and in a word takes care of all who are in need.

Justin Martyr, mid–second century[1]

Go in peace to love and to serve;
We will seek peace and pursue it.

Iona Abbey Worship Book[2]

Going forth is a brief but essential part of worship. Like our Möbius strip, in which mission and worship flow into and out of one another, this final action links worship as participation in God's mission and engaging in that mission

---

1. Justin, *I Apology* 67, in *The Apostolic Fathers with Justin Martyr and Irenaeus*, Vol. 1 of *Ante-Nicene Fathers*, ed. Alexander Roberts and James Donaldson, Christian Classics Ethereal Library, available at http://www.ccel.org/ccel/schaff/anf01.viii.ii.lxvii.html.

2. Morning Service, *Iona Abbey Worship Book* (Glasgow: Wild Goose Publications, 2001), p. 22.

in the world. As in the spinning top, the forces of worship are propelling us out of the center and into ministry in our daily lives.

Roman Catholic writer Gregory Augustine Pierce argues that the dismissal is the most important part of the mass. "When we are sent forth from the Mass," he says, "we are sent forth to go out and try again to help transform the world along the lines that God intended and Jesus preached." The dismissal is thus related to mission. Pierce reminds us that the word "mass" comes from the Latin phrase used for the dismissal, *Ite missa est,* meaning "Go, we are sent forth." Pierce comments, "Sometime in church history, some people thought this was an important enough part of the liturgy to name the entire thing after it."[3]

Although these are the final actions of a worship service, going forth is not an ending but a beginning. Describing the "liturgy after the liturgy," Orthodox theologian Ion Bria emphasizes the connection between what occurs in the Eucharistic liturgy and how worshipers live each day: "Since by the eucharistic event we are incorporated in Christ to serve the world and be sacrificed for it, we have to express in concrete *diakonia* [service], in community life, our new being in Christ, who is the servant of all."[4] Lutheran liturgical scholar Clayton Schmit argues that the final moment of worship is not a dismissal but a sending. "Dismissal at the close of worship," Schmit writes, "has the power of adjournment, where the activities of worship are suspended until the worshipers reconvene at a later time."[5] In contrast, "sending is the primary element of preparation for a demanding aspect of worship (action) that lasts typically from one Sunday morning to the next. During the week the faithful are engaged in outward worship, the work of God's people, which might be called 'the living liturgy of discipleship.'"[6] In the *Iona Abbey Worship Book,* the final rubric of the daily morning service underscores that the assembly is sent into action: "We remain standing to leave, the work of our day flowing directly from our worship."[7] For those

---

3. Gregory F. Augustine Pierce, *The Mass Is Never Ended: Rediscovering Our Mission to Transform the World* (Notre Dame, Ind.: Ave Maria Press, 2007), pp. 38-39.

4. Ion Bria, *Go Forth in Peace: Orthodox Perspectives on Mission* (Geneva: WCC Publications, 1986), p. 38.

5. Clayton J. Schmit, *Sent and Gathered: A Worship Manual for the Missional Church* (Grand Rapids: Baker Academic, 2009), p. 47.

6. Schmit, *Sent and Gathered,* p. 52.

7. Morning Service, *Iona Abbey Worship Book,* p. 22.

staying at the abbey, the connection between worship and work is further underscored by the scheduling of daily chores immediately after the morning service. Worshipers go forth to engage in liturgy, work for the common good. At the abbey, the immediate work for the common good might be sweeping floors or cleaning bathrooms, mundane tasks necessary for the good of those living in the same place.

In Justin Martyr's description of the Sunday service in the mid–second century, the final actions engage the assembly in work for the common good, not only the good of the Christian community but also the good of any who are in need. The deacons send communion to absent members of the assembly, and members of the assembly give from their means to provide for those in need, including orphans, widows, prisoners, and visitors. Over the course of the centuries, churches have used many other actions and ritual texts to conclude the Sunday assembly. What is essential is the commissioning, sending the assembly into the world to continue their participation in God's mission.

Going Forth to Other Members of the Community: Communion

Justin mentions almost in passing that the deacons send a portion of the communion bread and wine to those who are absent. Yet the action is significant because it strengthens the bonds of communion. Throughout Justin's account of the Sunday assembly, he highlights the importance of community. All who live in city or country gather in one place. After the sermon, everyone rises together to offer prayers. The people assent to the presider's thanksgiving over the bread and wine by saying "Amen." The elements are not just distributed; there is a "participation" in that over which thanks has been given.[8] Liturgical scholar Paul Bradshaw suggests that these practices manifest some of the "close sense of community" that the first followers of Jesus experienced in their meals eaten in memory of him, even though the meal had become a ritual sharing of a fragment of bread and a sip of wine.[9]

---

8. Justin, *I Apology* 67.

9. Paul F. Bradshaw, *Early Christian Worship: A Basic Introduction to Ideas and Practice* (Collegeville, Minn.: Liturgical Press, 2010), p. 48.

In addition to strengthening the ties of the community by sharing the blessed bread and wine with those who were absent, Christians also began to use the Eucharistic food as *viaticum,* taken for the passage from death to eternal life. Over the centuries, Christians have provided communion not only for the dying but also for those who are ill. In order to have the Eucharistic elements readily available, churches reserved some of the sacrament so it could be administered whenever needed. The sixteenth-century Council of Trent defended this practice: "The custom of reserving the Holy Eucharist in a sacred place is so ancient that even the period of the Nicene Council [325] recognized that usage. Moreover, the practice of carrying the sacred eucharist to the sick and of carefully reserving it for this purpose in churches . . . is also found enjoined in numerous councils and is a very ancient observance of the catholic church."[10] Martin Luther, though rejecting the practice of reserving consecrated bread and wine, nonetheless allowed the sacrament to be carried to the sick in their homes.[11]

For many centuries, clergy have been responsible for bringing communion to the sick and dying. The worldview of Christendom is evident in this practice: religious professionals, the clergy, are responsible for the "cure of souls," ministering to the laity, the recipients of ministry.[12] In recent decades, some churches have begun to permit laypeople also to bring communion to the sick. This is not a matter of relieving clergy of one of their responsibilities; rather, it is a way of having baptized Christians participate actively in Christian service.

In the Episcopal Church, the 1985 General Convention introduced a provision in canon law allowing lay Eucharistic ministers to take the sacrament to members of the congregation who, because of illness or infirmity, were unable to be present at a celebration. While clergy could take the sacrament to the sick at any time, lay Eucharistic ministers were required to go directly from the celebration to the sick person, a requirement subsequently

---

10. *The Canons and Decrees of the Council of Trent,* trans. H. J. Schroeder (St. Louis: Herder Book Co., 1941), p. 77.

11. Paul F. Bradshaw and Maxwell E. Johnson, *The Eucharistic Liturgies: Their Evolution and Interpretation,* Alcuin Club Collections 87 (London: SPCK, 2012), p. 243.

12. See, for example, the description of Christendom in *Worship and Mission after Christendom* by Alan Kreider and Eleanor Kreider (Scottdale, Pa., and Waterloo, Ontario: Herald Press, 2011), p. 39.

amended to allow the Eucharistic visitors to take the elements "in a timely manner."[13] Guidelines for this ministry call for the lay ministers to be sent from the assembly with these words: "In the name of this congregation, I send you forth bearing these holy gifts, that those to whom you go may share with us in the communion of Christ's body and blood. We who are many are one body, because we all share one bread, one cup."[14] Communion for the sick thus not only feeds them with the sacrament but also unites them in communion with their local assembly. Moreover, when the lay ministers are sent from the assembly, members of the assembly are reminded of their ties to those who are sick. This ministry with the sick is thus a form of participation in God's mission, restoring the absent members to union with God and with their sisters and brothers in the assembly.

Going Forth to Those in Need: The Collection

Collecting money, food, and other gifts for those in need has strong biblical foundations. Liturgical scholar Paul Bradshaw comments, "Not surprisingly, especially given Jesus' concern for the poor and outcasts in society, the sharing of food with the needy seems to have been a very important aspect of the early Christian movement."[15] After Greek-speaking disciples complained because their widows were being neglected, the apostles appointed seven men, sometimes considered the first deacons, to oversee the distribution of food (Acts 6:1-6). The apostle Paul counseled the church at Corinth to organize their meals so that no one would go hungry (1 Cor. 11:20-34).

In addition to providing food for the hungry, the early communities (some of them Gentile) contributed to a collection that Paul organized for the church in Jerusalem. J. G. Davies points out that Paul twice refers to this collection using the Greek word *koinonia* (Rom. 15:26; 2 Cor. 9:13), usually

13. Canon III.4.7, *Constitution and Canons Together with the Rules of Order for the Government of the Protestant Episcopal Church in the United States of America Otherwise Known as The Episcopal Church, Adopted and Revised in General Convention, 1789-2012* (New York: Church Publishing, 2012), p. 69.

14. Episcopal Church, *The Book of Occasional Services, 2003* (New York: Church Publishing, 2004), p. 325.

15. Bradshaw, *Early Christian Worship*, p. 43.

translated as "fellowship." The use of this term emphasizes that the gift is a form of communion, and Davies argues that the willingness of Gentile churches to contribute for the needs of the poor in Jerusalem "was proof positive of the actuality of the *koinonia,* that Jew and Gentile were one in Christ."[16] The collection was missional not only because it expressed care for those in need but also because it reflected reconciliation between formerly divided groups.

Justin places the collection in the context of worship. My students are always surprised to find that Justin says the collection occurred at the end of the service. While some churches place the collection of money at the time of the preparation of the table, offering money and other gifts along with bread and wine for communion, its place in the Sunday assembly as described by Justin invites us to consider the significance of the collection in itself.

James K. A. Smith proposes, "The liturgical practice of the offering indicates that Christian worship — which is a foretaste of the new creation — embodies a new economy, an alternative economy. . . . The Sunday offering in gathered worship is not disconnected from other systems of commerce, distribution, and exchange." Smith describes this as "kingdom economics."[17] In the earliest communities, those who were baptized and "devoted themselves to the apostles' teaching and fellowship, to the breaking of bread and the prayers" (Acts 2:42), also committed themselves to a new way of living: "All who believed were together and had all things in common; they would sell their possessions and goods and distribute the proceeds to all, as any had need" (Acts 2:44-45).

This may have been more of an idealized vision than a lived reality for many followers of Jesus, even in the first century, given the need to appoint ministers to distribute food to widows and the evidence from Paul's first letter to the Corinthians that that community was unable even to share their common meal equitably. But Acts also gives us the cautionary tale of Ananias and Sapphira, who sold a piece of property and retained some of the proceeds for themselves. When Ananias presented only a portion of the income

16. J. G. Davies, *Worship and Mission* (London: SCM Press, 1966; New York: Association Press, 1967), p. 137.

17. James K. A. Smith, *Desiring the Kingdom: Worship, Worldview, and Cultural Formation* (Grand Rapids: Baker Academic, 2009), pp. 204-5.

to Peter, Peter chastised Ananias, who dropped dead immediately. Just a few hours later, his wife likewise underreported the income from the sale, and she too promptly fell dead. This stark tale concludes, "And great fear seized the whole church and all who heard of these things" (Acts 5:11).

The biblical narratives lead James Smith to conclude, "The reconciled and redeemed body of Christ is marked by cruciform practices that counter the liturgies of consumption, hoarding, and greed that characterize so much of our late modern culture."[18] In her study of household economics as a Christian practice, Sharon Daloz Parks acknowledges the complexity of our contemporary context and proposes that Christians understand their economic practices in light of incarnation. She explains, "The whole of Creation is the place of God's presence. . . . Spirit is incarnate — within us, among us, beyond us, beneath us — in the motion and matter of Life Itself, giving dignity and value to every element of Creation. Every being participates in the household of God and is included in the economic imagination of God."[19] Our challenge is to discern and practice the economic implications of "God with us." Daloz Parks does not offer simple answers but rather seeks wisdom from different Christian traditions that attempt to align household economics with the economy of God. For example, some Quakers ask questions such as these related to economic life: "What are you doing as individuals or as a Meeting: To aid those in need of material help? To create a social and economic system which will so function as to sustain and enrich life for all? Do you keep to simplicity and moderation in your speech, your manner of living, and your pursuit of business?"[20] With regard to worship and economics, James Smith observes, "Sadly, in many contexts of worship in North America, the offering in worship is little more than a parody of such an alternative economics."[21]

How might our practices of offering in worship enact a vision of the reign of God, a place of abundance where all are fed? The apostle Paul wrote to the Corinthians regarding his collection for the church in Jerusalem: "Each of you must give as you have made up your mind, not reluctantly or under compulsion, for God loves a cheerful giver. And God is able to provide you

---

18. Smith, *Desiring the Kingdom*, p. 205.

19. Sharon Daloz Parks, "Household Economics," in *Practicing Our Faith: A Way of Life for a Searching People*, ed. Dorothy C. Bass, 2nd ed. (San Francisco: Jossey-Bass, 1997, 2010), p. 47.

20. Daloz Parks, "Household Economics," pp. 51-52.

21. Smith, *Desiring the Kingdom*, p. 205.

with every blessing in abundance, so that by always having enough of everything, you may share abundantly in every good work. . . . You will be enriched in every way for your great generosity, which will produce thanksgiving to God through us; for the rendering of this ministry not only supplies the needs of the saints but also overflows with many thanksgivings to God" (2 Cor. 9:7-8, 11-12). In missional churches, members of the assembly give generously and gladly, in thanksgiving for God's generosity and in trust that God continues to provide for their needs.

In some parts of the world, people offer their gifts with joyful singing and dancing, everyone in the assembly exuberantly carrying gifts to the altar.[22] The St. Giles Family Mass Community, a Roman Catholic congregation in Oak Park, Illinois, regularly includes an "almsgiving" designated for a particular ministry or charity. During the Sunday service, members of the assembly come forward to place their contributions in a basket on the floor in front of the altar, an informal procession that enacts their offering for those in need.[23] At my home congregation, All Souls Episcopal Parish in Berkeley, California, the offering on most Sundays is a more restrained passing of brass collection plates along the pews. But once a year, on the first Sunday in November (just after All Saints' Day), the parish celebrates its feast of title, an occasion for celebrating its identity as a community called and sent by God, in union with saints from ages past. It is the time of year when many congregations are planning budgets for the year ahead and asking members to make a financial commitment. At All Souls, on the first Sunday in November when the parish celebrates its identity, everyone is invited to come forward to present an envelope holding their commitment. Many couples and families process together, carrying just one envelope. The movement of so many in the assembly, though not with wild exuberance, is a witness to one another of our shared commitment.

In kingdom economics, all give willingly, recognizing that all we have is from God. All give generously, as each is able, in gratitude that God provides for everyone. The apostle Paul wrote to the Corinthian church about the practices of the church in Macedonia: "During a severe ordeal of affliction, their abundant joy and their extreme poverty have overflowed in a wealth of

---

22. Kreider and Kreider, *Worship and Mission after Christendom*, p. 214.
23. Stephen Bevans, e-mail message to the author, 29 November 2013.

generosity on their part. For, as I can testify, they voluntarily gave according to their means, and even beyond their means, begging us earnestly for the privilege of sharing in this ministry to the saints" (2 Cor. 8:2-4). The model for such generous giving is "the generous act of our Lord Jesus Christ, that though he was rich, yet for your sakes he became poor, so that by his poverty you might become rich" (2 Cor. 8:9). In kingdom economics, recognizing Christ's self-offering on behalf of the world, we gratefully participate in his work of mission for the common good.

Going Forth with Members of the Assembly: Welcoming Visitors

Congregations enacting God's mission will show hospitality to all who come to worship, outsider and regular alike. Although many people think of welcoming outsiders in the context of the gathering of the assembly, hospitality for strangers is also essential as the assembly goes forth. In his study of congregations that practiced an open communion table, Stephen Edmondson concluded, "True hospitality must be a programmatic effort in Christian communities, embraced by a majority of the members of that community. Only in this way does welcome extend from the pew into the parish hall."[24] Pointing out that "the church lives from the center with its eyes on the borders," Lutheran scholar Robert Hawkins urges that churches speak God's welcome to strangers who venture into worship at a time of crisis.[25] Some people who are strangers to church may choose to sit on the borders of the assembly, curious but wary, perhaps having been alienated by the church and cautiously seeking a way back, perhaps healing from past hurts.[26] Missional communities will listen attentively to the needs and concerns of those on the margins while being unafraid to speak prophetic truth, the peculiar story of God who is present and active in the world and makes claims on those who tell this story.[27]

24. Stephen Edmondson, "Opening the Table: The Body of Christ and God's Prodigal Grace," *Anglican Theological Review* 91 (2009): 232.

25. Robert D. Hawkins, "Occasional Services: Border Crossings," in *Inside Out: Worship in an Age of Mission*, ed. Thomas H. Schattauer (Minneapolis: Fortress Press, 1999), p. 187.

26. Stephen B. Bevans and Roger P. Schroeder, *Constants in Context: A Theology of Mission for Today* (Maryknoll, N.Y.: Orbis Books, 2004), pp. 365-66.

27. Kreider and Kreider, *Worship and Mission after Christendom*, pp. 67-69.

Communities that practice intentional hospitality will have a plan for following up with visitors to the Sunday assembly. After my husband and I moved to California in 2009, we began visiting congregations to discern where we would make our church home. After a few months, we decided to make a second visit to All Souls Parish in Berkeley. This time we completed the visitor card, giving our home address and telephone number. That afternoon, our doorbell rang. A woman from the parish had come with a small loaf of bread to welcome us and invite us to consider becoming members. We were surprised and touched by her hospitality. Recently, we had the opportunity to return the gesture when the coordinator of the newcomer ministry asked us to bring bread to a visitor to the Sunday assembly. The man we visited had just moved to the area and was as surprised and delighted as we had been; he has since become a member of the parish. Neither of these visits was lengthy, and the conversation was not especially profound. Yet the visits extended hospitality from pew to parish hall to home, and the simple act of taking time to acknowledge a stranger with a gift of food reflected God's generous love for all.

Following up with visitors, though vital, is only a first step. Edmondson explains that the parishes he studied had a process of integrating guests so that they could become members: "Orientation is that process whereby we help strangers learn to negotiate the intricate pathways through which our church life is structured. Welcome is what brings strangers from the doors that they access by those pathways into the room of service and fellowship to which these doors lead. Education is the means through which they learn the gospel context of that fellowship and service so that they might live more fully into it."[28] Missional congregations will work to incorporate guests into their community life and invite them to join in participation in God's mission in the world as well as in worship.

Alan Kreider and Eleanor Kreider emphasize the importance of education and formation in our contemporary post-Christendom context:

> In a Christendom context, people learned the Christian story and rudimentary Christian ethics by a process of osmosis, from parents and the wider culture as well as from the church. But in post-Christendom these

---

28. Edmondson, "Opening the Table," p. 233.

sources of learning have largely dried up. Today people are catechized by the global culture industries and by advertisers who prey without ceasing on our susceptibilities. If outsiders are to become followers of Jesus in post-Christendom, they need to engage in a process of deconstructing old assumptions and learning new ways of thinking and behaving. If they are to learn the elements of God's mission — love of God in Christ; love of the neighbor; love of God's reconciling work (including love of the enemy); and love of creation — they will need the support of the wider Christian family and of companions on the road.[29]

For guidance in fostering these new ways of thinking and behaving, some churches have looked to the example of pre-Christendom and fourth-century Christendom, when churches practiced an extended period of formation of converts called the "catechumenate." Although by the second century the infant children of believers were often baptized, adult baptism of believers was the normative practice. Converts seeking baptism underwent a process of formation intended to foster both a change of belief and a change of behavior, leading to their baptism and belonging in the Christian community.[30]

After the Second Vatican Council, the Roman Catholic Church introduced the Rite of Christian Initiation of Adults, largely modeled on what scholars had discovered about fourth-century catechumenal processes and rites. Roman Catholic liturgical scholar Aidan Kavanagh underscores the significance for the entire congregation of the introduction of this pattern of adult conversion and formation leading to baptism: "Members of an adult catechumenate must be secured through evangelization; they must be formed to maturity in ecclesial faith through catechesis both prior to baptism and after it; and there must be something to initiate them into that will be correlative to the expectations built up in them throughout their whole initiatory process. This last means a community of lively faith in Jesus Christ dead, risen, and present actually among his People."[31]

29. Kreider and Kreider, *Worship and Mission after Christendom*, p. 248.

30. Alan Kreider, *The Change of Conversion and the Origin of Christendom* (Harrisburg, Pa.: Trinity Press International, 1999), pp. xiii-xvii, 1-32.

31. Aidan Kavanagh, "Christian Initiation in Post-Conciliar Roman Catholicism: A Brief Report," in *Living Water, Sealing Spirit: Readings on Christian Initiation*, ed. Maxwell E. Johnson (Collegeville, Minn.: Liturgical Press, 1995), p. 8.

Although the Roman Catholic materials use many of the fourth-century terms, such as "pre-catechumenate," "election," "enlightenment," "scrutinies," and "mystagogy," other churches have adopted similar processes using different terminology. The Web site of the ecumenical North American Association for the Catechumenate describes the catechumenate as "an important tool for discipleship in today's church that not only prepares people for baptism but also for baptismal living."[32] Unofficial materials produced for the United Methodist Church identify three major movements in the process: evangelization (pre-catechesis), formation and instruction (catechesis), and the sacrament of initiation (baptism).[33]

More important than the particular terms is the catechumenal process itself. United Methodist pastor Daniel Benedict describes it as experience followed by reflection: "Storytelling, worshiping, doing the word in service to the poor and suffering, discovering opportunities for service in daily life, and reflecting on Scripture are the curriculum for learning to hear the distinctive voice to which disciples must first and finally listen. Continuous reflection on Scripture and the experiences of prayer, worship, gifts for ministry, and ministry in daily life are at the heart of the formational process of Christian initiation."[34] The process shapes people for Christian living, inviting them to become disciples who know the generous love of God and drawing them ever more deeply into God's mission of reconciliation.

James Smith describes formation as "a task of shaping and creating a certain kind of people."[35] Worship is one key place of formation: it is where the assembly experiences and enacts the good news of God's reconciling love. Drawing on the work of Craig Dykstra and Dorothy Bass, Smith calls for "practices beyond Sunday" that form Christians for participation in the reign of God: "When Christians engage in the practices of hospitality and Sabbath-keeping, singing and forgiveness, simplicity and fasting, they are engaging in a way of life that is formative and constitutive of Christian discipleship."[36]

32. "Welcome Ministry Practitioners and All Engaged in Spiritual Formation," North American Association for the Catechumenate, available at http://www.catechumenate.org/.

33. Daniel T. Benedict Jr., *Come to the Waters: Baptism and Our Ministry of Welcoming Seekers and Making Disciples* (Nashville: Discipleship Resources, 1996), p. 22.

34. Benedict, *Come to the Waters*, p. 61.

35. Smith, *Desiring the Kingdom*, p. 26.

36. Smith, *Desiring the Kingdom*, p. 212.

Far more than simply a gracious welcome to visitors in the Sunday assembly, missional hospitality is a practice of radical welcome in which members of the congregation engage in prophetic dialogue with visitors by journeying with them from pew to parish hall and beyond, inviting them into participation in God's mission in the world. Those who practice such hospitality will be in dialogue by listening carefully to the stories of those who sojourn with them, seeking to understand their experiences and perspectives and being willing to be changed through these encounters.[37] They will also be prophetic, telling the Gospel story of Jesus and the stories of God's work from creation to new creation, telling the stories of our participation in the new life of Christ. Stephen Edmondson describes this story-telling: "We tell [the Gospel story of Jesus] . . . for its power to illuminate and conform us to the true structure of love in our lives. It reveals love's paschal mystery — that we find life's fullness only by the gift of ourselves to the other, even as God gave Godself in Jesus. The gospel lies at the heart of our catechesis, then, not simply so that we might teach outsiders our ways, but so that we might ever learn more deeply God's ways in Christ."[38] Missional communities will seek opportunities in worship and in their common life outside worship to tell these stories to one another and to their guests, and so learn and follow God's ways in Christ.[39]

How the Assembly Goes Forth

The simple but essential function of going forth has taken various forms over the centuries. Roman Catholic liturgical scholar Michael Witczak comments, "The end of a service can be messy and even chaotic as the action winds down and ministers and people move to leave. Some would consider this a 'soft moment' point in the liturgy."[40] "Soft spots" in worship are moments

---

37. Stephanie Spellers, *Radical Welcome: Embracing God, The Other, and the Spirit of Transformation* (New York: Church Publishing, 2006), pp. 72-73.

38. Edmondson, "Opening the Table," p. 233.

39. For ideas about and examples of congregations telling God's story and the people's stories, see Kreider and Kreider, *Worship and Mission after Christendom*, pp. 120-33, 157-60.

40. Michael G. Witczak, "The Concluding Rites: History of the Latin Text and Rite," in *A Commentary on the Order of Mass of The Roman Missal: A New English Translation, developed*

when the action is primary, such as gathering or breaking bread or going forth. As rituals develop, these simple, functional actions may become highly elaborated and include multiple texts said or sung.

In missional worship, the action of going forth sends members of the assembly into the world as disciples of Christ. Although many congregations today include a formal blessing, and many consider it to be essential, this custom evolved over the course of many centuries. As we have seen, Justin describes sending communion to those who are absent and taking a collection for those in need, but he says nothing about any text or gesture over the assembly. In his survey of the development of this part of the service in the Western church, Witczak concludes that blessings were associated with celebrations at which bishops were present. "The desire to receive a blessing at the end of each mass, no matter who the presider," says Witczak, "evolved slowly during the Middle Ages," and the concluding prayers became more and more elaborate.[41]

J. G. Davies counsels against the use of a blessing and calls instead for a dismissal, which is "not a cozy rounding-off of a cultic act but part of the sending of God's servants in mission."[42] Other writers urge that the blessing explicitly send people into action for the good of the world. James Smith explains, "The blessing speaks of affirmation and conferral — that we go empowered for this mission, graced recipients of good gifts, filled with the Spirit, our imaginations fueled by the Word to imagine the world otherwise."[43] Clayton Schmit also understands the benediction as a form of sending: "The benediction is not a concluding prayer. It is a declarative statement of blessing spoken directly to those who are to go forth in action."[44]

Schmit argues against the term "dismissal" because "it suggests finality, rather than movement from one state to another."[45] Yet the word "dismissal" is linguistically related to the word "mission," both deriving from the Latin word meaning "to send." Understood in this way, a dismissal is not an end

---

under the auspices of the Catholic Academy of Liturgy, ed. Edward Foley et al. (Collegeville, Minn.: Liturgical Press, 2011), p. 627.

41. Witczak, "The Concluding Rites," pp. 628-29.
42. Davies, *Worship and Mission,* pp. 140-41.
43. Smith, *Desiring the Kingdom,* p. 207.
44. Schmit, *Sent and Gathered,* p. 53.
45. Schmit, *Sent and Gathered,* p. 47.

but another beginning, "a shift," says Roman Catholic liturgical scholar Susan Roll, "from one context to another, from worship within the church to living out one's Christian commitment in all other aspects of one's life."[46] However, the classical Roman Catholic dismissal *"Ite missa est"* is translated into English as "Go forth, the Mass is ended,"[47] diminishing a sense of continuity from the assembly for worship to their participation in God's mission in the world. At Holy Family Catholic Church, located in a Chicago suburb, after the blessing the assembly instead says together, "The Mass is never ended. Let us go forth in peace."[48]

Orthodox theologian Ion Bria reminds us that "the liturgy does not end when the eucharistic assembly disperses."[49] Rather, the dispersed assembly continues its liturgy in the world, working in mission for the common good, just as the liturgy of the gathered assembly is also work done for the common good. Whether the assembly is sent forth with a blessing or a dismissal or both, the text and action will propel members of the assembly into the world, like the energy flowing out of the center of a spinning top. If Eucharistic visitors are to take communion from the service to those who are ill or infirm, they may be formally sent out from the assembly before the dismissal, commissioned to carry holy gifts that unite those who are absent with the assembly that worshiped together. My home parish serves a meal for homeless people on one Sunday afternoon each month. On these Sundays, leaders in that ministry will come forward just before the dismissal with a large basket of fresh bread, which the presider blesses for the meal. The leaders, carrying the basket of bread, then join the worship ministers to process out of the church.

Some congregations make announcements just before the blessing or dismissal. Whether given at this point in the rite or earlier, the announcements are an important opportunity to relate worship and mission in the world, encouraging worshipers to look beyond themselves and the immediacy of the assembly.

In some assemblies, going forth includes a song, getting worshipers on

46. Susan K. Roll, "The Concluding Rites: Theology of the Latin Text and Rite," in *A Commentary on the Order of Mass of The Roman Missal*, ed. Foley et al., p. 636.

47. Witczak, "The Concluding Rites," p. 625.

48. Stephen Bevans, e-mail message to the author, 29 November 2013.

49. Bria, *Go Forth in Peace*, p. 38.

their feet and stirring their bodies to action. Clayton Schmit observes, "The music is often upbeat and the mood is one of anticipation and hope. Most appropriate are the songs and hymns that speak to God's empowerment of ministry as believers go forth."[50] The choir and other ministers might process out during the singing, and sometimes the entire assembly joins them in procession. At the parish of St. Mary in Islington, London, when Graham Kings was vicar, Kings would process down the aisle of the church as the final hymn was sung, and members of the assembly would turn around to face him at the doors of the church building. At the end of the hymn, Kings would fling open the doors, bless the congregation, and send them forth into the world.[51]

Immediately after the formal sending, worshipers gradually make their way into the world. It is not an abrupt move from worship to mission; rather, the adoration they have experienced in worship gradually moves them into action in the world. In some churches, a coffee hour or a meal follows worship, providing a time of fellowship for members of the assembly and an opportunity to begin to get acquainted with visitors and newcomers. Whether or not refreshments are provided, informal conversations as worshipers go forth are important expressions of hospitality and care for one another, enacting the reconciling love of God that the assembly has just celebrated.

Worship leaders will reflect on their experience in the assembly, perhaps having heard questions or comments as worshipers disperse. Intentional reflection on patterns and practices of worship, including the events of a specific worship service, is an important aspect of preparing for missional worship. In the next chapter, I will introduce a tool to assist in this preparation.

---

50. Schmit, *Sent and Gathered*, p. 158.
51. Stephen Bevans, e-mail message to the author, 29 November 2013.

CHAPTER 8

Preparing Missional Worship

The kingdom of God is justice and peace and joy in the Holy Spirit.
Come, Lord, and open in us the gates of your kingdom.

Songs from Taizé[1]

Celebrating worship as a locus of God's mission requires attention to preparing for worship. Worship is offered not only for members of the church but for the life of the world. All are welcome in an assembly that transcends age, class, race, ethnicity, gender, sexual orientation, and other categories that all too often divide humankind. All are invited to remember and celebrate God's work in creating the world; God's reconciling love made known in the incarnation, life, death, and resurrection of Jesus; and God's gift of the Spirit that continues to infuse the life of the Christian community. This story is an odd story. It tells us that God works through insignificant people and calls a tiny nation to be a light to the world; it assumes that God is at work in the world in mysterious and unpredictable ways; it makes claim on each of us who dare to tell this story. As the worshiping community remembers the odd story of God's love for the world, it also is re-oriented to our Christian hope for God's new creation.

Missional worship is not a technique or a recipe but rather an art that may take different forms. Reflecting on "organizing the assembly for mis-

1. *Songs from Taizé, 2013-2014* (Taizé, France: Ateliers et Presses de Taizé, 2013), #115.

sion," Lutheran liturgical scholar Gordon Lathrop asserts, "We should do word and sacrament in strength."[2] In missional worship, the assembly embodies and inhabits worship in such a way that texts and patterns come alive for people through speaking and singing, in symbols and actions. Drawing from the well of tradition, missional worship also attends to the context, incorporating elements of the local culture that are able to reflect the gospel. Missional worship will be countercultural when necessary, challenging injustice and oppression, critiquing and transforming cultural patterns in light of the gospel. Missional worship will also be cross-cultural, celebrating the diversity of the body of Christ in many different contexts and uniting worshipers with Christians in other places.[3]

In an analysis of the contemporary cultural context of the United States, Roman Catholic theologian Richard Gaillardetz identifies "a longing for transcendence and a longing for community, which have been rent asunder."[4] As a result, people seek either worship that is awe-inspiring, which transports worshipers to another spiritual realm, or worship that is relaxed, warm, and friendly. Gaillardetz argues that the two dimensions properly belong together: "The celebration of the liturgy is the privileged ritual expression of what is in fact true every moment of our lives: every authentic act of human communion is by that fact communion with God."[5] Gaillardetz does not take up the question of mission, yet his work has significant implications for the practice of missional worship. Those who prepare worship will consider both how the service will draw worshipers more deeply into the knowledge and love of God, and how it will foster communion among the members of the assembly. Communion with God and with one another enacts God's reconciling love that is God's purpose and desire for the world — indeed, for all creation. The assembly thus witnesses to and participates in God's mission. Moreover, even as preparation

---

2. Gordon W. Lathrop, "Liturgy and Mission in the North American Context," in *Inside Out: Worship in an Age of Mission,* ed. Thomas H. Schattauer (Minneapolis: Fortress Press, 1999), p. 207.

3. Lutheran World Federation, "Nairobi Statement on Worship and Culture."

4. Richard R. Gaillardetz, "North American Culture and the Liturgical Life of the Church: The Separation of the Quests for Transcendence and Community," *Worship* 68 (1994): 410.

5. Gaillardetz, "North American Culture and the Liturgical Life of the Church," p. 416.

for worship focuses on what will happen in the assembly, those preparing missional worship are always mindful of the interweaving of worship in the assembly and mission in the world, as in our Möbius strip and our spinning top.

A Worship Matrix

Worship engages the assembly in ritual action. The sights, sounds, and even smells of worship provide a rich experience that involves the whole person. Liturgical scholars Paul Bradshaw and Katharine Harmon point out that worship "is not made up of ideas, but things — words, materials, gestures, tastes, noise, sight and smell, and human persons. It is not only our brains that we take to worship but our whole selves." Moreover, they say, ritual is a "*social* behavioral pattern. . . . Doing things together is an important aspect of ritual: not just individuals, but communities act together, following a pattern that through routine repetition becomes a tradition."[6]

In the previous chapters of this book, we have explored a pattern of worship that has become a tradition for many churches. While the structure may vary and not every assembly includes every element all the time, these fundamental actions are transcultural aspects of worship; they unite believers across time, space, culture, and confession. The Nairobi Statement of the Lutheran World Federation explains, "The fundamental shape of the principal Sunday act of Christian worship, the eucharist or holy communion, is shared across cultures: the people of God gather, the Word of God is proclaimed, the people intercede for the needs of the church and the world, the eucharistic meal is shared, and the people are sent out into the world for mission."[7]

Every worshiping assembly embodies these primary activities in its particular worship space, with ritual objects and actions, in patterns of song and other music, speaking, and silence. To "map" the primary activities of

---

6. Paul F. Bradshaw and Katharine E. Harmon, "Ritual," in *The Study of Liturgy and Worship: An Alcuin Guide,* ed. Juliette Day and Benjamin Gordon-Taylor (London: SPCK, 2013), p. 26; emphasis in the original.

7. Lutheran World Federation, "Nairobi Statement on Worship and Culture," par. 2.1.

Worship Matrix

	people	space	time	objects	actions	texts	music	silence
Gather in the Name of God								
Proclaim and Respond to the Word								
Pray for the World								
Enact Reconciliation								
Celebrate the Communion Meal								
Go Forth in the Name of Christ								

worship with these dimensions of worship, I have developed a worship matrix. This matrix is a conceptual tool for preparing worship, encouraging attention to each dimension of worship for each major movement in the service. So, for example, as we prepare for the gathering, we do the following:

- we consider the *people* who will assemble, both regular members and outsiders, and we decide who will lead and serve the assembly in specific elements of the gathering;
- we decide how we will use the worship *space* and how the space will be decorated;
- we take account of liturgical *time,* both the season or feast of the church year as well as other events in the life of the congregation and the community, and the time of day;
- we determine what ritual *objects* we will use — for example, a processional cross — and what will be visible in the space — for example, the pulpit Bible;
- we plan the *actions* that will enable us to gather — for example, how people will enter the worship space and what postures they will be invited to assume;
- we select or write the *texts* that will be spoken, and decide what will be extemporaneous;
- we choose *music,* sung or instrumental, that will unite worshipers in praise; and
- we decide whether there is a moment during the gathering when *silence* would be suitable, perhaps after the presider bids "Let us pray," so that the assembly can focus its attention on God before the presider speaks the words of the prayer.

Having considered the missional significance of the main movements of worship, in this chapter I discuss each of the dimensions of worship in turn, cognizant that these dimensions interact with one another. Those who prepare missional worship will attend to all of the dimensions so that worship is a rich and evocative celebration of the mystery of God's love, one that draws worshipers into communion with God and with one another and that is offered for the life of the world.

People

As we discussed in Chapter 2, the assembly for worship is a baptismal community, knit together as the body of Christ through the ritual washing that is also a burial and a birth into new life. Yet in the post-Christendom context of North America, growing numbers of people have never participated in Christian worship, and some have never even entered a church building. Additionally, new waves of immigration and other population shifts challenge congregations to attend to their context. Who lives in the neighborhood? Who is not here in the assembly?

Lutheran liturgical scholar Gordon Lathrop acknowledges that many of our assemblies do not reflect their surrounding community: "We come into church and notice that the assembly is rather too much made up of people from one economic class or one race or one language."[8] Missional worship itself will challenge the assembly to recognize its own limitations, for in worship we learn of God, whose love embraces the whole human family and who through Christ calls together a community in which "there is no longer Jew or Greek, there is no longer slave or free, there is no longer male and female; for all of you are one in Christ Jesus" (Gal. 3:28). As we come to know God's wide embrace, we begin to recognize our failure to practice radical welcome, to open our hearts and our doors to those not like us and allow ourselves to be transformed through our encounter with them.

Episcopal priest Stephanie Spellers says that congregations that practice radical welcome value their history, traditions, and denominational heritage while also cultivating an identity "flexible enough to include The Other." The signs of radical welcome she identifies indicate that this is work not only for leaders but for the entire congregation: "Leaders have consciously studied the make-up of the surrounding community and intentionally invited those neighbors to join and help to shape their common life and common mission. The congregation is developing critical consciousness of who is inside, who is marginalized and who is outside, and why, and seeks to eliminate exclusionary barriers blocking The Other."[9]

8. Gordon W. Lathrop, *Holy Things: A Liturgical Theology* (Minneapolis: Fortress Press, 1993), p. 114.

9. Stephanie Spellers, *Radical Welcome: Embracing God, The Other, and the Spirit of Transformation* (New York: Church Publishing, 2006), p. 80.

The task of radical welcome extends far beyond worship, to every aspect of congregational life. Yet worship is one of the primary places where newcomers will enter a congregation, whether at their own initiative or in response to the witness and proclamation of members of the congregation. Hence those who prepare missional worship consider how it will be accessible and inviting to regular members and outsiders alike. For example, in the 1990s, Reba Place Fellowship in Evanston, Illinois, a community rooted in the Mennonite tradition, made an intentional effort to become a multiracial congregation. They quickly learned that their worship would need to change: they would need to utilize different musical idioms and bring in new leadership. Gradually, they have incorporated more African-Americans from their neighborhood.

In addition to attending to the long view, working over an extended period of time to effect systemic change that broadens the membership of the assembly, those preparing worship will be attentive to practices of hospitality for every service. Thomas Long, recognizing the contemporary yearning for God and yearning for community, calls for a practice of hospitality to the stranger rather than a false intimacy, whether intimacy with others or intimacy with God. Long points out that "most of the encounters with God in the Bible are not direct, face-to-face engagements at all but are mediated through prophets and priests, strangers and signs, dreams and visions, the practices of the community and the preaching of the apostles."[10] With regard to intimacy with others, Richard Gaillardetz describes an understanding of community "peculiar to our American culture," with several presuppositions: "A community is comprised of autonomous individuals, each possessing certain gifts and abilities, who voluntarily join with other individuals to form an association, a group, or what may loosely be called a community. The purpose of this association may be to pool resources, to share common interests, to find support in others, or to exercise acts of charity. These groups, when formalized, are bound by certain rules. . . . They are often sustained by a consumerist mentality: I will only remain a member as long as I derive some benefit from this group."[11] Gaillardetz calls this a "thin theory" of commu-

10. Thomas C. Long, *Beyond the Worship Wars: Building Vital and Faithful Worship* (Herndon, Va.: Alban Institute, 2001), p. 31.

11. Gaillardetz, "North American Culture and the Liturgical Life of the Church," pp. 407-8.

nity, one that "is prone to the consumerist, individualistic cult of intimacy which makes of community that sphere of relations which exist solely for the fulfillment of my personal needs."[12] In contrast, life with God in Christ is relational and communal. The Pauline concept of the body of Christ, in which believers are members of Christ, means not merely cooperation and coordination but organic unity in which we share life together. Our participation in this body transforms us and re-orients us, so that our identity is found in our unique contribution to the common life of believers.[13]

As members of the body of Christ, we practice hospitality that is not simply a warm welcome to worship but rather a recognition that in the stranger we meet, we are encountering Christ. Moreover, we welcome the stranger to worship knowing that Christ is the host of this assembly, and we are all guests. "We are beggars together," says Gordon Lathrop, adding, "Grace will surprise us both."[14]

As we prepare missional worship, we will be especially attentive to our practices of hospitality at the gathering of and the going forth from the assembly. Who will greet people, orienting them to the space and the service? Thomas Long found that vital and faithful congregations have a corps of gifted greeters, "people with the rare blend of memory, personality, generosity, alertness to the needs of others, and kindness who have the ability to recognize the stranger . . . to discern the proper level of greeting . . . and to make the stranger feel welcomed and at home."[15] Missional congregations will cultivate practices of hospitality that not only welcome outsiders to the assembly but also lead them from the pew to the parish hall and beyond, to the fullness of life in Christ. As we discussed in Chapter 7, missional congregations will develop processes that integrate newcomers, enabling them to join the congregation as it participates in God's mission in worship and in the world.

Among those to be integrated into worship are our children. In my own tradition, the Episcopal Church, I find that in many congregations, children

---

12. Gaillardetz, "North American Culture and the Liturgical Life of the Church," p. 410.

13. Jerome Murphy-O'Connor, "Eucharist and Community in First Corinthians," *Worship* 50 (1976): 372-74. See also Gaillardetz, "North American Culture and the Liturgical Life of the Church," pp. 412-13.

14. Lathrop, *Holy Things,* p. 121.

15. Long, *Beyond the Worship Wars,* p. 38.

do not participate fully in worship. Some assemblies do not welcome children because young children may cry, make other noises, or move around and so distract adults from their worship. Some parents keep their children out of worship because they are concerned that the children will disrupt the assembly. In some places, children do not participate in worship because adults believe that they cannot understand what is happening and so are developmentally not ready for the regular Sunday assembly. So children are placed in Sunday school or "children's chapel" for the entire duration of the principal Sunday liturgy, or they spend the service of the Word in their classrooms, the theory being that Christian education is equivalent to the service of the Word, presented at an age-appropriate level. In this model, children enter worship in time to receive communion. As they grow older, they begin to be invited into the assembly for the entire service. Yet rarely do children become regular members of the worshiping community. Sunday school continues through elementary or middle school, and then a youth group may be provided for teenagers. The youth group typically meets at a time other than Sunday morning, and very few teens have the inclination to come to worship on Sunday mornings unless their parents insist. From adults deciding to put their children in a classroom, the children, as they become teenagers, decide that Sunday worship is not for them. Perhaps they've learned their Sunday-school lessons only too well.[16]

Some congregations provide for children with a children's homily or simplified texts, but these address children primarily at a cognitive level. At the communion table, however, children are engaged not so much through cognitive understanding as through experience, the experience of movement to the altar rail or communion station, the experience of eating and drinking with other Christians. One mother of a two-year-old reported that she and her child sometimes do "cross-spotting" (finding crosses in the worship space) during the long Eucharistic prayer spoken by the presider, and sometimes her child raises his arms in prayer, imitating the *orans* ("praying") gesture of the presider.

16. For further discussion, see Ruth A. Meyers, "The Liturgical Formation of Children, Teens, and Young Adults," in *Worship-Shaped Life: Liturgical Formation and the People of God,* ed. Ruth A. Meyers and Paul Gibson (New York and Harrisburg, Pa.: Morehouse Publishing; Norwich, U.K.: Canterbury Press, 2010), pp. 106-24.

When people brought little children to Jesus for his blessing, Jesus told his disciples, "Let the little children come to me; do not stop them; for it is to such as these that the kingdom of God belongs. Truly I tell you, whoever does not receive the kingdom of God as a little child will never enter it" (Mark 10:14-15). How might children participate actively with adults throughout worship, from gathering through dismissal? How do we create respectful space for children as full members of the assembly? If we are to receive the reign of God as little children, what might children have to teach adults about how to enter God's reign? Anglican liturgical scholar David Holeton identifies several characteristics of children that might make them exemplary citizens of the reign of God. Children manifest "complete and unmitigated trust," the sort of trust Jesus asks us to place in God. Children are also natural and gracious receivers, able to accept, among other things, the awesome gift of God's grace eagerly, without protestation or embarrassment. Very young children are helpless to assure their own survival, an image of all people's ultimate dependence on the grace and mercy of God. Children also have a great capacity for mirth and wonderment.[17] Holeton concludes, "All the baptized, including infants and young children, have, because of their baptism, the right to claim a place within the Christian assembly. This is not something that we, as adults, give them as a concession or something that we do for them but, rather, something that is theirs by right of baptism."[18] Pointing out that "there is unlikely to be any liturgical celebration which finds all members of the community fully engaged at every moment," Holeton recommends that worship "be planned so that each member of the liturgical assembly will be fully engaged at some time."[19]

Engagement is key not only for children but for every member of the assembly. Anglican priest Mark Earey points out, "Active participation can very soon sound as if we simply want people to do 'jobs' in church: to read the Bible, lead the prayers, or help distribute communion. Or it can suggest that we only 'participate' when we are speaking or singing." Earey prefers the term "engagement," explaining, "We are 'engaged' when every part of our

17. David Holeton, "Welcome Children, Welcome Me," *Anglican Theological Review* 82 (2000): 97-101.

18. Holeton, "Welcome Children, Welcome Me," pp. 101-2.

19. Holeton, "Welcome Children, Welcome Me," p. 106.

being, body, mind, and spirit, is taken up with what we are doing. We are engaged in worship when we know ourselves to be part of what is going on; in silence, in awe, in joy, in listening, in speaking, in moving, in sharing news. . . . To be *formed* and transformed by God through liturgical worship, one has to be engaged by it."[20]

Attention to each of the dimensions of worship will help those preparing worship to design a service that is deeply engaging. Missional worship will also call upon many members of the assembly to serve the assembly. Lutheran scholar Gordon Lathrop asks, "Is there a variety of . . . ministries — doorkeepers, lectors, cantors and singers, leaders of prayer, ministers of communion — or does the event seem to consist only of clergy marching around and telling other people what to do? On the other hand, while using a variety of ministers and while encouraging a sense of participation, does the meeting avoid having the whole group do or speak what one person should do or speak for all?"[21] Not only will missional worship call upon a number of ministers; it will consider how those ministers represent the assembly in all its diversity of age, race, ethnicity, gender, and class, and in the diversity to which it aspires. For example, in the seminary communities I have served, we have invited clergy of different races and ethnicities to preside at worship because the ordained leadership within the community has been entirely Euro-American.

Space

Jewish liturgical scholar Lawrence Hoffman, writing for both Jewish and Christian worshiping communities, says that designing a space for worship "requires a fine balance among three elements: structures that are beautiful, structures that work, and structures that incorporate enough tradition to make them readily recognizable as appropriately Christian or Jewish."[22] For most congregations most of the time, the space for worship is a given, and

20. Mark Earey, "Liturgical Formation and Education of the People of God," in *Worship-Shaped Life*, ed. Meyers and Gibson, pp. 52-53.

21. Lathrop, *Holy Things*, p. 167.

22. Lawrence A. Hoffman, *The Art of Public Prayer: Not for Clergy Only*, rev. ed. (Woodstock, Vt.: SkyLight Paths Publishing, 1999), p. 209.

they have developed patterns for using that space. From time to time, it is useful to step back and consider how well the worship environment balances beauty, efficiency, and tradition. Thomas Long found that "vital and faithful congregations creatively adapt the space and environment for worship."[23]

Drawing upon biblical models of places for worship, Long proposes that a worship space incorporate elements of a tent, a temple, and a house. Remembering the Israelites wandering in the wilderness, the worship space "should allow for movement within worship, should convey the truth that God's people are constantly on foot serving God in the world, and should communicate that the place of worship is not a cul-de-sac but a way station for pilgrims on the move." The Israelites eventually moved from tent to temple as a place of worship, and a worship space that preserves the memory of the temple "should communicate wonder and the transcendence of God, prompting worshipers to bow before the presence of the Holy One." In the first century, the followers of Jesus worshiped in houses where they could gather at a table for the breaking of bread. Here "the emphasis of worship [shifts] to the gathered assembly and to the instruction, conversation, interaction, and fellowship that takes place among the participants."[24] These models help us conceive of a church building as both "a house of God" and "a house of the people of God," as Anglican liturgist Christopher Irvine proposes: "an ordered space in which people can deliberately place themselves before God in gathering with others among whom Christ has promised to dwell."[25]

Long's biblical models suggest function as well as beauty and a recognizable connection to Christian tradition. Our spaces for Christian worship must be suitable for the activities of Christian worship. United Methodist scholar James White identifies seven types of space and within them three liturgical centers — font, pulpit, and table — which are the focus of the primary actions of worship.[26]

Gathering space. The assembly needs a space where people enter and

23. Long, *Beyond the Worship Wars,* p. 67.

24. Long, *Beyond the Worship Wars,* pp. 67-71.

25. Christopher Irvine, "Space," in *The Study of Liturgy and Worship,* ed. Day and Gordon-Taylor, p. 108.

26. James F. White, *Introduction to Christian Worship,* 3rd ed., revised and expanded (Nashville: Abingdon Press, 2000), p. 86.

make a transition into the place of assembly. Long found that vital churches not only incorporated elements of a house, a place of "warmth, accessibility, and hospitality," but also emphasized the "tent" function of worship "by making it clear that the gathering place is not a park but a gateway, not a place to stop but a place to continue on the journey."[27] Some of these signs of a way station pointed outside the church, to activities of mission and service, while others emphasized congregational life, both its history and its current structures and activities. The gathering space is thus a liminal space, a threshold suggesting the dynamic interplay of worship and mission in the world.

Movement space. Movement space is necessary, White argues, not only because Christian worship requires movement but also because Christians are a pilgrim people.[28] While the fixed pews of a church may limit movement, it may be possible to remove pews in order to create more space. At Grace Church in Kirkwood, Missouri, where the new baptismal font was installed, several pews were removed near the entrance to the worship space, not only creating room for the font but also allowing the assembly to move to the font and gather around it for baptisms.

Congregational space. "Basically, a church is a people place," White reminds us.[29] Long observes that vital congregations incorporate elements of a "house" and of a "temple" in their provision for congregational space. These congregations foster communion with one another, as in a house, by arranging seating so that people can see one another or by roping off pews so that people sit more closely together. They also foster communion with God, as in a temple. Long gives an example: "Even those churches with seating in the semi-round took care to ensure that the chairs were tilted somewhat toward the chancel and not just aimed at each other."[30]

Choir space. Members of a choir, Long reminds us, are both worship leaders and members of the assembly. Placing them front and center can make them performers, not just leaders, while placing them in a balcony reduces their ability to serve as leaders because the assembly cannot see them. Long recommends placing the choir "in a 'borderline' position — that is, in a

27. Long, *Beyond the Worship Wars*, p. 72.
28. White, *Introduction to Christian Worship*, p. 86.
29. White, *Introduction to Christian Worship*, p. 86.
30. Long, *Beyond the Worship Wars*, p. 74.

spot that places them among the worshiping congregation and allows their music to come from the gathered assembly but also in a spot that allows them to be seen and heard easily so that they can exercise musical leadership." He found different arrangements of choir space in vital congregations.[31]

Baptismal space. The space for baptism will recognize the public nature of baptism as incorporation into the body of Christ and as a reminder to those present of their own baptisms. White describes baptismal space as "people space in concentric circles." The candidates for baptism and the ministers of baptism will be at the center, surrounded by family members and sponsors, and the rest of the assembly will gather around them.[32]

Pulpit space. White acknowledges that a pulpit is a convenience, not a necessity. Yet, he asserts, "If the reading and preaching of God's word is understood as a fresh theophany each time the people of God gather, then we need physical testimony to that belief in the form of a pulpit. . . . The visual aspects of this form of Christ's presence are not to be taken lightly."[33]

Altar-table space. White reminds us that the role of the table "is to serve, not to dominate. Thus we need to avoid such barriers as excessive height, the glare of too much direct light, over-scaled furnishings, enclosure, and other ways of making this space seem a remote and detached holy spot."[34] At All Saints' Episcopal Church in Chicago, a nineteenth-century church building, the table sits in the midst of the congregational space. Originally designed in a longitudinal arrangement with pews facing the same direction, a raised area for the choir, and a sanctuary with a high altar beyond, the space was rearranged near the end of the twentieth century. The nave (that is, the area originally designed for congregational seating) is nearly square. The pews are arranged into four sections, each angled to face the center of the room, and the table is set in the center. While this placement provides easy accessibility to the table and so in some ways has the character of a house, a member of the congregation assured me that they don't place their coffee cups on the table. Its use for the communion meal has given it a sacred character, one more associated with temple than with house. In contrast, at St. Gregory

31. Long, *Beyond the Worship Wars*, pp. 74-75.
32. White, *Introduction to Christian Worship*, p. 87.
33. White, *Introduction to Christian Worship*, p. 88.
34. White, *Introduction to Christian Worship*, pp. 87-88.

of Nyssa Episcopal Church in San Francisco, where the table is also in the center of the room, the congregation intentionally uses the same table for communion and then afterwards for refreshments in order to underscore the connection between the communion meal and our daily bread. Yet here, too, the assembly distinguishes their uses of the table. When the table is covered with a cloth for the celebration of communion, they show respect by taking care not to place worship books on it or lean on it. When the cloth is not on the table, members of the assembly relate to it more casually as a coffee table or a work table.

Considering the functions of worship will enable those preparing worship to determine the most effective way to use their space so that members of the assembly can be engaged in the actions of worship. Attention to lighting and sight lines as well as acoustics are important considerations. But our places for worship must not only be functional; they must also be beautiful. Clayton Schmit argues that art is necessary in worship because it enables us to express our adoration of God: "We need the windows of art and the perspectives of artists to provide us a glimpse of God and a means by which to respond to God's goodness."[35] The decoration of a worship space might well incorporate elements of the local culture as well as materials from other cultures. For example, Alan Kreider and Eleanor Kreider have found that some Western Christians have imported Salvadoran painted crosses to adorn their churches: "These crosses have become part of the fabric of worship, revealing the themes of God and Christ involved in the lives and struggles of the people."[36]

Time

As discussed in Chapter 3, many churches keep the feasts and seasons of the church year, enabling them to encounter much of the biblical narrative of salvation history from creation to new creation. The liturgical calendar

35. Clayton J. Schmit, *Sent and Gathered: A Worship Manual for the Missional Church* (Grand Rapids: Baker Academic, 2009), p. 85.

36. Alan Kreider and Eleanor Kreider, *Worship and Mission after Christendom* (Scottdale, Pa., and Waterloo, Ontario: Herald Press, 2011), p. 213.

allows assemblies to focus on different aspects of the paschal mystery while also celebrating the totality of God's mission of reconciliation each time they worship. For churches that follow a lectionary, the appointed lessons each week give particular shape to the character of the feast or the season.

Those preparing worship will take account of the calendar in every aspect of worship. "Time" on the worship matrix intersects with other dimensions of worship and with each major movement of worship. The season or feast of the year is a consideration when planning the decoration of the worship *space* and perhaps also its arrangement. Many churches follow the pattern of liturgical colors that became set during the Middle Ages and have paraments (hangings for altar, pulpit, etc.) in these colors. As the congregation becomes familiar with them, the colors signal seasonal changes and help set the tone for the service. During the late 1990s, St. Nicholas Episcopal Church in Elk Grove Village, Illinois, re-ordered its worship space so that the congregational seating as well as the table and lectern were easily movable. For each major season, they moved the furniture into different configurations, creating different experiences of their space and so establishing a different atmosphere for worship each season.

In a similar way, the church season might be evident in a particular ritual *object* such as an Advent wreath or a paschal (Easter) candle. A congregation might also use *actions* to reflect seasonal change — for example, adopting different postures, kneeling more during the penitential season of Lent but not at all during the festal season of Easter, or processing outside, through the neighborhood, on Palm Sunday as they remember Jesus' triumphal entry into Jerusalem.

Some *texts* and especially *music* have long been associated with particular feasts and seasons, and their use is an important marker of the liturgical time. Those who prepare worship will take account of the liturgical calendar for each movement of worship — for example, selecting a song for gathering that marks the season, or using a text specific to the feast in the Eucharistic prayer.

Other aspects of time might also affect preparation for worship. National holidays such as the birthday of Martin Luther King Jr. might be recognized in worship, and some congregations have their own calendars. Alan Kreider and Eleanor Kreider point out that congregations can remember their particular history and identity in different ways. Commemoration of a patronal

saint, a practice used especially in Anglican and Roman Catholic congregations, can recognize the saint's charism and how it shapes the congregation's
participation in God's mission. Some churches remember their founders
and celebrate their contributions to the community. Kreider and Kreider
comment, "These [practices] can help Christians enter into God's story and
. . . ask useful questions: What does God call us to cherish as 'provisions'?
What does God call us to offload as 'baggage'?"[37]

The time of day is less often a factor in preparing worship for the Sunday
assembly, but it may be a consideration when preparing other services. Since
the early centuries of the church, Christians have marked the beginning and
the end of the day with prayer. At the end of the day, as night falls and lamps
are lit, Christians remember Christ as the light of the world. An ancient
Greek hymn written for Christian evening prayer expresses this clearly: "O
gracious Light, pure brightness of the ever-living Father in heaven, O Jesus
Christ, holy and blessed!"[38] In addition, during evening prayer Christians
have asked for protection during the coming night. At the beginning of the
day, Christians offer praise and thanksgiving for the new day, the rising sun
rather than candles reminding the assembly of Christ the light.

Objects

Christian worship is not just a cerebral activity involving our brains. In
Christian worship we gather around things, objects which are filled with
meaning. Water, bread, wine, and the Bible are the primary symbols of our
worship.

Anglican liturgist George Guiver explains, "The word 'symbol' comes
from two Greek words meaning 'thrown together.' Two realities are set in
relationship: the symbol itself and the deeper and richer reality it evokes."[39]
While we can reflect on symbols and ponder their meaning, a symbol cannot

---

37. Kreider and Kreider, *Worship and Mission after Christendom*, pp. 80-81.

38. *The Book of Common Prayer and Administration of the Sacraments and Other Rites
and Ceremonies of the Church, Together with The Psalter or Psalms of David* (New York: Church
Hymnal Corp., 1979), p. 118.

39. George Guiver, "Sign and Symbol," in *The Study of Liturgy and Worship*, ed. Day and
Gordon-Taylor, p. 33.

be fully explained: "there is a surplus [of meaning] that cannot be identified or described with precision."[40] Our Christian symbols are associated
with stories: the water of baptism with Jesus' baptism; the bread and wine
of communion with Jesus' table fellowship. These stories, though, do not
exhaust the meaning but rather add depth and complexity as they intersect
with other stories of Scripture — for example, the Exodus account of the
Israelites' safe passage through the Red Sea and God's provision of manna
in the wilderness.

Abundant use of symbols allows them to speak vividly. Gordon Lathrop
points out, "We are given by the risen Christ the use of a book, bread and
wine, water. If we use these gifts in such a way as to let them stand in clarity,
undiminished and unobscured, they will show us the remarkable connections that exist between our worship and daily life, between the center of
worship and its cultural context."[41] Baptism with a copious amount of water,
enough to drown in, will evoke the central meanings of burial, birth, and
bathing. Reading Scripture from a Bible of significant size and dignity, rather
than from a page of the worship leaflet, will convey the awesome strength of
the peculiar story of God's love for the world. Celebrating communion with a
large loaf of baked bread and an ample cup of wine will evoke the sustenance
of a meal more clearly than a tiny communion wafer and individual-sized
cup of wine. Lathrop suggests that attention to a rich, vivid communion
celebration will enable the assembly to make connections to daily life, to
understand food as a gift from God that is to be received with thanksgiving
and shared with those in need: "As long as a meal remains the primary act
of Christian worship and as long as Christian believers see the connection
between that meal and our daily tables, issues of world hunger and of the
distribution of resources that people need to live will not disappear from the
agenda of Christian daily life."[42]

Of course, the Bible, bread, wine, and water are not the only objects we
use in worship. Recognizing these as primary, however, enables those preparing worship to consider how other objects are used. Sometimes these other
objects assume a more significant place. For example, a paschal candle might

---

40. Guiver, "Sign and Symbol," p. 33.
41. Lathrop, "Liturgy and Mission in the North American Context," pp. 208-9.
42. Lathrop, "Liturgy and Mission in the North American Context," p. 209.

be prominent not only for the great fifty days of Easter but also at baptism and at funerals, reminding us of the light of Christ that gives light to all creation. In most worship spaces, a cross will be prominent. Clayton Schmit urges, "Let there be a single, large cross that stands *iconically* at the frontier between our need for salvation and God's satisfaction of that need on such an instrument of death. And let a single, visible cross stand *symbolically* as a magnet for shared and expanding perceptions of God's grace."[43]

Reflection on symbols can deepen their meaning for people and so is an important element of Christian formation, as George Guiver points out: "Most symbols benefit from the attempt (always only partially successful) to analyze and explain their significance." Yet, he continues, "Simultaneous explanation kills symbols, silences them, truncates their complex evocations. It is a golden liturgical rule never to explain things while we are doing it."[44] When we attempt to explain a symbol in the midst of worship, we close down meaning, as Clayton Schmit acknowledges: "Once we tell people what a symbol means, our *stated* meaning crowds out or masks any other meanings that might otherwise occur to the participant."[45] Those preparing worship will consider carefully how to use symbols so that they are clear and evocative, inviting rich associations with Scripture and with human experience, engaging people in wonder and awe at God's gracious love for the world.

Actions

Gestures, postures, and movement in worship involve the whole person in the activities of worship. In addition, writes Jeremy Haselock, they "affirm the incarnation, confirming the sanctity of our bodies, involving them in prayer and declaring them to be our primary instrument for worship."[46] Some bodily activity expresses our relationship with God — for example, arms uplifted in praise or heads bowed in reverence. Other activity expresses relationship with the gathered assembly, says Haselock: "By the deliberate use

43. Schmit, *Sent and Gathered*, p. 121.
44. Guiver, "Sign and Symbol," p. 35.
45. Schmit, *Sent and Gathered*, p. 123.
46. Jeremy Haselock, "Gestures," in *The New Westminster Dictionary of Liturgy and Worship*, ed. Paul Bradshaw (Louisville: Westminster John Knox Press, 2002), p. 227.

of a common body-language in the worshipping assembly, unity in ritual, belief, and community is affirmed and through the discipline of ceremonial action, minds are focused on the words and actions of the liturgy and people learn to pray with the totality of their being."[47]

In this post-Christendom era, shared assumptions for Christian behavior are diminishing, including assumptions about behavior in the assembly. Bridget Nichols, citing French liturgical scholar Patrick Prétot, describes "consequences of a vanishing familiarity with liturgical behavior: the loss of a common memory; general uncertainty about how to behave in gatherings for public prayer; and the lack of any sort of gestural vocabulary that marks the transition from everyday life to a setting which requires concentration on the presence of God."[48] Unfamiliarity with liturgical behavior is true particularly of those with little or no experience of Christian worship. Those preparing worship will consider how to welcome newcomers and orient them to the behaviors of the assembly, behaviors that cultivate both relationship with God and relationship with the people of God.

Anglican bishops Mary Gray-Reeves and Michael Perham describe their experience of the Sunday assembly at St. Paul's Episcopal Church in Seattle, where they "experienced most fully the power of shared gesture for building up a sense of the body of Christ and of a community intent on God." They describe a service that "was well-ordered Anglican liturgy of a familiar kind, entirely conventional in its shape and text." Three elements "contributed to its being a stunning and moving experience":

> First . . . there was a deep spirit of engagement by the entire congregation. They did indeed "carry you in worship," as their service sheet said, by their prayerfulness and attentiveness. . . . The second element was "performance" and as part of it, very significantly, "pace." Clearly everything had been carefully choreographed and rehearsed, yet it did not feel precious or stilted; the whole liturgy was a beautiful "dance" in which the performers were entirely caught up. . . . The third element was the non-verbal participation by the entire community — the turning west at the beginning

47. Haselock, "Gestures," p. 228.
48. Bridget Nichols, "Prayer," in *The Study of Liturgy and Worship*, ed. Day and Gordon-Taylor, p. 45.

and the end, the reverencing of the cross at the entry, the mutual bowing between ministers and congregation — creating a sense of a community engaged in something entirely corporate and significant for them.[49]

Assemblies in different worshiping traditions will have different sensibilities about appropriate posture, gesture, and movement. Those preparing worship will consider how best to foster the full engagement of the assembly through bodily activity. Over time, the core members of an assembly can learn a shared set of worship behaviors that will provide a model for visitors. In so doing, the assembly will begin to convey a sense both of the building up of the body of Christ and of a community growing in the knowledge and love of God.

Texts

Worship is more than purposeful action and the use of ritual objects. The texts of worship also play a significant role in the congregation's missional work for the common good. Anglican liturgical scholar Juliette Day points out, "Christianity has placed a great emphasis on words: Jesus Christ is the 'Word of God' made intelligible by the Incarnation; the gift of the Spirit was publicly demonstrated by the apostles' preaching in all the languages of those present; when in the Gospels, the disciples ask Jesus how to pray, he gives them the example of the Lord's Prayer as a text in itself and as a model for the content of prayer in general."[50]

In worship, people address God and one another, and God speaks to the people of God. The language of the texts in which people address God and one another is "collective speech," which means "that in syntax, rhythm, and vocabulary it may be easily spoken; and that the meaning conveyed has the potential to be assented to by all."[51] This is true not only of the words that members of the assembly speak, but also of the words that leaders speak. Liturgical scholar Ruth Duck makes this point with an example from a con-

49. Mary Gray-Reeves and Michael Perham, *The Hospitality of God: Emerging Worship for a Missional Church* (New York: Seabury Books; London: SPCK, 2011), pp. 100-101.

50. Juliette Day, "Language," in *The Study of Liturgy and Worship*, ed. Day and Gordon-Taylor, p. 65.

51. Day, "Language," p. 66.

fession of sin in *The Book of Common Prayer.* The text "We have followed too much the devices and desires of our own hearts"[52] uses alliteration and rhythm in a manner that makes it easy to speak aloud, and the image of "devices and desires of our own hearts," though not common speech today, is a vivid metaphor that enables us to ponder our sins. Duck suggests an alternative that has a similar meaning: "The direction for our perambulations is provided by our defense mechanisms and libidinal urges." This text, she says, would be unsuitable for public prayer because of the complexity of the words and the awkward phrasing of the sentence.[53]

Learning texts by heart. It is not enough for the words of our worship to be easy to speak aloud. Thomas Long found that vital and faithful congregations have "a significant repertoire of worship elements and responses that the congregation knows by heart."[54] Just as a congregation can learn a shared set of worship behaviors that draw the assembly into communion with God and with one another, so also learning texts "by heart" enables those words to be engraved on our hearts, creating "a deep memory of how we are to be in the presence of God."[55] As members of the assembly learn the words, they become less dependent on printed text, whether in a worship leaflet or a service book, and more able to engage the experience of worship. In the vital congregations that Long studied, "The bulletins were mainly for visitors, and they were crafted as such. . . . The goal was to wean regular worshipers away from the bulletin. . . . When prayers and other elements of worship move from the page to the memory, they gain the capacity to gather experiences unto themselves and to become expressions of a full and rich devotion."[56]

The language of the people. The importance of selecting or crafting texts that the assembly can easily speak aloud and learn by heart as one body is not the only criterion for the language of worship. In some multicultural congregations, the assembly may regularly include worshipers for whom English is

---

52. "The Order for Morning Prayer, Daily throughout the Year," *The Book of Common Prayer* 1662, available at http://www.eskimo.com/~lhowell/bcp1662/daily/morning.html. See also *The Book of Common Prayer* 1979, p. 41.

53. Ruth C. Duck, *Finding Words for Worship: A Guide for Leaders* (Louisville: Westminster John Knox Press, 1995), p. 25.

54. Long, *Beyond the Worship Wars,* p. 86.

55. Long, *Beyond the Worship Wars,* p. 86.

56. Long, *Beyond the Worship Wars,* pp. 92-93.

a second language or even a third or fourth language. Some congregations hold regular worship services in different languages and on occasion come together for one service with worshipers fluent in different languages. Sometimes a larger assembly comes together for a special occasion.

The experience of the Taizé community is instructive. Because the first members of the community were French-speaking, the language of worship, including the proclamation of Scripture, was French. New members of the community were required to learn the language. By the late 1960s, large numbers of people from different countries were visiting the community, and they tried valiantly to participate fully in the community's worship, even though many of them did not speak French. To include these pilgrims, the brothers began reading Scripture in different languages.[57] At most services today, with thousands of people from throughout the world visiting the community each week, Scripture is proclaimed in two languages. Then one or two sentences that encapsulate the essence of the passage are read in several other languages. The brothers take care to select passages that do not require explanation so that worshipers can hear the heart of the scriptural message and ponder its significance for their lives.[58]

In the reformations that swept through Europe during the sixteenth century, proclaiming Scripture and worshiping in the language of the people were both important and costly. (Some of those who dared to translate the Bible lost their lives for this offense.) The preface to the first English prayer book explained that, "whereas St. Paul would have such language spoken to the people in the Church, as they might understand, and have profit by hearing the same, the Service in the Church of England (these many years) hath been read in Latin to the people, which they understood not; so that they have heard with their ears only; and their hearts, spirit, and mind have not been edified thereby."[59] Reading Scripture in the language of the people has a missional purpose, serving to build up the assembly in the knowledge and love of God, enabling its members to be shaped by the peculiar stories of God's work in human history.

57. Jason Brian Santos, *A Community Called Taizé: A Story of Prayer, Worship, and Reconciliation* (Downers Grove, Ill.: IVP Books, 2008), pp. 105-6.

58. Santos, *A Community Called Taizé*, pp. 113-14.

59. "Historical Documents," *The Book of Common Prayer* 1979, p. 866.

The Taizé community's use of multiple languages for the proclamation of Scripture reflects several aspects of the dynamic interplay of worship and culture identified in the Nairobi Statement of the Lutheran World Federation. The practice of proclaiming Scripture at worship is transcultural, and the worship at Taizé assumes the significance of Scripture for all worshipers, regardless of the language(s) they know. By using the language of pilgrims from different places, the brothers contextualize worship for visitors who understand those languages. Even for worshipers fluent in multiple languages, there is usually a heart language, the language at the core of one's being that most fully expresses the yearning for God. Hearing Scripture in this language, even just a sentence or two, can create opportunity for a profound connection with God as the Scriptures speak to one's innermost being. At the same time, for those not fluent in a particular language, the proclamation of Scripture in a foreign tongue can become a cross-cultural experience, a reminder of the marvelous diversity of the human community and of God's work in many different places. It is also an act of hospitality, as worshipers hear unfamiliar languages and yield space for others in the assembly to hear and understand.

At Taizé, the proclamation of Scripture in different languages is complemented by chants sung in different tongues. The 2013-2014 book of chants for use in worship in the Church of Reconciliation includes texts in fifty different languages, and many of the 153 songs in the book can be sung in several languages. The texts are short and are repeated multiple times as each chant is sung, enabling many worshipers to learn texts by heart and so engage deeply in the prayer. The memorability of the texts is evident as pilgrims sing the texts at other times during the day — for example, as grace before a meal or at the beginning of a Bible study.

Few assemblies include worshipers who speak as many diverse languages as do the Taizé community's pilgrims. But the Taizé practice of proclaiming Scripture suggests ways that multilingual assemblies can engage worshipers who understand different languages. A passage of Scripture can be read in two or more languages. If more than one reading is included in worship, each passage can be read in a different language. Reading a brief excerpt in different languages expands the reach of Scripture to individual worshipers and invites the assembly to recognize God's work among diverse people. The assembly can also include other worship texts in different languages, and if short texts are used repeatedly, an assembly can learn them by heart — for example, *Kyrie eleison* ("Lord, have mercy") as a response to intercessory prayer. Providing a translation, whether written or projected on a screen, allows worshipers to understand a text in a language they do not know. Even when the assembly does not include people who speak different languages, using another language can be a significant cross-cultural experience. Alan Kreider and Eleanor Kreider point out that many people in the West "have lived in monolingual settings. . . . A gift to us Westerners from worldwide Christians can be the reminder that it is important to learn another language and to incorporate words of another language in our services."[60]

Inclusive language. In recent decades, English-speaking Christians have been addressing another aspect of the language of worship that involves not only the translation of Scripture but also other texts written or selected for worship: the use of inclusive language. The English Language Liturgical Consultation, an international and ecumenical body, has translated liturgical texts commonly used by major Christian churches throughout the English-speaking world — for example, the Nicene Creed and the Apostles' Creed. During the 1980s, when this body revised translations that were published in the early 1970s, one of its guiding principles was the use of inclusive language. They explained, "The Consultation recognized that, because of changes in the received meaning of the words, the use of 'man' or 'men' for 'human being(s)' can be misleading and is no longer generally acceptable in liturgical texts."[61] In the Nicene Creed, for example, an earlier translation read, "For *us men* and for our salvation he [Jesus Christ] came down from heaven." The Consultation retranslated this as "For *us* and for our salvation he came down from heaven."[62]

More recent translations of Scripture have also attended to changing English usage, enabling congregations to use inclusive language for the proclamation of Scripture in the assembly. For example, the Contemporary English Version of the Bible, published in 1995, explains,

60. Kreider and Kreider, *Worship and Mission after Christendom,* pp. 214-15.

61. English Language Liturgical Consultation, *Praying Together* (Norwich: Canterbury Press, 1988), p. xii.

62. English Language Liturgical Consultation, *Praying Together,* pp. 9, 12. For the earlier translation, see International Consultation on English Texts, *Prayers We Have in Common* (London: Geoffrey Chapman, 1970, 1971), p. 11; emphasis added.

In everyday speech "gender generic" or "inclusive" language is used, because it sounds most natural to people today. This means that where the biblical languages require masculine nouns or pronouns when both men and women are intended, this intention must be reflected in translation. . . . The Greek text of Matthew 16:24 is literally, "If anyone wants to follow me, *he* must deny *himself* and take up *his* cross and follow me." The Contemporary English Version shifts to a form which is still accurate, and at the same time more effective in English: "If any of *you* want to be my followers, *you* must forget about *yourself*. *You* must take up *your* cross and follow me."[63]

Other recent translations, such as the New Revised Standard Version (1990) and the Common English Bible (2011), have made similar decisions about translation.

The missional implications of inclusive language are significant. Our language must reflect the truth that God's reconciling love embraces all, that in Christ "there is no longer male and female" (Gal. 3:28). As norms of English language shift, the language of worship must also shift.

The language we use to speak to and about God is more complicated. Liturgical scholar Gail Ramshaw points out, "Like Judaism and Islam, Christianity has denied that God is a sexual being; yet Christian texts, including the Hebrew and Greek of the Bible, have spoken as if God were of the masculine gender. Male terms for God, such as 'Father' and 'King,' have predominated in many Christian pieties."[64] Hymnwriter Brian Wren agrees: "The systematic and almost exclusive use of male God-language, in a faith in which God is revealed as incarnate in a male human being, gives a distorted vision of God and supports male dominance in church and society."[65] Wren, like Ramshaw and other Christians, advocates the use of many names for God.

The ways we address God and refer to God in worship must offer us

63. Preface to *The Holy Bible: The Contemporary English Version* (Nashville, Atlanta, London, Vancouver: Thomas Nelson Publishers, 1995), p. x; emphasis in the original.
64. Gail Ramshaw, "Inclusive Language," in *The New Westminster Dictionary of Liturgy and Worship*, ed. Bradshaw, p. 244.
65. Brian Wren, *What Language Shall I Borrow? God-talk in Worship: A Male Response to Feminist Theology* (New York: Crossroad; London: SCM Press, 1989), pp. 4-5.

multiple ways to imagine the breadth of God's love and the promise of new creation. Scripture tells us that God created us, male and female, in the image of God (Gen. 1:27). When the only nouns and pronouns used in worship to speak of God are male, it is difficult for women to imagine themselves as created in the image of God, much less to claim their full and equal dignity with men. Expanding our language about God is thus a missional concern.

One approach, evident in the psalter in the 1993 Presbyterian *Book of Common Worship,* employs felicitous translations that do not use masculine pronouns in reference to God. In this psalter, as well as in the English Language Liturgical Consultation's alternative translations of the canticles *Magnificat* (the Song of Mary; Luke 1:46-55) and *Benedictus* (the Song of Zechariah; Luke 1:68-79), God is addressed as "you" rather than "he," even though "he" is the literal translation of the Hebrew and Greek. The English Language Liturgical Consultation explained, "In Hebrew prayer God is praised indirectly in the third person ["he"] as well as by direct address ["you"]. The third and second persons may alternate, as for instance in the Song of Hannah (1 Samuel 2) and frequently in the psalms. There is also ancient liturgical precedent for converting an original third-person address to the second person, as in the *Sanctus,* where the original 'his glory' [Isaiah 6:3] has long been rendered as 'your glory.' In contemporary English, direct address is more natural."[66]

Another approach to worship language about God is to expand the range of names, metaphors, and images that are used. A bishop of the Anglican Church in Aotearoa, New Zealand, and Polynesia once told me that *A New Zealand Prayer Book,* published in 1989, uses over two hundred different names and designations for God. For example, the service of Night Prayer includes an alternative to the Lord's Prayer that addresses God as "Eternal Spirit, Earth-maker, Pain-bearer, Life-giver, Source of all that is and that shall be, Father and Mother of us all, Loving God, in whom is heaven."[67]

The seventeenth-century hymn "O Sacred Head, Sore Wounded" asks,

66. English Language Liturgical Consultation, *Praying Together,* p. 34. Some recent translations of Scripture — for example, the Contemporary English Version — render the Hebrew of Isaiah 6:3 as "your glory" rather than "his glory."

67. Anglican Church in Aotearoa, New Zealand, and Polynesia, "Night Prayer," in *A New Zealand Prayer Book* (Christchurch, New Zealand: Genesis Publications, 1989), p. 181.

"What language shall I borrow to thank thee, dearest friend . . . ?"[68] What language shall we borrow to speak of the all-embracing love of God, to tell the odd story of God's love affair with the world? The language of our liturgy must enable all who worship to understand themselves as beloved children of God, created in the image of God, and so called to participate in God's mission of reconciling love for the world.

Music

Vital and faithful congregations, writes Thomas Long, "emphasize congregational music that is both excellent and eclectic in style and genre."[69] Decisions about music for worship can be divisive, a fact that reflects the power of music. Long comments, "A person's music is a powerful alloy of memory and emotion, experience and conviction, expression and aspiration. No wonder feelings are aroused, defenses mounted, and passionate arguments ignited whenever the topic of music and worship is raised."[70] Yet the congregations that Long studied had found a way through the "worship wars" engendered by the selection of music. In these congregations, the music was congregational, carrying the assembly along through the entire worship service, "the thread that ties the flow of the service together."[71] The music in these congregations was also excellent, "as measured by inherent musical standards," and effective, "as measured by how well it actually works in a given congregation to give voice and expression to praise."[72] Finally, in these vital congregations, the music was eclectic, widely varied in style and genre, which Long describes as a broad bandwidth, using a wide range of musical idioms.[73]

While Long emphasizes congregational music, he also recognizes a place for choral or instrumental music. In the vital congregations that he studied,

---

68. Paul Gerhardt, "O Sacred Head, Sore Wounded," trans. James Waddell Alexander, in *The Hymnal 1982* (New York: Church Hymnal Corp., 1985), #168, 169.

69. Long, *Beyond the Worship Wars*, p. 60.

70. Long, *Beyond the Worship Wars*, p. 55.

71. Long, *Beyond the Worship Wars*, p. 61.

72. Long, *Beyond the Worship Wars*, p. 63.

73. Long, *Beyond the Worship Wars*, pp. 63-64.

such music was not a performance but part of the worship, integral to the flow of the service and expressing thoughts and emotions of members of the assembly.[74] I recently worshiped with a seminary community in the midst of a "quiet day": classes were suspended, which allowed time for reflection and prayer. The Eucharist offered several opportunities for silence, and the preacher emphasized the significance of silence, telling us that we would listen after communion to a recording of the hymn "Let All Mortal Flesh Keep Silence," sung to the seventeenth-century tune "Picardy."[75] I was initially disappointed that the assembly would not be allowed to sing. But the voices and the instrumentation in the recording blended together to create a rich and haunting sound that gave new depth to the hymn, and I was drawn into wonder and praise.

The criteria that Long identifies are helpful, yet there is more to consider when preparing missional worship. Music is an opportunity to blend voices, literally bringing them into harmony with one another and so embodying our communion with one another. Music also draws us more deeply into communion with God, as Augustine of Hippo explained in his commentary on Psalm 72: "Those who sing praise do not only praise, but praise joyfully; those who sing praise not only sing, but also love the one to whom they sing. In the praise of one who is confessing [God] there is a public proclamation, in the song of the lover, affectionate love."[76] By drawing worshipers into communion with God and one another, music enables the assembly to participate in the mission of God, to enact God's reconciling love for the world.

Music can also build communion beyond the members of the assembly. Eleanor Kreider and Alan Kreider recount a visit of two Zimbabwean Christians to their church in Indiana: "They brought us a song that captured for

74. Long, *Beyond the Worship Wars*, p. 62.

75. "Let All Mortal Flesh Keep Silence," in *The Hymnal 1982*, #324.

76. *Qui enim cantat laudem, non solum laudat, sed etiam hilariter laudat: qui cantat laudem, non solum cantat, sed et amat eum quem cantat. In laude confitentis est praedicatio: in cantico amantis affectio.* Augustine, *Enarratio in Psalmum 72*, in *S. Aurelii Augustini Opera Omnia — editio latina, Patrologia Latina* 36, available at http://www.augustinus.it/latino/esposizioni_salmi/index2.htm. My translation is based on that of John Zuhlsdorf, "St. Augustine: He Who Sings Prays Twice," 20 February 2006, http://wdtprs.com/blog/2006/02/st-augustine-he-who-sings-prays-twice/.

them the character of their church back home: *Som'landela, som'landel'u-Jesu* ('We will follow, we will follow Jesus'). We learned the song on the spot, and it has become precious to us. As we use this Zulu song in our own worship, we remember our two Zimbabwean brothers and the churches they represent, and we too pledge ourselves to follow Jesus anew."[77] By strengthening commitment to the gospel, such cross-cultural song is an expression of mission, bearing witness to God's redemptive love revealed among diverse Christian communities and uniting Christians from different parts of the world.

Cross-cultural music can also express solidarity with the oppressed, as Graham Maule from the Wild Goose Resource Group explains.[78] In the early 1980s, at the time that black South Africans were living under the strictures of apartheid, a friend had given his colleague, John Bell, a collection of South African freedom songs. Bell began introducing these into the repertoire of their worship group, a voluntary group of sixteen young people who met weekly to sing new songs and work on new liturgical material and approaches. The songs were sung in many places — at youth events, workshops, and festivals. And, in the years before the overthrow of apartheid, the songs were sung weekly outside the South African consulate in the center of Glasgow. Thereafter the songs were incorporated in Wild Goose books, recordings, and other resources.

In 1987, some of the Wild Goose Worship Group visited the *Kirchentag*, a huge church festival in Germany. One night at a service in a suburban church, the Reverend Allan Boesak of South Africa, one of the foremost Christian leaders opposing the apartheid regime, preached the sermon. Afterwards a woman from the Wild Goose Group approached Boesak and told him that people in Scotland were singing the freedom songs in their churches and on the streets. Visibly moved, his eyes filling with tears, he told her to send the thanks of his people to the people of Scotland, to let them know how important it would be to his people to know that their songs were being sung, even though they themselves were often abused, beaten, and imprisoned for doing the same at funerals and on marches, if they weren't prevented from singing altogether.

77. Kreider and Kreider, *Worship and Music after Christendom*, p. 211.
78. Graham Maule, e-mail to the author, 8 October 2013.

Later, other South Africans who visited Scotland would echo the same sentiment. They, like Boesak, were stunned to find their songs being sung in such a different cultural context. That Christians from an entirely different part of the world would sing their songs was a concrete message of hope for these South Africans. Because other Christians used and embraced their music, they knew they were not alone in their struggle and so were encouraged to continue their efforts to end apartheid in their homeland.

The cross-cultural use of music is important, say Eleanor Kreider and Alan Kreider, "for worship that reflects only one culture misses the opportunity to prefigure the cosmic reconciliation that is the goal of God's mission; it makes it hard for the worshippers to glimpse heavenly worship in which people from every tribe and territory are worshipping God and the Lamb."[79] United Methodist musician C. Michael Hawn, while encouraging the use of music from other cultures, does, however, sound a note of caution that churches which do so need to take care not to stereotype or denigrate the sending culture.[80] When done respectfully, the cross-cultural use of music in worship, as well as in other contexts, is an important expression of mission, bespeaking our connections to one another as well as expressing the yearning for justice and the promise of new life that are integral to the gospel.

Silence

Describing their experience of worship at St. Paul's Episcopal Church in Seattle, Anglican bishops Michael Perham and Mary Gray-Reeves report that the assembly repeatedly throughout the service was invited to keep a time of "silence and stillness."[81] The parish Web site explains this use of silence: "An important part of our worship is punctuation of the liturgy with periods of silence. Our brief or sometimes lingering moments of silence focus our attention on the present, rather than rushing to the next thing. We listen, we

79. Kreider and Kreider, *Worship and Music after Christendom*, p. 20.

80. C. Michael Hawn, "Praying Globally: Pitfalls and Possibilities of Cross-cultural Liturgical Appropriation," in *Christian Worship Worldwide: Expanding Horizons, Deepening Practices*, ed. Charles E. Farhadian (Grand Rapids: Wm. B. Eerdmans, 2007), pp. 219-24.

81. Gray-Reeves and Perham, *The Hospitality of God*, p. 80.

engage, we reflect, we move on, we stay grounded."[82] For Gray-Reeves and Perham, these periods of silence were an essential element of the pacing and the "deep spirit of engagement" they experienced in the assembly that morning.[83]

In Chapter 3, we discussed the use of silence as a form of response to the Word. In the silence after the Word in worship in the Taizé community, pilgrims have the freedom to encounter God or the Scripture in their own ways. Jason Brian Santos describes his experience of adjusting to these silences in worship:

> In retrospect, I . . . struggled with what I was supposed to be doing during the silence. . . . I'm so used to living a life that is full of tasks that need to be accomplished. As a young person, I was taught to actively pray. . . . Words, whether in my head or out loud, were the medium I used to communicate to God. . . . What I failed to learn how to do was to sit before God and listen and remain in the stillness of the moment and allow God to penetrate my soul.[84]

In addition to its use as a response to Scripture, silence can be effective at several other points in worship. A time of silence after the presider bids "Let us pray" enables the assembly to gather itself in prayer, ready to say "Amen" in response to the presider's prayer. Silence after the confession of sin is introduced offers an opportunity to reflect on one's own sins before joining the assembly in a shared liturgical text. Clayton Schmit finds that the "music of silence . . . is too infrequently provided. Sometimes we need to be surrounded by an aural vacuum so that it can be filled with silent prayer and so that, through it, we can perceive that still small voice."[85] Like shared body language and memorized texts, members of the assembly can learn, over time, to enter the silence in communion with one another and so also tune their hearts to God.

---

82. "Worship and Music," St. Paul's Episcopal Church, Seattle, Washington, available at http://www.stpaulseattle.org/worship-and-music/.

83. Gray-Reeves and Perham, *The Hospitality of God*, p. 80.

84. Santos, *A Community Called Taizé*, pp. 117-18.

85. Schmit, *Sent and Gathered*, p. 104.

Embodying a Gospel Vision

When worship is prepared thoughtfully and creatively, the various dimensions of worship — people, space, time, objects, actions, texts, music, and silence — work together to engage the community in its common work and to foster communion with God and with the people of God, and so enact and signify the mission of God. Since all worship is a response to God, good preparation leaves room for the Spirit to work among the assembly. Carefully prepared worship is also open to the world, making space for outsiders to enter and participate and to offer their gifts and wisdom.

Well-crafted worship reflects a gospel vision, an understanding that God is at work in the world, seeking to restore all people to harmony with God, with one another, and with all of creation. Well-designed worship proclaims and celebrates the peculiar story of God's ways with the world, so that members of the assembly remember not only who God is but also God's claims on them, that God sends them in mission to work for the common good.

Concluding Reflections: Missional Worship as Work for the Common Good

Through Christ, then, let us continually offer a sacrifice of praise to God, that is, the fruit of lips that confess his name. Do not neglect to do good and to share what you have, for such sacrifices are pleasing to God.

Hebrews 13:15-16

For Christians, participation in the assembly for worship is essential. In the assembly, the people of God celebrate and participate in God's self-giving love for the life of the world. The members of the assembly remember Jesus incarnate, crucified, and risen, and they embody a sure and certain hope for God's reign of justice, peace, and love, the reign that Jesus proclaimed and enacted. Through the Spirit, the Crucified and Risen One is present in the assembly. Worship establishes the assembly's distinctive identity as the body of Christ and sends the assembly forth to be the body of Christ in the world. Worship and mission flow into and out of one another, as they do in our Möbius strip and in our spinning top, so that worship is missional and mission is worshipful.

I was vividly reminded of the significance of worship at the beginning of Advent 2013, when I attended a production of *War Horse* on the London stage, then two days later participated in the Advent Carol Service at Canterbury Cathedral. *War Horse,* based on a novel by Michael Morpurgo, tells the story of World War I from the perspective of a horse reared on a farm in

England, sent to the front as a cavalry horse in the British army, then captured by German soldiers and used to pull ambulances and weaponry. It is a gripping and moving account of the horror and futility of war. The Advent Carol Service begins with a bidding prayer, calling the assembly to intercede for all who are in need, for justice and peace throughout the world, and for the unity and witness of the church. Then Scripture is proclaimed in a series of readings that tell the story of salvation, focusing on God's promises of new creation and the incarnation of Jesus. After each reading, the choir sings an anthem or the assembly sings a hymn.[1] As the service unfolded on that cold December day in Canterbury, each worshiper held a candle, providing a warm glowing light as the darkness fell outside.

As I listened and sang and prayed, I found myself drawn into God's love for the world. "Comfort, comfort, O my people, says your God" (Isa. 40:1). "Waters shall break forth in the wilderness, and streams in the desert; and the ransomed of the Lord shall return. . . . They shall obtain joy and gladness, and sorrow and sighing shall flee away" (Isa. 35:6, 10). And so it went, promises piled upon promises. The music expressed yearning and hope. We concluded with the classical Anglican Advent prayer that echoes Romans 13:12: "Almighty God, give us grace that we may cast away the works of darkness, and put upon us the armor of light."[2] In a world still torn by war and scarred by injustice, the Advent Carol Service oriented the assembly to God, enabling us to remember God's promises and claim them for ourselves, giving us a reason to hope as we aligned ourselves with God's desires and God's reconciling love for the world.

All Christian worship enacts and celebrates God's reconciling love for the world and so is a form of participation in God's mission. Nonetheless, it is quite possible for worshipers to approach worship as a means of individual

---

1. The Advent Carol Service at Canterbury Cathedral included these prophetic texts: Isaiah 40:1-5; Isaiah 35:1-6, 10; Isaiah 11:1-9; Ezekiel 11:14-20; Jeremiah 31:31-34; and Isaiah 60:1-5a. The New Testament passages were Mark 1:1-8 (John the Baptist) and Luke 1:26-38 (the Annunciation). See "Carol Services in the Advent Season," in *Common Worship: Times and Seasons* (London: Church Publishing, 2006), pp. 44-49. For background about the service, see "History of A Festival of Nine Lessons and Carols," King's College, Cambridge (U.K.), available at http://www.kings.cam.ac.uk/events/chapel-services/nine-lessons/history.html.

2. "The First Sunday of Advent," *Book of Common Prayer* 1662, available at http://www.eskimo.com/~lhowell/bcp1662/communion/xmas.html.

salvation that meets their needs for connection with God, assuming that other members of the assembly likewise are there to have their needs met. It is quite possible for worship leaders to perform worship as a dull routine, a duty to be observed. It is quite possible to view worship and mission as entirely separate spheres of action.

Yet it is equally possible to envision worship and mission as integrally related. In worship, the assembly participates in the mission of God by praising God, remembering God's mighty acts in the creation and redemption of the world, embodying God's reconciling love for the world, proclaiming the good news that Jesus announced and performed, engaging the context, praying for justice and peace, embodying justice and peace in interactions with other worshipers in the assembly, showing respect and care for creation by the way material things are used in worship, and bearing witness and listening to those outside the assembly. In communion with God and with one another, the assembly proclaims and enacts the reconciling love that is God's purpose and desire for the world — indeed, for all creation. Such missional worship is true liturgy, turned outward toward the world and offered for the common good.

Missional worship is a matter of perception and attitude rather than technique. Hence, developing missional worship requires a shift in the community's approach to worship. Missional worship happens in a missional congregation, one that proclaims and enacts the reign of God in all aspects of its life, one that *expects* to encounter God's mercy and judgment both in the assembly for worship and in daily life.

As we in twenty-first-century churches leave Christendom behind, we have a new opportunity to bear witness to the gospel of the crucified and risen Christ, to reclaim the biblical story of God's creative and redemptive love for the world and God's promise of a new creation. As churches seek to be conformed more and more to Christ, to *be* the body of Christ both in the assembly for worship and in the world, they will be reborn through the Spirit.

Churches that are missional are beacons of hope, confident that the Spirit provides all that is needed to face the challenges they encounter. Members of these churches know that worship is a primary locus of God's mission, a place and a time where the assembly celebrates and enacts God's reconciling love for the world. These churches live ever more fully into their call to participate in the mission of God in the world. We can imagine worship in these churches as Möbius strips in which mission and worship flow into and out of one another. From this perspective, worship is mission is worship . . . Yet the assembly's gathering for worship is just one component of a multidimensional approach to mission. We can also imagine missional worship as the core of our spinning top, drawing the assembly together to offer a sacrifice of praise, then sending the assembly into the world to engage in other dimensions of the mission of God — to do good and share what they have, as a sacrifice to God (Heb. 13:16).

Missional worship is thus true liturgy, work for the common good, in which the assembly responds to God's self-giving acts for the life of the world. Gathered by the Spirit, the assembly is drawn into Christ's liturgy, his self-offering for the sake of the world. In this public service, the assembly enacts and signifies God's gracious desire, merciful judgment, and abundant love for the world. Going forth from this worship in the power of the Spirit, members of the assembly continue to participate in God's mission, living as the body of Christ in the world. They then return, again and again, bringing the hopes and hungers of the world into the encounter with God in Christian worship.

Nairobi Statement on Worship and Culture: Contemporary Challenges and Opportunities

This statement is from the third international consultation of the Lutheran World Federation's Study Team on Worship and Culture, held in Nairobi, Kenya, in January 1996. The members of the Study Team represent five continents of the world and have worked together with enthusiasm for three years thus far. The initial consultation, in October 1993 in Cartigny, Switzerland, focused on the biblical and historical foundations of the relationship between Christian worship and culture, and resulted in the "Cartigny Statement on Worship and Culture: Biblical and Historical Foundations." (This Nairobi Statement builds upon the Cartigny Statement; in no sense does it replace it.) The second consultation, in March 1994 in Hong Kong, explored contemporary issues and questions of the relationships between the world's cultures and Christian liturgy, church music, and church architecture and art. The papers of the first two consultations were published as *Worship and Culture in Dialogue*.[1] The papers and statement from the Nairobi consultation were published as *Christian Worship: Unity in Cultural Diversity*.[2] In 1994-1995, the

---

1. *Worship and Culture in Dialogue* (Geneva: Lutheran World Federation, 1994). This volume was also published in French, German, and Spanish.

2. *Christian Worship: Unity in Cultural Diversity* (Geneva: Lutheran World Federation, 1996). This volume was also published in German.

Study Team conducted regional research, and prepared reports on that research. Phase IV of the Study commenced in Nairobi and will continue with seminars and other means to implement the learnings of the study, as LWF member churches decide is helpful. The Study Team considers this project to be essential to the renewal and mission of the Church around the world.

1. Introduction

1.1. Worship is the heart and pulse of the Christian Church. In worship we celebrate together God's gracious gifts of creation and salvation, and are strengthened to live in response to God's grace. Worship always involves actions, not merely words. To consider worship is to consider music, art, and architecture, as well as liturgy and preaching.

1.2. The reality that Christian worship is always celebrated in a given local cultural setting draws our attention to the dynamics between worship and the world's many local cultures.

1.3. Christian worship relates dynamically to culture in at least four ways. First, it is transcultural, the same substance for everyone everywhere, beyond culture. Second, it is contextual, varying according to the local situation (both nature and culture). Third, it is counter-cultural, challenging what is contrary to the Gospel in a given culture. Fourth, it is cross-cultural, making possible sharing between different local cultures. In all four dynamics, there are helpful principles which can be identified.

2. Worship as Transcultural

2.1. The resurrected Christ whom we worship, and through whom by the power of the Holy Spirit we know the grace of the Triune God, transcends and indeed is beyond all cultures. In the mystery of his resurrection is the source of the transcultural nature of Christian worship. Baptism and Eucharist, the sacraments of Christ's death and resurrection, were given by God for all the world. There is one Bible, translated into many tongues, and biblical preaching of Christ's death and resurrection has been sent into all the world. The fundamental shape of the principal Sunday act of Christian worship, the

Eucharist or Holy Communion, is shared across cultures: the people gather, the Word of God is proclaimed, the people intercede for the needs of the Church and the world, the eucharistic meal is shared, and the people are sent out into the world for mission. The great narratives of Christ's birth, death, resurrection, and sending of the Spirit, and our Baptism into him, provide the central meanings of the transcultural times of the church's year: especially Lent/Easter/Pentecost, and, to a lesser extent, Advent/Christmas/Epiphany. The ways in which the shapes of the Sunday Eucharist and the church year are expressed vary by culture, but their meanings and fundamental structure are shared around the globe. There is one Lord, one faith, one Baptism, one Eucharist.

2.2. Several specific elements of Christian liturgy are also transcultural, e.g., readings from the Bible (although of course the translations vary), the ecumenical creeds and the Our Father, and Baptism in water in the Triune Name.

2.3. The use of this shared core liturgical structure and these shared liturgical elements in local congregational worship — as well as the shared act of people assembling together, and the shared provision of diverse leadership in that assembly (although the space for the assembly and the manner of the leadership vary) — are expressions of Christian unity across time, space, culture, and confession. The recovery in each congregation of the clear centrality of these transcultural and ecumenical elements renews the sense of this Christian unity and gives all churches a solid basis for authentic contextualization.

3. Worship as Contextual

3.1. Jesus whom we worship was born into a specific culture of the world. In the mystery of his incarnation are the model and the mandate for the contextualization of Christian worship. God can be and is encountered in the local cultures of our world. A given culture's values and patterns, insofar as they are consonant with the values of the Gospel, can be used to express the meaning and purpose of Christian worship. Contextualization is a necessary task for the Church's mission in the world, so that the Gospel can be ever more deeply rooted in diverse local cultures.

3.2. Among the various methods of contextualization, that of dynamic equivalence is particularly useful. It involves re-expressing components of Christian worship with something from a local culture that has an equal meaning, value, and function. Dynamic equivalence goes far beyond mere translation; it involves understanding the fundamental meanings both of elements of worship and of the local culture, and enabling the meanings and actions of worship to be "encoded" and re-expressed in the language of local culture.

3.3. In applying the method of dynamic equivalence, the following procedure may be followed. First, the liturgical ordo (basic shape) should be examined with regard to its theology, history, basic elements, and cultural backgrounds. Second, those elements of the ordo that can be subjected to dynamic equivalence without prejudice to their meaning should be determined. Third, those components of culture that are able to re-express the Gospel and the liturgical ordo in an adequate manner should be studied. Fourth, the spiritual and pastoral benefits our people will derive from the changes should be considered.

3.4. Local churches might also consider the method of creative assimilation. This consists of adding pertinent components of local culture to the liturgical ordo in order to enrich its original core. The baptismal ordo of "washing with water and the Word," for example, was gradually elaborated by the assimilation of such cultural practices as the giving of white vestments and lighted candles to the neophytes of ancient mystery religions. Unlike dynamic equivalence, creative assimilation enriches the liturgical ordo — not by culturally re-expressing its elements, but by adding to it new elements from local culture.

3.5. In contextualization the fundamental values and meanings of both Christianity and of local cultures must be respected.

3.6. An important criterion for dynamic equivalence and creative assimilation is that sound or accepted liturgical traditions are preserved in order to keep unity with the universal Church's tradition of worship, while progress inspired by pastoral needs is encouraged. On the side of culture, it is understood that not everything can be integrated with Christian worship, but only those elements that are connatural to (that is, of the same nature as) the liturgical ordo. Elements borrowed from local culture should always undergo critique and purification, which can be achieved through the use of biblical typology.

4. Worship as Counter-cultural

4.1. Jesus Christ came to transform all people and all cultures, and calls us not to conform to the world, but to be transformed with it (Romans 12:2). In the mystery of his passage from death to eternal life is the model for transformation, and thus for the counter-cultural nature of Christian worship. Some components of every culture in the world are sinful, dehumanizing, and contradictory to the values of the Gospel. From the perspective of the Gospel, they need critique and transformation. Contextualization of Christian faith and worship necessarily involves challenging all types of oppression and social injustice wherever they exist in earthly cultures.

4.2. It also involves the transformation of cultural patterns which idolize the self or the local group at the expense of a wider humanity, or which give central place to the acquisition of wealth at the expense of the care of the earth and its poor. The tools of the counter-cultural in Christian worship may also include the deliberate maintenance or recovery of patterns of action which differ intentionally from prevailing cultural models. These patterns may arise from a recovered sense of Christian history, or from the wisdom of other cultures.

5. Worship as Cross-cultural

5.1. Jesus came to be the Savior of all people. He welcomes the treasures of earthly cultures into the city of God. By virtue of Baptism, there is one Church; and one means of living in faithful response to Baptism is to manifest ever more deeply the unity of the Church. The sharing of hymns and art and other elements of worship across cultural barriers helps enrich the whole Church and strengthen the sense of the *communio* of the Church. This sharing can be ecumenical as well as cross-cultural, as a witness to the unity of the Church and the oneness of Baptism. Cross-cultural sharing is possible for every church, but is especially needed in multicultural congregations and member churches.

5.2. Care should be taken that the music, art, architecture, gestures and postures, and other elements of different cultures are understood and respected when they are used by churches elsewhere in the world. The criteria for contextualization (above, sections 3.5 and 3.6) should be observed.

6. Challenge to the Churches

6.1. We call on all member churches of the Lutheran World Federation to undertake more efforts related to the transcultural, contextual, counter-cultural, and cross-cultural nature of Christian worship. We call on all member churches to recover the centrality of Baptism, Scripture with preaching, and the every-Sunday celebration of the Lord's Supper — the principal trans-cultural elements of Christian worship and the signs of Christian unity — as the strong center of all congregational life and mission, and as the authentic basis for contextualization. We call on all churches to give serious attention to exploring the local or contextual elements of liturgy, language, posture and gesture, hymnody and other music and musical instruments, and art and architecture for Christian worship — so that their worship may be more truly rooted in the local culture. We call on those churches now carrying out missionary efforts to encourage such contextual awareness among themselves and also among the partners and recipients of their ministries. We call on all member churches to give serious attention to the transcultural nature of worship and the possibilities for cross-cultural sharing. And we call on all churches to consider the training and ordination of ministers of Word and Sacrament, because each local community has the right to receive weekly the means of grace.

6.2. We call on the Lutheran World Federation to make an intentional and substantial effort to provide scholarships for persons from the developing world to study worship, church music, and church architecture, toward the eventual goal that enhanced theological training in their churches can be led by local teachers.

6.3. Further, we call on the Lutheran World Federation to continue its efforts related to worship and culture into the next millennium. The tasks are not quickly accomplished; the work calls for ongoing depth-level research and pastoral encouragement. The Worship and Culture Study, begun in 1992 and continuing in and past the 1997 LWF Assembly, is a significant and important beginning, but the task calls for unending efforts. Giving priority to this task is essential for evangelization of the world.

Bibliography

WORSHIP

Baptism, Eucharist, and Ministry. Geneva: World Council of Churches, 1982.

Bradshaw, Paul F. *Early Christian Worship: A Basic Introduction to Ideas and Practice.* Collegeville, Minn.: Liturgical Press, 2010.

————. *Eucharistic Origins.* New York and Oxford: Oxford University Press, 2004.

Bradshaw, Paul, ed. *The New Westminster Dictionary of Liturgy and Worship.* Louisville: Westminster John Knox Press, 2002.

Bradshaw, Paul F., and Maxwell E. Johnson. *The Eucharistic Liturgies: Their Evolution and Interpretation.* Alcuin Club Collections 87. London: SPCK, 2012.

————. *The Origins of Feasts, Fasts, and Seasons in Early Christianity.* London: SPCK; Collegeville, Minn.: Liturgical Press, 2011.

Carson, D. A., ed. *Worship: Adoration and Action.* Grand Rapids: Baker Books, 1993.

Chupungco, Anscar. *Liturgies of the Future: The Process and Methods of Inculturation.* New York and Mahwah, N.J.: Paulist Press, 1989.

Day, Juliette, and Benjamin Gordon-Taylor, eds. *The Study of Liturgy and Worship: An Alcuin Guide.* London: SPCK, 2013.

Duck, Ruth C. *Finding Words for Worship: A Guide for Leaders.* Louisville: Westminster John Knox Press, 1995.

————. *Worship for the Whole People of God: Vital Worship for the 21st Century.* Louisville: Westminster John Knox Press, 2013.

Foley, Edward, John F. Baldovin, Mary Collins, and Joanne M. Pierce, eds. *A Commentary on the Order of Mass of The Roman Missal: A New English Translation, developed under the auspices of the Catholic Academy of Liturgy.* Collegeville, Minn.: Liturgical Press, 2011.

Hawn, C. Michael. *One Bread, One Body: Exploring Cultural Diversity in Worship.* Bethesda, Md.: Alban Institute, 2003.

Hoffman, Lawrence A. *The Art of Public Prayer: Not for Clergy Only.* Second edition. Woodstock, Vt.: SkyLight Paths Publishing, 1999.

Johnson, Maxwell E., ed. *Living Water, Sealing Spirit: Readings on Christian Initiation.* Collegeville, Minn.: Liturgical Press, 1995.

———, ed. *Sacraments and Worship: The Sources of Christian Theology.* Louisville: Westminster John Knox Press, 2012.

Kreider, Alan. *The Change of Conversion and the Origin of Christendom.* Harrisburg, Pa.: Trinity Press International, 1999.

Lange, Dirk G., and Dwight W. Vogel. *Ordo: Bath, Word, Prayer, Table: A Liturgical Primer in Honor of Gordon W. Lathrop.* Akron, Ohio: OSL Publications, 2005.

Lathrop, Gordon W. *Holy Things: A Liturgical Theology.* Minneapolis: Fortress Press, 1993.

Long, Thomas C. *Beyond the Worship Wars: Building Vital and Faithful Worship.* Herndon, Va.: Alban Institute, 2001.

Mitchell, Leonel L. *Praying Shapes Believing: A Theological Commentary on The Book of Common Prayer.* Minneapolis: Winston Press, 1985.

Saliers, Don E. *Worship as Theology: Foretaste of Glory Divine.* Nashville: Abingdon Press, 1994.

Satterlee, Craig A. *When God Speaks through Worship: Stories Congregations Live By.* Herndon, Va.: Alban Institute, 2009.

Schmemann, Alexander. *For the Life of the World: Sacraments and Orthodoxy.* Second edition, revised and expanded. Crestwood, N.Y.: St. Vladimir's Seminary Press, 1973.

Underhill, Evelyn. *Worship.* London: James Nisbet & Company, 1936. Reprint edition: New York: Crossroad, 1982.

Wainwright, Geoffrey, and Karen B. Westerfield Tucker. *The Oxford History of Christian Worship.* New York and Oxford: Oxford University Press, 2006.

White, James F. *Introduction to Christian Worship.* Third edition, revised and expanded. Nashville: Abingdon Press, 2000.

———. *Protestant Worship: Traditions in Transition.* Louisville: Westminster John Knox Press, 1989.

MISSION

Barrett, Lois Y., ed. *Treasure in Clay Jars: Patterns in Missional Faithfulness.* Grand Rapids: Wm. B. Eerdmans, 2004.

Bevans, Stephen B., and Roger P. Schroeder. *Constants in Context: A Theology of Mission for Today.* Maryknoll, N.Y.: Orbis Books, 2004.

Bolger, Ryan, ed. *The Gospel after Christendom: New Voices, New Cultures, New Expressions.* Grand Rapids: Baker Academic, 2012.

Bosch, David. *Transforming Mission: Paradigm Shifts in Theology of Mission.* Maryknoll, N.Y.: Orbis Books, 1991.

Bria, Ion, ed. *Go Forth in Peace: Orthodox Perspectives on Mission.* Geneva: WCC Publications, 1986.

Gibbs, Eddie, and Ryan K. Bolger. *Emerging Churches: Creating Christian Community in Postmodern Cultures.* Grand Rapids: Baker Academic, 2005.

Guder, Darrell L., ed. *Missional Church: A Vision for the Sending of the Church in North America.* Grand Rapids: Wm. B. Eerdmans, 1998.

Newbigin, Lesslie. *The Open Secret: An Introduction to the Theology of Mission.* Revised edition. Grand Rapids: Wm. B. Eerdmans, 1995.

————. *Trinitarian Faith and Today's Mission.* Richmond, Va.: John Knox Press, 1964.

Spellers, Stephanie. *Radical Welcome: Embracing God, The Other, and the Spirit of Transformation.* New York: Church Publishing, 2006.

Van Gelder, Craig. *The Ministry of the Missional Church: A Community Led by the Spirit.* Grand Rapids: Baker, 2007.

WORSHIP AND ETHICS

Bass, Dorothy C., ed. *Practicing Our Faith: A Way of Life for a Searching People.* Second edition. San Francisco: Jossey-Bass, 1997, 2010.

Hauerwas, Stanley, and Samuel Wells, eds. *The Blackwell Companion to Christian Ethics.* Oxford and Malden, Mass.: Blackwell Publishing, 2004.

Scharen, Christian. *Public Worship and Public Work: Character and Commitment in Local Congregational Life.* Collegeville, Minn.: Pueblo Books, 2004.

Smith, James K. A. *Desiring the Kingdom: Worship, Worldview, and Cultural Formation.* Grand Rapids: Baker Academic, 2009.

Volf, Miroslav, and Dorothy C. Bass, eds. *Practicing Theology: Beliefs and Practices in Christian Life.* Grand Rapids: Wm. B. Eerdmans, 2002.

WORSHIP AND MISSION

Bria, Ion. *The Liturgy after the Liturgy: Mission and Witness from an Orthodox Perspective.* Geneva: WCC Publications, 1996.

Dally, John Addison. *Choosing the Kingdom: Missional Preaching for the Household of God.* Herndon, Va.: Alban Institute, 2008.

Davies, J. G. *Worship and Mission.* London: SCM Press, 1966; New York: Association Press, 1967.

Gray-Reeves, Mary, and Michael Perham. *The Hospitality of God: Emerging Worship for a Missional Church.* New York: Seabury Books, 2011.

Kreider, Alan, and Eleanor Kreider. *Worship and Mission after Christendom.* Scottdale, Pa., and Waterloo, Ontario: Herald Press, 2011.

Pierce, Gregory F. Augustine. *The Mass Is Never Ended: Rediscovering Our Mission to Transform the World.* Notre Dame: Ave Maria Press, 2007.

Schattauer, Thomas H., ed. *Inside Out: Worship in an Age of Mission.* Minneapolis: Fortress Press, 1999.

Schmit, Clayton J. *Sent and Gathered: A Worship Manual for the Missional Church.* Grand Rapids: Baker Academic, 2009.